GOVERNING CHILDHOOD

Issues in Law and Society
General Editor: Michael Freeman

Governing Childhood

Edited with an Introduction by

ANNE McGILLIVRAY
Faculty of Law, University of Manitoba

Dartmouth

Aldershot • Brookfield USA • Singapore • Sydney

Published by
Dartmouth Publishing Company Limited
Gower House
Croft Road
Aldershot
Hants GU11 3HR
England

Dartmouth Publishing Company
Old Post Road
Brookfield
Vermont 05036
USA

British Library Cataloguing in Publication Data
Governing childhood. - (Issues in law and society)
    1.Children - Legal status, laws, etc.
    I.McGillivray, Anne
    342.4'327

Library of Congress Cataloging-in-Publication Data
Governing childhood / edited with an introduction by Anne McGillivray.
        p.   cm.
        ISBN 1-85521-833-X (hardback : alk. paper). -- ISBN 1-85521-840-2
(pbk. : alt. paper)
        1. Children--Government policy. 2. Juvenile justice,
    Administration of. 3. Children--Legal status, laws, etc.
    I. McGillivray, Anne.
    HQ789.088   1996
    305.23--dc20   96-32163
                                                                                         CIP

ISBN 1 85521 833 X (Hbk)
ISBN 1 85521 840 2 (Pbk)

Printed and bound in Great Britain by
Biddles Ltd, Guildford and King's Lynn

Contents

Debates of French lawmakers in the early 1870s about the regulation of
child street performers and professional child beggars reveal the erosion
of the public-private opposition by concerns about the ability of the family
to maintain its own moral order. By collapsing the physical and moral
bodies of the 'abused' young performer, the 1874 law protecting children
in the itinerant trades would point toward the possibility of regulating the
most juridically sacrosanct of all nineteenth-century spaces: the private
space of parent-child relations.

Sex delinquency as constructed by the early juvenile court is presumed to
reflect middle class sexual morality. The Denver Juvenile Court of Judge
Ben Lindsey articulated a less traditionalist conception, indicting not the
sexually precocious girl but the repressive conventions that stigmatized
her. Lindsey's constitution of the female delinquent, and complementary
analysis of Denver Juvenile Court and Colorado State Industrial School
for Girls records, substantiate this revisionist thesis.

Contributors

JANET AINSWORTH is Associate Professor of Law at Seattle University, where she teaches criminal procedure and children and the law. Her research focuses on sociolinguistic aspects of the criminal justice system. Her critique of the law on police interrogation practices recently appeared in the Yale Law Journal.

PAUL COLOMY is Associate Professor of Sociology at the University of Denver. He has published articles in sociological theory, social change and social psychology. His current research is concerned with the constitution of delinquency and the development of the juvenile justice system.

MICHAEL FREEMAN is Professor of English Law at University College London and the author of numerous books and articles on childhood and the family, rights theory and jurisprudence. He is editor of *The International Journal of Children's Rights*. Recent works include *Children's Rights, A Comparative Perspective* and *Divorce: Where Next?*

ALICE HEARST is Assistant Professor of Government at Smith College, where she teaches public law. She is presently a visiting faculty member at Cornell, teaching family law and feminist legal thought. She is at work on her manuscript *Good Families/Good Citizens: The Anxiety of Reimaging the Domestic Sphere.*

MARTIN KRETZMANN is a doctoral candidate in sociology at the University of Denver. He has published in the areas of political litigation, deviance, delinquency and the juvenile court. His dissertation examines the legal and political influence of Denver Judge Ben Lindsey on the juvenile court during the Progressive Era, and subsequent developments in the United States.

SHEILA MARTINEAU is a doctoral candidate in educational studies at the University of British Columbia. She is author of 'The Eugenics Movement and the Educational State in Canada' in Juanita Ross Epp, ed., *Schools, Complicity, and Sources of Violence* (1996). Her dissertation is a critical discourse analysis of the multidisciplinary concept of teaching resiliency to at-risk youth in inner-city schools.

ANNE McGILLIVRAY is Associate Professor of Law at the University of Manitoba. She has written on children's rights, the criminalization of child abuse, child sexual assault and corporal punishment, and was guest editor of Mosaic, *Adversaria: Literature and the Law* (1994). She is completing a study of Aboriginal women as victims of intimate violence and investigating eurocolonial images of Aboriginal childhood.

MARTHA MINOW is Professor of Law at Harvard University, where she is involved in efforts to establish courses and interfaculty initiatives in Children's Studies throughout the university. Her books include *Making All the Difference: Inclusion, Exclusion, and American Law* (1990) and *Family Matters: Reading on Family Lives and the Law* (1993).

SYLVIA SCHAFER is Assistant Professor of History at the University of Wisconsin - Milwaukee. Her publications include 'When the Child is the Father of the Man: Work, Sexual Difference and the Guardian State in Third Republic France' in Ann-Louise Shapiro, ed., *Feminist Revision History* (1994). She is completing her book on 'moral danger', the family and the state in nineteenth-century France.

Introduction

Governing Childhood

ANNE McGILLIVRAY

Childhood is unknown. Starting from the false idea one has of it, the farther one goes, the more one loses one's way.

Rousseau, 1762

Child training everywhere seems to be in considerable part concerned with problems which arise from universal character- istics of the human infant and from universal characteristics of adult culture which are incompatible with the continuation of infantile behaviour ...

Whiting and Child, 1953

The only steady linear change over the last four hundred years seems to have been a growing concern for children, although their actual treatment has oscillated cyclically between the permissive and the repressive.

Lawrence Stone, 1979

Childhood is the most intensively governed sector of personal existence.

Nikolas Rose, 1989

HOW CHILDHOOD IN THE MODERN WEST is understood has taken a distinct shape in the last twenty years. Governing the self may once have been a matter between man and god. It is now and has been for the last two centuries or more a matter for the state as well. What had seemed accidental by-product of law and social policy aimed elsewhere, or random quasi-charitable intervention to control children who risked the public order, or a private matter of culture, taste and privilege is now seen as a central concern of the state: the shaping of childhood in the production of citizenship. The emergence of childhood redefined the private, reconditioned motherhood (and fatherhood) and inspired and fuelled the enormous complex of therapeutic disciplines, Foucault's 'strange sciences' which now define for us the conditions of normality.

While nature and childhood are closely associated, little about childhood is 'natural'. Childhood is by definition a condition which requires intimate mediation and constant surveillance. Government — or governance — is the tutored mediation of the intimate. 'Governing childhood' is the theme chosen for this book for its connotations of social construction and intimate management both within and 'outside' state regulation, a concept which embraces the diverse forms and nuances of the conduct of childhood. How we envision and regulate childhood tells us as much about ourselves as a people or a state as it does about the lives of children. The work of Foucault and his followers has shaped and defined the way we understand the government of individuality. This project, however, is not 'about' Foucault.

'Governing childhood' is a concept which invites the centring of childhood in social and legal studies. There are two reasons why we might want to do this. First, childhood is not just a socio-legal construct of the modern West but a condition of life universally defined by special limits and unique obligations. That childhood is outgrown does not resolve the need to evaluate its condition and its boundaries. Second, childhood offers a novel perspective on the nature of the social order, on questions of regulation, culture and subjectivity. As feminism's centring of 'womanhood' and women enables radical and reformative critique of law and society, so does centring childhood and the child in law and society studies, rights discourse and historical analysis.

Childhood is a submerged geography of pastoral or volcanic landscapes neither outgrown nor fully known despite the gaze of an astonishing variety of disciplines into its psychology, history, mores and management. The modest monograph collection of the University of Manitoba, for example, includes 11,338 works indexed to 'children', 7515 to 'child', 2619 to 'childhood' and 140 to childhood history. The Legal Periodicals Index lists 4765 articles on children and law. Childhood scholars write from the disciplinary perspectives of sociology, history, literature, psychology, psychiatry, law, criminology, anthropology, medicine, pediatric medicine, social work, education. Yet it is worth remembering, as Foucault and others remind us, that the disciplinary gaze may be focused on the deviant in the identification and regulation of the norm, and that the 'therapies of freedom' reflected in his later body of work, best framed in the context of childhood by Nikolas Rose, do not apply to children in the same way as to adults.

What follows is a selective and eclectic overview of works which exemplify certain themes and directions in the study of governance and childhood. The first of these is the government of the private, illustrated by the Ariès school of childhood history and the work of Foucault, Donzelot and Rose. The second is the relationship between childhood and society, a concept originating with Freud and launched by Erik Erikson, reflected in works which examine broad linkages between the construction or management of childhood and the ethos, legal paradigms and 'psychology' of a society or state.

I. DISCIPLINING THE PRIVATE: HISTORIES AND GOVERNMENTALITIES

THE WORK OF MICHEL FOUCAULT which most strongly resonates with the government of childhood is *Discipline and Punish* (1975). His dark portrayal of the 'normalizing' disciplines is accompanied by numerous textual hints and associations relating this darkness to childhood. Technologies of normalization — the creation of docile bodies and governed souls — 'over'-determine subjectivity and focus on the corporal as well as the corporeal. Yet these technologies, justly questioned in the adult context, are seemingly irreducibly associated with the fragility of childhood, the apparently inherent structuring of learning and physical maturation and the centrality of the child's body in the management of childhood. Childhood is metaphor and essence of repression, domination and (futile) resistance, a view of power which permeates *Discipline and Punish*.[1]

For Foucault, modern techniques of discipline (*surveillance*) produce an effect, a 'soul', in those supervised, trained, corrected, in children at home and at school. This soul is a corporeal prison which constrains the body by its very constitution. It results from 'a certain type of power and the reference of a certain type of knowledge ... aimed at the governance of the individual' (29). In an important historical shift, 'the normal took over from the ancestral and measurement from status' to create a political anatomy of the body mapped out by new disciplines, practices and analyses. In this coercive individualization, 'the child is more individualized than the adult' and the 'internal search for childhood' became the mark of the new disciplinary society (193). The basic methodology is straightforward. By gathering together and observing classes of people   (soldier, student, delinquent, prisoner, worker, child), difference can be observed, measured and effaced through techniques perfected by the 'psy' disciplines. Examination of school discipline, for example, shows that progression is less about aspiration or ability than a conformity impelled by the 'perpetual penalty' of status or defect which 'supervises every instant' and 'compares, differentiates, hierarchizes, homogenizes, excludes. In short, it *normalizes*' (183). Difference is not lost. Its measure becomes the measure of the norm, 'a useful imperative' in the reinforcement of hierarchy.

The discipline of childhood is for Foucault a powerfully linked theme with the disciplinary technologies of the prison. Like the prison, the family is a primary institutional support of the disciplined society, part of a carceral archipelago of linked mechanisms of normalization, 'a multiple network of diverse elements — walls, space, institution, rules, discourse' (307) which is site and machinery of the production of the soul. The family, 'essentially in the parents-children cell', has become disciplined, having absorbed 'external schemata, first educational and military, then medical, psychiatric, psychological', making the family 'the privileged locus of emergence for the disciplinary question of the normal and abnormal' (216). We are not to be misled, Foucault admonishes, by the promise of one disciplinary authority to relieve us from the rigours of another, from the promise of educational psychology, for example, to 'correct the rigours of the school'. We are merely referred from one to another schema of power-knowledge. The docile body, the disciplined soul, is created out of 'the petty, malicious minutiae of the disciplines and their investigations'. These disciplines — 'psychology, psychiatry, pedagogy, criminology and so many other strange sciences'[2] — are to the humanity of those scrutinized what 'the terrible power of investigation' is to 'the calm knowledge of the animals, the plants or the earth': 'Another power, another knowledge' (226).

Whose body is rendered more docile, whose geopolitics are more controlled, whose 'calm knowledge' is more rigorously investigated than that of the child? The child is matrix of the norm. Foucault's child lurks in the interstices of a vast yet intimate power-knowledge equation in which she is to be remade in accordance with an external and vicious schemata, her 'calm knowledge' destroyed. In configurations of childhood in the modern West, there is a recurrent tension between visions of childhood as innocent embodiment of singular virtues, and childhood as innately evil or at best deeply antisocial. Socialization corrupts or saves. Foucault's corrupted child is a child of Rousseau.

Rousseau's *Emile* (1762), a novelized treatise on education, imaged a new childhood, innocent, even divine. Innocence being unsustainable and bookish education corrupting, *Emile* promoted a tutored mediation of childhood experience, close to nature, learning from experience. The work had a revolutionary impact on upper-middle and upper-class English families newly interested in domesticity and disenchanted with puritan childhood theory, which emphasized the child's sinfulness and its elimination through rigorous training.[3] Despite John Wesley's denunciation of *Emile* as 'the most empty, silly, injudicious thing that a self-conceited infidel wrote',[4] Rousseau's vision was reflected in over two hundred treatises on education published in England between 1762 and 1800, although the notion of original sin was never satisfactorily tied off. (The illuminated poems of William Blake were a reminder throughout this period of 'other' childhoods and of inadequacies in Rousseau's ideas about the tutoring of children.)[5]

Philippe Ariès' *Centuries of Childhood* (1962) inaugurated a new era in childhood study. Childhood is to be understood as a changing social construct (*conception*). Ariès in effect projected a Rousseau view of the child onto history. The pre-modern child was a miniature adult moved as quickly as possible from infancy to adult society and childhood was a blissful state in an undifferentiated world. A major shift in thinking about childhood was reflected in late seventeenth- and early eighteenth-century regimes for child segregation and instruction. This entailed increasingly strict parental and tutorial surveillance and heightened pressure on the child to perform according to external pedagogic and social standards. Childhood, in effect, was now explicitly about itself. Childhood became a bounded social construct defining and constraining children, rather than a seamless transition from infancy to adulthood. Ariès took care to say that his thesis is about ideas and not about the actual treatment of children but this distinction was often missed in the new history of childhood.

Centuries of Childhood was published in the same year as 'The Battered Child Syndrome' (1962), the groundbreaking pediatric study by Kempe and his colleagues which revolutionized contemporary thinking about childhood. The dark side of Ariès' 'new childhood' was about to receive a name: child abuse.[6] Historians of the Ariès school argued that, prior to the 'invention' of childhood, the child was anonymous. Family size and high infant mortality precluded lavishing affection on the individual child and parents were at best indifferent to their children, at worst abusive (*cf.* Shorter 1975). Others wrote histories of childhood as histories of child abuse, a nightmare from which we have now just begun to awaken (*cf.* deMause 1974). Such histories may mistake the idea for the substance — but what is the substance?

Lawrence Stone's *The Family, Sex and Marriage in England 1500-1800* (1977) was inspired by Ariès, whose laudatory comments appear on the jacket of the paperback edition. Ariès drew much of his evidence from seventeenth-century Dutch portraits, a slippery problem in view of the stylistic conventions of portraiture, and Heoward's diary record of the childhood of a French king. Stone drew on a wider array of sources — cultural ephemera such as letters, diaries, tracts, tombstones; shifiting ideas about individuality and sensibility; broader social and demographic change — to identify shifts in procreation, parenting practices and the idea and ideology of the family. His is in some ways the most compelling account of childhood in the modern era despite (or perhaps because of) the complexities of class, gender, sensibility and taste for which the work could not fully account. These precluded a uniform childhood and contributed to the invisibility of substandard ones. Stone concluded that the treatment of children oscillates between 'the repressive' (the sixteenth- and nineteenth-century emphasis on filial piety, ritual beating and the 'utter subordination of the child') and 'the permissive' (the affective individualism of the seventeenth and twentieth centuries which, in emphasizing individual happiness, threatens parental bonds and social cohesion). While treatment of children oscillates (and varies within those oscillatations), concern for children steadily increased throughout the modern period.[7] Corporal punishment was for Stone a touchstone of child-rearing mores. How often, how hard, for what and by whom children were beaten, a Stone theme, became a *motif* of the post-Kempe era of childhood study.[8]

Forgotten Children (1983) offered a steady-state view of childhood, the antithesis of Ariès-Stone hypotheses of change or fluctuation. Linda Pollock's diary, autobiography and newspaper sources disclosed a continuity in parent-child relations and child treatment throughout the medieval and modern periods, characterized by close, caring, individualized and not particularly punitive child rearing. Her review of 385 child abuse trials reported in *The Times* between 1785 and 1860 is compelling in its demonstration of contempo-rary judicial and social condemnation of brutal child treatment. While hers is an intuitively 'right' view of child-rearing, she does not account for presumed effects of social change on childhood and many of the children among her English and American middle-class diarists are writing to order.

Family size and infant mortality statistics do not support the Ariès school, as Pollock later demonstrated (1987). The English family household varied within a much smaller range — between 4.18 and 4.57 members throughout the periods canvassed — than the more dramatic shrinkage posited in claims about the rise of the nuclear family. Infant mortality rose between 1650 and 1750, the era of the 'emergence' of childhood to which a declining infant mortality was supposed contributory, to a nineteenth-century peak. Nor is it possible to demonstrate the impact of child-rearing advice, like that of Rousseau and others, on the actual treatment of children. The 'emergence' of childhood, Pollock suggested, represented only an increasing emphasis on child-centred family reorganization and family privacy,[9] while the treatment of children remained much the same.

Jacques Donzelot began the examination of family government urged by Foucault[10] with *The Policing of Families* (1979). The nineteenth century saw a series of shifts in the state regulation of childhood in which the family, in particular the working class family, became the site of projects of citizenship focused on the normalization of deviant, difficult and potentially dangerous children. Powers, agencies and practices constituting a 'tutelary complex' operated through youth court, schools, medico-hygienic clinics and social agencies. The 'familialization of society' would 'return' to the family its primacy in the rearing of children. It did so by engaging and manipulating maternal aspirations and by regulating the images of mother, father and family. The family was now accountable, at no risk to its authority or autonomy, for implanting in the child a self-governing citizenship. Exhortations to conform to ideals of family relations and good children were familiar in the moralizing of earlier decades but the images of normality were now generated by the new family expertise of the tutelary 'psy' disciplines. Foucault's terrible disciplines were now the familiar.

Donzelot advanced a Foucauldian model of intimate government while retreating from the correlation of normalization with repression and punishment. The haunting abstractions of disciplinary wrongness which permeates *Discipline and Punish* is echoed only faintly in Donzelot.[11] The echo is more faint still in *Governing the Soul* (1989), Nikolas Rose's account of the management of subjectivity in the twentieth century. Mapping the 'dark continent' of the family and investigating the 'attitudes, behaviours, and beliefs of the natives who dwelt there' has made childhood 'the most intensively governed sector of human existence' (103). What is good for children is inextricably twined with the social good.

In different ways, at different times, and by many different routes varying from one section of society to another, the health, welfare, and rearing of children have been linked in thought and practice to the destiny of the nation and the responsibilities of the state.

The 'complex apparatus' of welfare, schooling, juvenile justice, parental education and surveillance is only the 'most obvious manifestation' of this linkage (2). Governing the subjectivity of the child is a socialization into adulthood which is not an 'anthropological universal' but 'the historically specific outcome of technologies for the government of the subjectivity of citizens' (130). Governing the child is a logical extension of post-1700 statist concerns with population measure, control and citizenship. Conceptions, inventions, explanations and expertise of the psychological sciences are now at the centre of the measure and manipulation of subjectivity.

Rose's 'therapies of freedom' are not the repressive surveillance of *Discipline and Punish* but the more benign governmentality explored in Foucault's later works. This vision of governance differentiates between consensual relations and violent or violating exercises of social control. It accommodates the subtleties of modern techniques of government which determine subjectivity while freeing individuality. The making of the self is no longer a coercive exercise of power. It is a reflexive reinvention of the soul, a healthy self-government by which, Rose wrote, 'we evaluate ourselves according to the criteria provided for us by others' and 'adjust ourselves by means of the techniques propounded by the experts of the soul' (5). The psyschometrics of childhood — the 'great project' which mapped out each microstage of childhood and every occasion for correction — was a knowledge advanced by the 'psy' sciences in multiple ways and places. Tutelary messages about passages, stages and the psychic and phsyical health of children and parents are broadcast in advice columns, television programs, government advertising, self-therapy manuals and child care books; communi-cated in school, clinic and agency offices and home visits; institutionalized in the discourse of juvenile and family courts: above all, internalized in 'the unceasing reflexive gaze of our own psychologically educated self-scrutiny'. In the remaking of the soul, the child is at the centre. The adult subject must reinvestigate childhood but the child is an overt target. 'The soul of the young citizen has become the object of government through expertise' (131).

The meaning of privacy in the familial society has undergone another shift. 'No longer do experts have to reach the family by way of the law or the coercive intrusion of social work.' The campaign to construct a family which will accept the duties of socialization and 'live them as its own desires' is a success. The programs are installed. The family is now intensively governed

through the promotion of subjectivities, the construction of pleasures and ambitions, and the activation of guilt, anxiety, envy, and disappointment. The new relational technologies of the family are installed within us, establishing a particular psychological way of viewing our family lives and speaking about them, urging a constant scrutiny of our inherently difficult interactions with our children and each other, a constant judgement of their consequences for health, adjustment, development and intellect. The tension generated by the gap between normality and actuality bonds our personal projects inseparably to expertise (208).

Family privacy is the emblem and the reward of the successful (psychologized) government of the soul. 'Each normal family will fulfil its political obligations best at the very moment it conscientiously strives to realize its most private dreams' (208).

But normal families may have odd dreams and family dreams may not be the dreams of childhood, as Freud and his followers remind us. Relations between childhood and society also work the other way. As society makes childhood, so does childhood mark society.

II. (PSYCHO) ANALYSING THE PUBLIC: CHILDHOOD AND SOCIETY

CHILDHOOD AND SOCIETY are cross-linked in central ways. The perception and regulation of childhood reflects the nature of the society whose childhood it is, while insights derived from psychoanalisis and psychological study of childhood are applied to the constitution and functioning of law and the social. Erik Erikson made the point in *Childhood and Society* (1950, 1963), a study of 'the ego's roots in social organization'.

This is a book on childhood. One may scan work after work on history, society, and morality and find little reference to the fact that all people start as children and that all peoples begin in their nurseries. It is human to have a long childhood; it is civilized to have an ever longer childhood. Long childhood makes a technical and mental virtuoso out of man, but it also leaves a lifelong residue of emotional immaturity in him. While tribes and nations, in many intuitive ways, use child training to the end of gaining their particular form of mature human identity, their unique version of integrity, they are, and remain, beset by the irrational fears which stem from the very state of childhood which they exploited their specific way (16).

Society is 'beset' by the irrational fears of exploited childhood and extended childhood has left a residue of emotional immaturity. Tribes and nations use childhood to gain collective identity, their 'unique version' of integrity. This is the stuff of social psychoanalysis. Childhood experience or 'psychological evolution' illuminates 'the fact that the history of humanity is a gigantic metabolism of individual life cycles'.

Erikson's case studies canvassed childhood disturbances and child development, with the reminder that 'a chart is only a tool to think with, and cannot aspire to be a prescription to abide by'; Aboriginal child-rearing; the childhood of Adolf Hitler; and 'American' childhood. His introduction to his study of Sioux and Yurok childhood regimes categorically stated that 'Even anthropologists living for years among aboriginal tribes failed to see that these tribes trained their children in some systematic way'.[12] Erikson's psychoanalysis of society and childhood opened an important conceptual door. Although dated, this was an immensely popular work which played a symbolic freeing role in civil rights movements of the 1960s (Coles 1970). Childhood matters. Childhood is shaped by and conditions society. Child-rearing practices reinforce and reflect the social structure. The 'deadliest sin is the mutilation of a child's spirit'. These Erikson themes are amplified or deconstructed in later works exploring the relations of childhood and society.

In *For Your Own Good* (1984), Alice Miller drew on psychoanalysis to connect child-rearing practices with social violence. Western European child-rearing is a 'poisonous pedagogy' deriving from a 'pathological' parental need for control.

The former practice of physically maiming, exploiting, and abusing children seems to have been gradually replaced in modern times by a form of mental cruelty that is masked by the honorific term *child-rearing*. Since training in many cultures begins in infancy during the initial symbiotic relationship between mother and child, this early conditioning makes it virtually impossible for the child to discover what is actually happening to him. The child's dependence on his or her parents' love also makes it impossible in later years to recognize these traumatizations, which often remain hidden behind the early idealization of the parents for the rest of the child's life (4).

A variety of practices aimed at the enforcement of parental control, few of which would attract the attention of child protection agencies and many of which bore the *imprimatur* of the 'child expert', internalize at once love, violence and hierarchy. The analysis resonates with the Foucauldian shift from corporal to corporeal discipline and a carceral family which is 'not the daughter of laws, codes or the judicial apparatus' but of 'repression, rejection, exclusion, marginalization ... the formation of insidious leniencies, unavowable petty cruelties, small acts of cunning (307-8)'. Miller's psychoanalysis rooted public violence (war, genocide, mass murder) and self-directed violence (addiction, suicide) in parenting practices and social norms. Technologies of transference of 'poisonous pedagogy' implied cross-effects of gender: Christianne F. is a drug addict and Sylvia Plath committed suicide; Bartsch is a mass murderer of infants and Hitler and Hess of infantilized (as substandard riduculed) adults. The implication is that women exposed to such a pedagogy punish their child selves; men punish real children and infantalized adults. Miller's work, like Erikson's, had a wide readership and a subtle freeing effect for those captured by Foucault's disciplinary net.

Post-Erikson anthropological studies of childhood draw relationships between childhood and society in a cross-cultural context. Jill Korbin's *Child Abuse and Neglect* (1981) examined the relationship of cultural values and child-rearing practices to (idiosyncratic) child abuse. European cultures are at the wrong and dangerous end of scales which measure factors implicated in abuse: infant indulgence, maternal-infant contact, obedience training, expectations of compliance, kin involvement in child-raising. Corporal punishment values, cultural valuation of children and of certain kinds of children (healthy, male versus damaged or twin or female), and availability of social supports are implicated in child abuse, while methodologies associated with lower risks of idiosyncratic abuse in non-Western cultures are in somewhat short supply in the modern West. Korbin set out a three-tiered scheme for evaluating practices in a cross-cultural context which seeks to overcome the limits of emic and etic perspectives. She concluded that the outstanding feature of child abuse across cultures is its discovery and that assignment of causation varies widely. This strangeness about child abuse — its cyclical emergence, cultural reconstruction, differential disciplinary response and political manipulation — suggests that the construction of child abuse (and childhood) as a social problem is deeply conditioned by cultural mores and preoccupations (*cf.* Wolff 1988, McGillivray 1992).

Mariana Valverde's *The Age of Light, Soap, and Water* (1991) looked at social work during the major transitional age of Canadian society, the period from the 1880s to the first world war. This was the era of the evangelical social purity movement which in practice and discourse united moral, physical and social hygiene, religion and science, state and moral philanthropy, in a virtually seamless web. Social purity visions of childhood and the new Canada were intimately connected and symbolically identical. As a Vancouver 'race' agitator said, 'we must remember we are trying to evolve a Canadian race as well as a Canadian nation' (113). Child welfare social work, although state-funded and increasingly regulated and empowered (Ursel 1992; Chunn 1992), was entirely private, reflecting the reliance on 'private' moral initiative central to the liberal state. By constructing and ignoring a private moral realm, the liberal state can then claim to regulate what transpires within only where invited to do so by its constituents or their experts. The disciplinary divisiveness of United Kingdom and United States purity associations was not a feature of the Canadian movement. Canadian charity work had from the beginning of the period internalized a 'scientific' perspective and discourse (51). As almost everything was a 'moral' problem, the fields of social purity were boundless, the public-private line moveable at moral will.

While the movement imported ideas from abroad, sometimes without sufficient reflection on Canadian conditions — counting Winnipeg bedrooms for example, in the London slum 'lodger evil' construct of child sexual abuse — 'social purity' had a uniquely Canadian flavour. The popular discourse of natural and national purity provided powerful metaphors. The opening speaker at the 1896 meeting of the National Council of Women praised '[t]his vast Dominion, stretching as it does from ocean to ocean, endowed by nature so lavishly' and prophesied that 'surely by every sign and token, whether of natural resource or racial heritage, the future of Canada will be, must be, the golden future of a great and mighty nation' (45). The racial heritage was of course white, like the 'lavish' natural resources of pure water, untouched wilderness and a glacial empty North.

Despite close correlations of post-1870s child welfare and juvenile justice reforms in Canada with those of other jurisdictions, Canadian reform discourse was less about child protection than about regulating sexuality and eliminating vice and degeneracy. 'If Canada is to rear an imperial race, it will not be by children raised in slums', an Anglican clergyman stated in 1912 (138). In the regulation of childhood, sexuality, 'race' and 'blood', protection and coercion were indistinguishable. Valverde's study is an important reminder that the relations of childhood and society — expert tutelage, the regulatory role of the complex of bodies and agencies which comprise the state, the 'problem' of childhood, moral regulation, and the constitution of race, class, sexual and gender relations — are conditioned by social structures, cultures, geographies and nationalist aspirations. Childhood 'is' nationhood.

Psychoanalysis and cultural studies have begun to inform the critique of law. Law's mediative and repressive functions, modes of thought and production of subjectivity (the rational autonomous self which chooses compliance or noncompliance; the structuring of desire as legal or illegal, normal or deviant) invite analyses which account for relations between the self and the social. The psychoanalysis of law's subject is the project of David Caudill in his adaptation of the work of Jacques Lacan to the legal context. Caudill asked 'how are the hidden materials of culture and law like the hidden conflicts of personality disclosed by Freud?' (1995). As law is 'a major repository of our demands, and a major producer of gratification and frustration with respect to social desires', who 'we' are is of central significance. Law's subject is conditioned by childhood.

Cultural psychoanalysis as exemplified in the work of Lacan is 'analogous to bringing the unconscious into consciousness', thus integrating structuralist social analysis and psychoanalysis (Caudill 1991). The unconscious (which, as Freud and his followers taught, bears the residue of childhood) functions in '[e]veryday thought and clinical disorder'. Ego formation begins with an infant's recognition of an external image of her self. This 'mirror moment' forecloses direct contact with reality for contact forever mediated by the imaging of the Other integrated into the self. The child is in this moment and through this image bound to the social structure. To this idealized image or subject are addressed legal constructs of autonomy and freedom (*cf.* Caudill 1993). The subject is 'a subject of the unconscious, of psychoanalysis, of desire, of knowledge, of language, and of culture' which embraces internal and external, self and other. The self is 'decentred, split, and perhaps splintered', an objective 'I' set in opposition to the Other and confused with the subject, which includes it. The grammar of the first person places the 'I' or self as 'determinant or instrumental of action', 'an impossible mirage'. In *The Alchemy of Race and Rights* (1991), Patricia Williams, as Caudill observed, drew upon the Lacanian subject in her analysis of the subjectivity of race: 'The distancing does not stop with the separation of the white self from the black other ... [Blacks are] conditioned from infancy to see in themselves only what others, who despise them, see.' Recognizing 'hidden subjectivities and unexamined claims', Williams suggested, will lead to 'a more nuanced sense of legal and social responsibilities'.

Erikson, Miller, Lacan and others have applied knowledges and techniques of psychoanalysis and related discourse analysis to make connections between childhood and the constitution or ethos of a society. The focus of psychoanalytic and linguistic studies is not childhood or its management *per se*. Such studies are concerned rather with deep structures of law, society, language and subjectivity embedded in childhood, and with the relatedness of social structures to biosocial structures inherent in, or mediated by, the experience of childhood. Childhood 'is' society.

Directly concerned with legal discourse in the production of knowledge about children, the legal construction of childhood and the child as legal subject is King and Piper's *How the Law Thinks About Children* (1995). Teubner's theory of autopoiesis is used to examine the tension between legal discourse and child welfare discourse. Law is an autopoietic social system, recursively producing its elements from the network of its elements in the paradoxical self-referencing which characterizes all organizational discourse. Knowledge is internally produced and tested in procedures which ultimately are merely internal comparisons of different world views. Truths are differently generated and received by different autopoietic systems. While 'psychic' and 'social' systems are co-evolved and synchronistic, there is no overlap: the persons dealt with by law are 'mere constructs, semantic artifacts produced by the legal discourse itself', 'internal products of legal communications'. Legal discourse 'modifies the meaning of everyday world constructions and in case of conflict replaces them with legal constructions' (24-8).

Science, as a knowledge external to law, must support and legitimate law's normative accounts in order to be admitted into legal discourse. From a legal perspective, child welfare science lacks the necessary objectivity. Child welfare accounts are case-based, derived from psychoanalytic methods in which external validity or 'generalizability' is lost (45). Law produces 'not only versions of children, childhood, parents and parenthood as epistemic subjects, but also versions of child psychology'. These versions are 'reinforced by those self-selecting experts whose daily concerns and theoretical orientations ... draw them into law and then trap them within the legal discourse' (59). The hybrid discourse of law and psychology has produced six mutually exclusive constructs of the child: victim, witness, needs-bundle, rights-bearer (of 'limited practical utility'), object in custody disputes, criminal offender. Law's child is a semantic artifact.

The concerns raised by Teubner — that law colonizes other systems or creates hybrid discourses which violate other knowledges — are addressed in two ways. First, this may be a transitional stage in which other systems have raised awareness of the damage done to children by legal proceedings; the 'psy' sciences mitigate the damage. Second, Teubner may be read as referring only to legal judgments and not to their production, a much leakier epistemic exercise. Alternatively, encouraging 'child-responsiveness' by decentring legal discourse may be the answer to Teubner, through mediation, hearings in which child welfare discourse dominates, independent advocacy for the child and legal specialization.

As these varied works suggest or imply, forgrounding childhood in social and legal analysis, as the 'new child' was foregrounded in eighteenth-century portraiture, frees childhood discourse from its kiddie-law boundaries and sentimentalized separated discourses which ignore or obscure the dimensions of childhood. We gain critical perspectives which enrich the understanding of law, its claims and its tropes, and which illuminate the intimate relations of the social and the personal.

III. OBSERVATIONS

INTERNALIZING THE CIVILIZING DISCOURSE of the 'psy sciences' has not decreased occasions for the direct intervention of law and social work into childhood. Such interventions have continued to increase. These disciplines have contributed to the divided childhood reflected in public, judicial and agency discourse, deepening the gap between the innocent perishing child and the blameworthy offending child, between child as object in custody and protection disputes and child as legal subject, as rights-bearer, witness, victim, criminal. Such divisions are easily manipulated. Childhood is a lightning-rod for social problems. Children are scapegoats for events which are not of their making. 'Childhood' is a ready substitutes for 'race' in right-wing discourses of national desuetude. Reform agendas, particularly in juvenile justice, disclose the susceptibility of child law and the construction of childhood to political pressure, even as the 'psy' childhood sciences now struggle to close the gap.

Few of the works surveyed discuss the twin themes or driving forces of the post-1960s resurgence of childhood. These are child abuse and children's rights, the dark and bright sides of reform, the moral panics and the claims of moral entitlement which in one way or another have constituted the bulk of recent childhood discourse and fuel the controversy over the ownership of childhood. If childhood is the most intensively governed sector of human existence, its government is also the most contested.

It cannot be right that children's rights is a concept to be dismissed as lacking legal utility, as King and Piper stated. 'Children's rights' is an intentionally challenging discourse which is both intrinsic and extrinsic to law. Its claims have influenced ordinary legal discourse and added a new and provacative dimension to legislative reforms. Nor can it be right, as Rose intimates, that child abuse response is only a small, although highly visible, part of the tutelage of childhood. 'Child abuse' has informed that tutelage and given it the moral valence required to make tutelage a priority for parent and state. Nobody wants to be a child abuser, certainly not by mistake, as Rose himself has demonstrated. Ideas about child abuse and children's rights have gripped the public imagination, fed law reform, informed constitutional interpretation and international convention and ensured that childhood remains not only an open public matter but a matter open to more than one point of view, disciplinary or otherwise.

If there is an immediate point to childhood studies, it is the improvement of childhood conditions. Child abuse, however understood, has provided the impetus and children's rights the context for evaluating the government of childhood. If the wider aim is to gain insight into social ethos, structure, regulation and law, then the novel standpoint of childhood has proven a fertile ground of inquiry into historical regimes, economic theory and practices, family structuring, the constitution of subjectivity and desire, crime and punishment, colonization and resistance. Childhood provides the metaphors of innocence and experience, the duality which informs our understanding of morality and our construction of the social good.

'Governmentality' conveniently captures the conception and the regulation of childhood, drawing attention away from 'grand acts' of 'the state' to more intimate regimes, nuanced bilateral relations between childhood and society and the experience of everyday life. Instances of such government I leave in the capable hands of the contributors to this volume.

These include early intimations of state management of childhood, in the regulation of nineteenth-century French child street performers; a Denver court's unusual response to the gendering of delinquency in the Progressive Era; the impact of essentialism on the United States juvenile justice system and implications for the wider administration of justice; the creation of moral panic over a child killing in England, and the demonization of children for political ends; the colonization of Aboriginal childhood in Canada, its resonance with nineteenth-century modes of childhood governance and its political consequences; moral reasoning and the construction of the child citizen in United States judicial discourse on the family; and a rights-based tutorial strategy for a new politics of childhood which includes children in adult endeavours.

The essays by Schafer, Ainsworth, Freeman and Martineau were presented at panels titled 'Constructing Childhood: Ideologies of Governance' which I convened at meetings of the United States Law and Society Association and the Canadian Law and Society Association held respectively in Toronto and Montreal in June of 1995. Martha Minow was discussant on the Toronto panel and contributed the evocative Afterword to this book. The essay by Colomy and Kretzman was separately presented at the Toronto sessions. An earlier version of the essay on Aboriginal childhood was presented at the 1994 Phoenix meetings of the United States Law and Society Association.

Manuscript preparation was made possible by a grant from the Legal Research Institute of the University of Manitoba, the able and intelligent assistance of *Manitoba Law Journal* editors Michael Colborne and John-Paul Bogden, and the patience of Law School computer technician Ken Drewniak.

This book would not have come into being without the invitation and encouragement of Michael D.A. Freeman, a tireless scholar of childhood and the family, and longstanding champion of children and their rights.

Notes

1. The changes described were accompanied by reforms to statutory and judge-made law which resulted in greater procedural fairness for accused persons, legal certainty and other guarantees of civil liberty, and a general liberalizing of law antecedent to legal measures for the protection of children as victims, witnesses and offenders. The liberalizing of law and extension of rights made it possible to talk about rights for children.

2. Foucault also lists the disciplines of medicine, education, public assistance and social work as recipients of 'the ever more massive transference of judicial functions' and an 'ever greater share of the powers of supervision and assessment'. Power is materialized at the level of disciplinary technique, practice, observation, examination and investigation. These technologies are rooted in the methods of the Inquisition which gave rise to the scientific method for the examination of natural phenomena. When turned back on human study, these technologies are, for Foucault, inquisitorial in the worst sense. 'What Great Observer', he asks rhetorically, 'will produce [a less destructive] methodology for the human sciences?' 'Unless', he adds, 'such a thing is not possible'.

3. Rousseau was in exile in England shortly after the publication of *Emile*, from 1765 to 1767, which contributed to the work's popularity there. Locke's *Some Thoughts Concerning Education* (1693), which emphasized obedience training and the role of education as preparation for adult society, was highly influential in France, where it was read as equating 'the good' with personal pleasure and happiness. Locke thus encouraged a French belief in natural goodness, reflected in Rousseau's images of the innocent child and noble savage. 'The French response to Locke ultimately proved to be a vital factor in English childhood' (Steward 1995, 143). The segregation of the child in the English boarding school (which embodied Locke's theories of education) encouraged the 'cult' of childhood while facilitating its control and domination. On Locke's theories of childhood generally, see Archard (1993).

4. Cited in Steward (1995). One's own parenting will of course influence such evaluations. Wesley's mother Susannah was a strong advocate of corporal punishment and wrote of her children's infancy, '[w]hen turned a year old (and some before) they were taught to fear the rod and to cry softly, by which means they escaped abundance of correction which they might otherwise have had: and that most odious noise of the crying of children was rarely heard in the house, but the family usually lived in as much quietness as if there had not been a child among them.' Rousseau deposited his five infants by Therese Lavasseur one by one on the steps of the local foundling hospital. On protestantism and parenting, see Grevin (1991).

5. Blake's 'The Rose', for example, speaks to an intimate corruption which may be analogized to child sexual abuse. More famous depictions of the chimney sweep and the demonized, because unwanted, newborn speak directly to social conditions of the day.

6. The designation 'battered child syndrome' was a deliberate choice. The authors believed that to label as 'child abuse' the patterned bruising and bone fractures visible not only (as formerly) on autopsy, but through the x-ray of living children,

was an invitation to criminal sanctions. 'Abuse' suggests an 'abuser'. 'Syndrome' is by contrast a medical term, reflecting the authors' view that the appropriate intervention was medical and therapeutic rather than criminal. Politicization of domestic violence, and identification and study of other forms of parentally- and institutionally-induced harm to children favoured the more evocative term 'child abuse' (McGillivray 1992). Child abuse is, as many observers have pointed out, a term without specific meaning in medicine, child protection or criminal law, an unbounded category of blameworthy behaviour, thus quintessentially political.

7.   Two recent contributions of the 'Ariès school' should be mentioned here. In *Children in the House: The Material Culture of Early Childhood, 1600-1900* (1992), Karin Calvert uses artifacts of childhood — child furniture, toys, swaddling customs, Godeys Ladies Book and the like — to examine ideas about childhood and the treatment of young children in the United States, concluding that the 'conception' or 'sentiment' of childhood has undergone the shifts posited by Ariès. James Christen Steward's (1995) *The New Child: British Art and the Origins of Modern Childhood, 1730-1830,* deserves more than this brief note. The text is the thesis of an exhibition of works which I viewed at Berkeley in October 1995. Text and exhibition illustrate and contextualize the origins and nature of the 'new' childhood of the eighteenth century. Steward has redeemed the structural inadequacies of Ariès' study and brought it full circle in the context of family portraiture, in a sensitive and compelling depiction of the emergence of childhood and the contradictions exposed in that pictorial centring and celebration of the child and childhood.

8.   Corporal punishment in practice and law continues to define childhood in dangerous ways. This 'discipline' of childhood confuses necessary interference with the child's 'person' with darker parental conflicts. I cannot argue with this branch of child study. While it is limiting and ultimately self-defeating to define childhood in terms of ill-treatment and damage, the damage of such values and practices is real.

9.   We see hints of the complexity of family privacy in the works of Stone, Pollock, Foucault and Rose. Tutelage as a form of governmentality is private in that it is directed at the individual conscience; it is also public, a linking system of state and subject which reinforces the ideology of privacy from state intervention at each moment it is most thoroughly breached. The architecture of surveillance is captured in Jeremy Bentham's Panopticon, an arrangement of space which centres and exposes the subject to the hidden observer, a reverse of the dungeon and *oubliette* (and of the private attic spaces which housed the nursery and hid the mad). Prisons, schools and juvenile institutions adopted the new panoptical architecture as its reverse was reflected in the design of private housing. The

architecture of privacy is inversely related to the architecture of surveillance. The hallway and dumbwaiter were seventeenth-century inventions which kept the servants out of the bedroom and dining room, decreasing surveillance (Stone 1979), as did central heating later; detached housing for the lower classes decreased the surveillance of neighbours. Implications for domestic violence are clear. 'It's hard to beat your wife when the neighbours are around', as anthropologist Richard Lee remarked to me in a discussion of the 'remarkable' invention of privacy. Childhood was notably exempt from the new privacy. Much expert attention was given to sleeping arrangements. Children should sleep separately from each other and all adults, but should their rooms surround those of their parents for ready observation? How is one-way observation to be achieved, protecting the parental bed? (The Fisher-Price baby monitor is the modern technocratic solution.) In the 'new childhood', Bentham's Panopticon was represented by a tutored parental omnipresence which was to let no accomplishment or transgression of the child go unmarked. The ideology of privacy gained political ascendence with John Stuart Mill's demarcation of state interests in his essay *On Liberty*, in an age which saw the emergence of mandatory universal schooling which would inculcate common moral values, the legal and disciplinary enhancement of charitable intervention into childhood, and an increasingly tutored interest in the minutiae of childhood. Architectural privacy contributed to the appearance of a private governance of childhood; this privacy, conversely, is implicated in child abuse and other forms of intimate violence.

10. Some links are in parentheses: '(one day we should show how intrafamilial relations have become 'disciplined' ...)' and '([a] whole study remains to be done of the debates that took place during the Revolution concerning family courts, paternal correction and the right of parents to lock up their children)'. (Foucault 1979, 216; 297).

11. Donzelot closed with the account of the prisoner who read his dossier. It listed his psychological problems and bad deeds but said nothing of his aspirations or of what he had loved. He wrote a note to that effect and killed himself.

12. These studies were commissioned as part of a series for the United States Bureau of Indian Affairs. The Bureau was concerned about 'demoralization' and 'degeneration' of Indian tribes and their 'obstinate' resistance to re-education (Rose 1989). Erikson's observations do not seem to advance this assimilationist agenda.

References

I. Works Referenced

Archard, David (1993) *Children, Rights and Childhood* (Routledge).

Ariès, Philippe (1962), *Centuries of Childhood: A Social History of Family Life* (Jonathan Cape).

Calvert, Karin (1992), *Children in the House: The Material Culture of Early Childhood, 1600-1900* (Boston).

Caudill, David (1991), 'Freud and Critical Legal Studies: Contours of a Radical Socio-Legal Psychoanalysis' 66 Indiana Law Journal 65.

_____. (1995), 'Lacanian Ethics and the Desire for Law' 16 Cardozo Law Review 793.

_____. (1993), 'Pierre Schlag's 'The Problem of the Subject': Law's Need for an Analyst' 15 Cardozo Law Review 707.

Chunn, Dorothy E. (1992), *From Punishment to Doing Good: Family Courts and Socialized Justice in Ontario 1890-1940* (University of Toronto Press).

Coles, Robert (1970), *Erik H. Erikson: The Growth of His Work* (Little, Brown).

deMause, Lloyd (1974), *The History of Childhood* (Psychohistory Press).

Donzelot, Jacques (1979), *The Policing of Families* (Hutchinson).

Eekelaar, John (1986), 'The Emergence of Children's Rights' 6 Oxford Journal of Legal Studies 161.

Erikson, Erik (1963), *Childhood and Society* (2d) (Norton).

Foucault, Michel (1979), *Discipline and Punish: The Birth of the Prison* (Vintage).

Kempe, C. *et al.*(1962), 'The Battered Child Syndrome' 181 Journal of the American Medical Association 17.

King, Michael and Christine Piper (1995), *How the Law Thinks About Children* (2d.) (Arena).

Korbin, Jill (1981), *Child Abuse and Neglect: Cross-Cultural Perspectives* (University of California Press).

McGillivray, Anne (1992), 'Reconstructing Child Abuse: Western Definition and Non-Western Experience' in M.D.A. Freeman and P. Veerman (eds.), *The Ideologies of Children's Rights* (Martinus Nijhoff) 213.

Miller, Alice (1984), *For Your Own Good: Hidden Cruelty in Child-Rearing and the Roots of Violence* (Farrar, Straus and Giroux).

Pollock, Linda (1987), *A Lasting Relationship: Parents and Children Over Three Centuries* (Fourth Estate).

_____. (1983), *Forgotten Children: Parent-Child Relations from 1500-1800* (Cambridge University Press).

Rose, Nikolas (1989), *Governing the Soul: The Shaping of the Private Self* (Routledge).

Rousseau, Jean-Jacques (1762), *Emile, or On Education*.

Shorter, Edward L. (1975), *The Making of the Modern Family* (Basic Books).

Steward, James C. (1995), T*he New Child: British Art and the Origins of Modern Childhood* (University of California Press).

Stone, Lawrence (1975), *The Family, Sex and Marriage in England 1500-1800* (Penguin).

Ursel, Jane (1992), *Private Lives, Public Policy: 100 Years of State intervention in the Family* (Women's Press).

Valverde, Mariana (1991), *The Age of Light, Soap and Water: Moral Reform in English Canada, 1885-1925* (McClelland & Stewart).

Williams, Patricia J. (1991), *The Alchemy of Race and Rights: The Diary of a Law Professor* (Harvard University Press).

Wolff, Larry (1988), *Postcards from the End of the World: Child Abuse in Freud's Vienna* (Atheneum).

II. Works Considered

Finkelhor, David and Jill Korbin (1988), 'Child Abuse as an International Issue' 12 Child Abuse & Neglect 3.

Freeman, Michael D.A. and Philip Veerman, eds. (1992), *The Ideologies of Children's Rights* (Martinus Nijhoff).

Freeman, Michael D.A. (1992), 'The Limits of Children's Rights' in Freeman and Veerman, *supra.*

_____. (1983), *The Rights and Wrongs of Children* (Pinter).

Grevin, Philip (1991), *The Religious Roots of Punishment and the Psychological Impact of Physical Abuse* (Knopf).

McGillivray, Anne (1990), 'Child Abuse in the Courts: Adjusting the Scales after Bill C-15' 19 Manitoba Law Journal 549.

_____. ' "He'll learn it on his body": Disciplining Childhood in Canadian Law' (unpublished).

_____. (1991), 'Forgetting Children, Forgetting Truth' 6 Criminal Reports (4th) 325.

_____. (1993), 'Legitimating Brutality' 16 Criminal Reports (4th) 125.

_____. (1994), 'Why Children Do Have Equal Rights: In Reply to Laura Purdy' 2 International Journal of Children's Rights 243.

McNay, Louise (1994), *Foucault: A Critical Introduction* (Continuum).

Nedelsky, Jennifer (1993), 'Reconceiving Rights as Relationship' 1 Review of Constitutional Studies 1.

Olsen, Fran (1983), 'The Family and the Market: A Study of Ideology and Legal Reform' Harvard Law Review 1497.

_____. (1985), 'The Myth of State Intervention in the Family' 18 Journal of Law Reform 835.

Parton, Nigel (1985), *The Politics of Childhood* (Macmillan).

Smart, Carol, ed. (1992), *Regulating Womanhood: Historical Essays on Marriage, Motherhood and Sexuality* (Routledge).

Straus, Murray A. (1994), *Beating the Devil Out of Them: Corporal Punishment in American Families* (Lexington).

Sullivan, Terrence (1992), *Sexual Abuse and the Rights of Children: Reforming Canadian Law* (University of Toronto Press).

I

Law, Labour and the Spectacle of the Body: Protecting Child Street Performers in Nineteenth-Century France

I. INTRODUCTION

'CHILD ABUSE', philosopher Ian Hacking reminds us, 'is not one fixed thing'.[1] Indeed, understandings of 'abuse' have been articulated in quite distinct ways in different historical and geographical settings. This is particularly true where conceptions of 'abuse', that is, conceptions of the moral limits of adult power over children, emerge in the terrain of law. Reading 'abuse' as inexorably shaped by a bounded universe of possible meanings and institutional frames, reveals more than the term's historical instability, however. It also reveals the very concrete ways in which the juridical redefinition of these limits transforms fundamental relationships between adults, children and the state. Re-marking the limits of adult power, or recasting the 'truth' of 'abuse', Hacking notes, also transforms the individuals involved in these relationships.

There is not strictly a truth of the matter that, once discovered, will remain the truth, for once it is counted as true and becomes common knowledge, it will change the very individuals — abusers and children — about whom it was supposed to be the truth.[2]

By the late nineteenth century, reformers in many western nations had seized upon these questions about the multivalent relationships between the state, adults and children as central to their quest to regulate children's experiences of home, school and workplace.[3] Perhaps nowhere were these issues raised with greater intensity — and greater ambivalence — than in

France in the early 1870s. The shock of the rapid German victory in the Franco-Prussian War of 1870, the horror aroused by the radicalism of the Paris Commune, and the recent discovery of France's low birth rate combined to persuade observers from across the political spectrum that state intervention in the family might be the only solution to the nation's precarious geopolitical, social and demographic situation.

The government of the French Third Republic, formed when Emperor Napoleon III was captured by the Germans in September 1870, took the regulation of childhood as one of its first arenas of action.[4] Between January and December of 1874, the National Assembly passed three child protection laws that together comprised a powerful new challenge to the long-standing legal and cultural sanctity of paternal authority in France.[5] Until that moment, apart from the brief interlude of the revolution of 1789, adult authority over children, and especially the legal consecration of 'natural' paternal authority, remained essentially unchallenged in the French juridical tradition.[6] By questioning the inherited logic that grounded paternal autonomy in natural right, the new child protection laws of 1874 and the debates they engendered served to open a new discursive field. They provided the arena and the conceptual foundation for developing a notion of protective governmental intervention within the context of a nascent liberal order. In doing so, they recast essential understandings of parental identity, authority and responsibility, and significantly expanded the borders of the social terrain in which the state could legitimately act 'in the interest of the child'.

The first of these laws, enacted in May, addressed the employment of children in industry, setting new standards for the length of the child's workday and the conditions of his or her labour.[7] The second, promulgated in early December 1874, imposed new restrictions on the employment of children in the 'itinerant professions', a rough grouping of outdoor, performance-based occupations ranging from street musician to acrobat to 'professional beggar'. The third law, passed later that same month, addressed the treatment of infants, an issue of vital concern in a country terrified of the effects of its declining birthrates and high rates of infant mortality. This law imposed a new regulatory structure on the wet nursing industry.[8]

All three of the 1874 protection laws contributed essential elements to the wider effort to develop new notions of 'danger' and 'responsibility' that might in turn redescribe the boundaries between children, parental authority and the authority of the state. All three of the new laws also raised critical questions about the child's body as the object of an inappropriate use of adult power, that is, as the object of possible abuse or exploitation. Finally, all three forged important new connections between the moral status of the parent who exposed his or her child to 'danger' — be it in the factory, the performative arena of the street, or the home of the wet nurse — the physical vulnerabilities of the child's body, and the child's present and future moral character. In short, all three laws cast the child's body as the site of two intersecting sets of conflated dangers: first, the danger of physical harm and the danger of moral degeneration; and second, the dangers posed to the child's body and those posed to the social body.[9]

While the three laws worked in concert to begin to redefine the parent, the child, and the nature of governmental authority, as well as the relationships between them, each one also delineated a distinctive terrain of regulation and a set of unique concerns. This essay focuses on the second of the three protective laws enacted in 1874: the law on the employment of children in the 'itinerant professions'. This measure and the debates it engendered crystallized many of the themes raised in the discussion of the two other laws that year. The discussions surrounding it similarly threw contemporary questions about the limits of parental authority, as well as the limits of the state's capacity — and right — to regulate that authority, into especially sharp relief.

The discourse on children in the itinerant professions also reveals its own quite particular features. The proposal and promulgation of the law served to articulate a common juridical understanding of the dangers threatening children whose work was essentially defined as 'performative' rather than productive. Further, in their focus on popular entertainment and its effects, the debates on the law provide an especially revealing window onto the legislative efforts to contain broader contemporary anxieties about a moral order increasingly seen as tied both to the proper exercise of parental power and the policing of public space.

The issues that emerged in the debates around the law on the employment of children in the itinerant professions were thus critical to the juridical recasting of the family, the state and their respective protective duties in the later nineteenth century. Most importantly, the debates about the possible 'abuse' of child performers reveal how the opposition between public and private, a distinction firmly embedded in Napoleonic law, was eroding under the concern about the demoralizing influence of public spectacle — including street performance — and the concurrent anxiety about the ability of the 'modern' family to maintain moral order in the 'private' space of the home.

By drawing these new distinctions in 1874, and by challenging established legal boundaries between public and private life, lawmakers and social reformers would lay an important part of the groundwork for articulating later notions of 'abuse' that would resituate the scene of 'abuse' from the public space of the street and the world of contractual relations to the more intimate space of the family and the world of domestic relations.

II. PATERNAL AUTHORITY AND THE NAPOLEONIC NORM

EFFORTS TO RETHINK PARENTAL AUTHORITY and its limits in late nineteenth-century France brought legislators into direct confrontation with their Napoleonic legacy. In the first decades of the nineteenth century, Emperor Napoleon Bonaparte had overseen the rationalization of the diverse legal traditions inherited from pre-revolutionary and revolutionary France into 'modern' written code.[10] The codes, and especially the civil code, or *Code Napoléon*, served as the bedrock of family law in nineteenth- century France, as well as in several nations conquered by France during the Napoleonic Wars.[11] In France, the codes stood as the inescapable frame of reference for all subsequent legislative reform; they described the horizon of legal thought from the early nineteenth-century forward.

The Napoleonic codes also imposed structural limits on reform. In the context of a written code, those who sought to remake the field of French justice inevitably had to return to the language and the logic of the law itself in order to construct arguments for new legislation that might override original Napoleonic statutes. Precedent and custom, so crucial to the elaboration of law in the Anglo-American tradition, had no place in the strictly ordered realm of the French codes.[12] Most important for considering the sketching of early notions of abuse, Napoleonic law — and the more general discourse it generated — inscribed powerful notions of 'natural' parental authority, paternal power, and the proper relations between parents and children against which reformers had to cast their arguments for change.

What did these naturalized notions of authority and familial relations look like? Drawing with particular vigour on Roman law traditions, Napoleonic law described a family where a barely-regulated exercise of paternal power, founded in the laws of nature, served as the foundation of domestic and civil order.[13] While mothers were explicitly included in a few articles defining 'parental' powers and filial duties, moreover, a reading of the civil code as a whole makes clear that in the case of married couples, 'parental authority' (*l'autorité parentale*) was in fact identical with '*paternal* authority' (*la puissance paternelle*). To paraphrase article 373, the parental powers vested in married couples were in practice to be wielded by the father and the father alone.[14]

French civil law placed few restrictions on the exercise of parental power, at least where male heads-of-household were concerned. One of the primary limits on this authority was temporal rather than qualitative: the age of majority. According to the *Code Napoléon*, sons and daughters remained fully subject to paternal authority until the age of twenty-one, except when parents voluntarily emancipated them earlier in their lives, for example, when parents approved an underage child's marriage.[15]

Elsewhere, the Civil Code firmly underscored the authority of the male head-of-household over his offspring. For example, the Code forbade minors to leave their father's household without his permission. In the case of a child's 'extreme insubordination', the father of the family could invoke his 'right of correction', that is, the right to have his progeny incarcerated for a fixed period of time upon simple demand to the local justice. The father also maintained control of his children's property, excepting wages and goods earned independently of the family, or those given to the child under the express condition that they *not* be subject to paternal control. In exchange for the juridical guarantee of his paternal rights, the father was obliged to support his children and to provide an upbringing appropriate to the family's social rank. He had also to accept legal responsibility for the debts his children incurred while underage, and for expenses resulting from their illness or death.[16]

Despite the articulation of these few parental responsibilities, the bulk of the Civil Code's sections on family law embodied a secular consecration of a paternal power founded in 'nature' and serving the social good by assuring an ordered domestic sphere. In this way, the French Civil Code crystallized the nexus of natural right and social exigency into enforceable — and culturally viable — statutory justice for the nineteenth century.

The Napoleonic criminal code, promulgated several years after the *Code Napoléon*, affirmed by its reticence the Civil Code's notion of extensive paternal power protected in most areas from the sanctioning authority of the state.[17] Indeed, only three articles out of the several hundred comprising the body of French criminal law cast the ties between parents and children as a unique type of legal relationship or signalled familial relations as a special area of criminal justice. The first of these articles allowed the court to remove minors who had been acquitted of crimes from the physical custody (*la garde*) of their parents when the paternal household appeared to provide an unacceptable moral environment for their rehabilitation.[18]   While this provision did not strip parents of their formal legal authority over their children, it transferred the ultimate determination of the child's best interest from parent to magistrate, and positioned the parent as the direct object of legal regulation.

The second and third articles to suggest a special juridical category for the parent-child relationship allowed the state to bring criminal charges against parents who had been implicated in the prostitution of their own children (*'l'excitation habituelle des mineurs à la débauche'*).[19]   As part of a comprehensive written penal code, these articles also described the range of possible punishments. If convicted, parents had to serve two to five years of a prison sentence and pay a fine of three hundred to one thousand francs. In addition, the second article empowered magistrates to suspend all rights of custody and trusteeship from parents convicted of prostituting their own children. The suspension could last for a period of ten to twenty years. Finally, the measures called for the court to strip these mothers and fathers of all rights of parental authority (*la puissance paternelle*) and allowed for extended periods of discretionary police surveillance to ensure that the sentence was being observed.

Although limited in their scope and rarely applied, these criminal measures would become important weapons in the arsenal of precedents collected by the reformers of the early 1870s.[20]   In particular, this handful of articles from the Napoleonic penal code permitted the further elaboration of two critical questions: the question of the parent's relationship to the body of the child, and especially to the body as the material site of the child's moral development; and the question of how moral environment might figure into new definitions of 'endangerment' or 'abuse'.

Equally important, these early nineteenth-century measures suggested the possibility that the exercise of parental authority could, in certain circumstances, be subject to external assessment and regulation. In other words, Napoleon criminal law provided the thin edge of the wedge that would eventually dislodge its own foundational notions of natural and inviolable parental rights and posit instead an understanding of parental power — and the possible abuse of that power — set firmly in the realm of the social.

III. CHILDREN IN THE ITINERANT PROFESSIONS: THE DEBATES OF 1874

OVER THE COURSE OF 1874, the French legislature devoted several of its sessions to discussing a report and bill on 'children in itinerant trades' presented by Deputy Eugene Tallon in March.[21] Tallon, following the lines of debate laid out in the discussions of children in industrial labour earlier in the year, focused on the importance of state protection as a means of restricting 'abusive' or exploitative labour practices. In this instance, however, the proposed legislation addressed a quite different type of work: children's labour as street musicians, acrobats, carnival performers and 'professional' beggars.

Although children's work experiences were at issue in the debates on both industrial and performative labour, recognizing the contemporary resonances of the distinction between them is essential for understanding both the course of the debate on child performers and its historical significance. Where productive labour in manufacturing and agriculture represented the essence of 'work' for many middle and working-class observers in nineteenth-century France, street performance denoted an unsavoury disruption of this under-standing: it presented an opaque spectacle of 'work' that might easily mask the face of dangerously 'immoral' mendicancy.[22]

The paradoxical concern about the hypervisibility of public performance and its concurrent moral illegibility ran through the assembly's debates about protecting children in the itinerant trades. Four main themes emerged in the course of the debates: the extent of the state's right to regulate 'private' commercial activity; the extent of parents' moral responsibility in the 'exploitation' of their own children; the legal — and moral — differences between a *patron* unrelated to his child workers and a parent who employed his own offspring; and finally, the difference between the legitimate and illegitimate extraction of labour power from a child's body.

According to Tallon's report, children in the itinerant trades comprised a special category of child labourers and were thus in particular need of protection. The risks they faced were not identical to the risks of industrial production so vilified earlier in the year in the debates on protecting child industrial workers. Instead, child street performers appeared to confront the physical and moral 'perils' of 'abandonment, ignorance, and demoralization' that defined traveling performance as a distinctive, non-productive form of labour.[23]   Their lives were marked not by the persistent and debilitating exhaustion that accompanied productive work within the enclosed space of the factory, but by a lack of geographical fixity, by the moral dangers at large in public space. 'The actions, the examples, the spectacles that the mature and experienced adult sees each day without paying them any attention', Tallon declared, 'profoundly strike the child's spirit, penetrating his heart and leaving there the germ of his future sentiments.'[24]   In the public byways, child performers were exposed to physical and moral risk, not in the name of production, but in the name of entertainment; their work was to satisfy popular appetites for spectacle, or, in the case of 'intentionally' maimed or disfigured children who accompanied beggars, 'to draw compassion' — and coins — from passersby.[25]   For Tallon and his committee, corrupting dissimulation defined the essence of children's public performance and distinguished its dangerous qualities from those enumerated earlier by the critics of industrial production.[26]

The issue of how to attribute responsibility for endangerment comprised another central element in the debate on child street performers and beggars. Although Tallon asserted that the majority of children involved in the itinerant trades were not in fact employed by their own parents, he nevertheless blamed parents for the dangers their children faced in the hands of others. In his view, employment by adults other than one's own relatives constituted a common and more or less accepted structure of industrial production. In the professions centred on human display, however, it signalled an unnatural commerce in bodies. Parents who 'sold' their children into the ambulant trades, or who simply allowed them to be used as performers or as props for adult beggars, turned their offsprings' bodies into marketable commodities.[27]   They engaged in a human traffic that violated the 'natural' protective law of parental affection. Tallon could barely contain his disgust for this sort of commerce: 'the sale of children [is] the greatest abuse of paternal authority that the legislator could ever repress'. To underscore his point, Tallon invoked the authority of Marcel Du Camp's widely-read account of the Parisian under-classes, *Paris et ses organes*, directly quoting Du Camp's assessment of these employment practices as comprising a 'monstrous commerce'.[28]

In stressing the immoral trade in children between parent and *patron*, Tallon and other reformers in the assembly struggled to uncouple the proposed law from the discourse of danger and protection that had underpinned the new law protecting children in industrial production. Most important, they reassigned the positive and negative moral valences among industrial *patron*, itinerant *patron* and biological parent. Looking back at an early but extremely limited effort towards the protection of child industrial workers dating from the 1840s, one legislator compared street performance to factory labour in these terms. In the case of manufacturing, he argued, 'it was a matter of children entrusted to industries that constituted the glory and wealth of the country'. In the itinerant trades, on the other hand, 'it is a matter of miserable wretches who are, in contrast, ... the object of an odious specula-tion'.[29] Tallon likewise differentiated here between 'respectable' industrial labour and labour in the service of travelling performers, even when those performers were the child's own parents. Where ordinary 'honest' labour in industrial production might allow the child 'to raise his condition through thriftiness', in performative labour the child's good qualities 'are lost in base occupations, where, after long years of suffering, he finds nothing but demoralization and degradation'.[30]

The inversion of the arguments and valuations that had paved the way for the passage of industrial labour legislation earlier in the year extended still further. As lawmakers thinking about itinerant labour and abuse recast industrial employment as the poor child's salvation, so arguments that once had protected paternal territory from external regulation in matters of child labour became the objects of protest and derision. For example, when one Deputy Chévandier stated his fear during the debates on protecting children in the itinerant professions that '[in the] name of freedom itself you would commit, simultaneously, a double offense against the freedom of labour and the freedom of the *père de famille*', an argument that had essentially won the day in the limiting the reach of industrial regulation, he was roundly booed by many of his fellow members of the assembly.[31]

Tallon and the legislative commission he represented, on the other hand, were adamant about the importance of applying the proposed law directly to the *père de famille*. 'It is legitimate', Tallon wrote in his report, 'to protect the child against all those who would turn him from the path of morality, utility, and hard work', even the child's own parents, if the child's interests were threatened and the good of society was at stake.[32] Initiating a child into such 'immoral' professions as the itinerant trades, he added, was a violation of one of the Civil Code's most fundamental definitions of parental duty: 'the obligation to feed, support, and raise [one's] children.'[33] When the aforemen-tioned Chévandier contended that the force of natural 'paternal feeling' would ensure that no father would do intentional harm to his own children, Tallon replied that sentiment was no longer an acceptable guarantee against abuse:

'Sadly, the facts are there to prove to you that affection is not always strong enough, although I'd like to believe it exists in the hearts of all fathers.'[34] In putting the 'natural' benevolent paternal instinct to the test of empirical observation, Tallon also implicitly invoked the logic of the developing social sciences, suggesting that it was in debates such as these that the ahistorical 'natural' family was coming to be supplanted in legislative discourse by a family rooted in the empirically-constructed — and hence governable — realm of the social.[35]

Anxiety about the father's legitimate rights over his children's bodies resonated with particular force in the sub-debate about acrobatics and contortionism as 'family trades'. Chévandier, for example, ever the advocate of the free market and paternal authority within it, contended that fathers had the right to train their children for work in the family occupation even if that occupation was contortionism and the training in question entailed the 'unnatural' manipulation of limbs (*'exercices de dislocation'*). The child's body, he argued, was naturally flexible; such training entailed no pain so long as the contorted positions were achieved gently and gradually. Again he asserted his faith in the father's ability to govern himself and his family. 'Paternal feeling', Chévandier declared, 'keeps watch as much under the poor saltimbanque's tent as in the house of the artisan or the rich man. I am convinced that the family father does not expose his child to dangerous maneuvers out of sheer wantonness ...'[36]

Chévandier's suggestion that protective paternal feeling effectively patrolled the border between painful abuse and honourable training in a family tradition inspired other legislators to make their own distinctions and, in the end, helped draw protective boundaries around the state's power to limit paternal power where fathers passed a performative 'skill' on to their offspring. Thus French lawmakers revised the draft of the bill to focus exclusively upon 'maneuvers of such a violence and brutality that they risk the safety and even the lives' of the child performers. In this category, they put high wire acts and acrobatic performances where children were tossed high in the air. Against Chévandier's wishes, they also included contortionism in this category. 'We cannot', a more liberal legislator argued, 'confuse contortionism, a violent assault on childhood, with exercises like those practiced in music ...'[37]

Amid the articulation of these types of oppositions, the final draft of the proposal also created a set of distinctions that permitted parents some degree of exclusion from the regulatory force of the law. Their exclusion was not as definitive, however, as it had been in the case of regulating children's labour in industry. There legislators explicitly omitted parents who employed their own children from the category of employers subject to the protective law's provisions. By contrast, the law on the itinerant professions held parents directly accountable, at least under certain conditions. Equally important, it subjected those found guilty of exploiting or endangering their children to punishments that struck squarely at their civil identities as parents. The law enacted in December 1874 thus prohibited the use of children under sixteen for performance in the travelling professions, but allowed parents to employ their own children in their performances once they reached the age of twelve. Parents would violate the law, however, if they employed any of their own children under age twelve or allowed their children to work as street performers for other adult *patrons*. As possible punishment for these infractions, the law empowered the court to strip parents or legal guardians of all parental rights in those cases where magistrates saw fit to do so.[38]

Despite the heated exchanges between Tallon and Chévandier, the proposed measures regulating children's work in the itinerant professions aroused surprisingly little contestation in the National Assembly as a whole. The relative lack of controversy may have been produced through a strategy of pre-emptive argument; in his initial report, Tallon engaged in an elaborate defense of the state's right — embodied in the court's prerogative — to evaluate the fulfillment of parental duty. According to Tallon, the legislature could treat parental authority and obligation only as legally-defined attributes, assimilated into an undiscriminating system of juridically-based civil rights. '*La puissance paternelle*', he argued, 'is, like all other rights, governed in modern legislation by civil law ... law which, in consecrating parental right, also defines its duties...'. Tallon further stressed the legal precedents for denying parents custody of and authority over their children. 'If the father neglects his duty', he argued, citing article 203 of the Civil Code, 'a verdict from the court may dispossess him of his authority.' Tallon also noted the first child labour law of 1841, an 1851 law regulating the apprenticeship of minors, as well as recent legislation in Italy on the itinerant professions, as products of the 'legislator's right to intervene' in order to protect the intersecting interests of children and society as a whole.[39]

The rendering of the relationship between parent and society embedded in Tallon's narrative of legislative innovation was crucial for the justification of expanding the state's right to participate in parenthood. In Tallon's analysis, the limits of parental authority extended only so far as parents fulfilled their social duty to raise their offspring and no further. When the balance between authority and duty became skewed by parental 'cupidity' or self-interest, it constituted a 'criminal excess' and required external redress. 'As for the deprivation of the rights of *la puissance paternelle* and the removal from guardianship', Tallon argued, 'it would seem the appropriate sanction ... against those who have violated the laws of nature, of affection and of duty'.[40] Thus, although Tallon accorded 'paternal feeling' the status of a natural attribute, he suppressed the possibility of a natural origin that might imply that parental rights superseded civil law.   Instead, he argued that '*la puissance paternelle*' was essentially a social attribute, and as such, subject to socially-encoded moral standards. In his reading, nature could be admitted to the discussion of paternal rights only insofar as it did not contradict the social and juridical definition of parental obligation.

IV.   CONCLUSION: 'ABUSE' AND 'NATURAL' RIGHT

THE ENACTMENT OF LEGISLATION regulating children's labour in the itinerant trades in 1874 marked an important moment of transition from the 1804 Civil Code's consecration of 'nature' to new juridical understanding of the proper government of the family. In this new order, the stamp of nature would appear only as a rhetorical shadow in the articulation of a social order based on and regulated by laws for which society, not nature, provided the crucial frame of reference. It was this shift that made it possible for legislators to embark on their project of redefining the limits of adult authority, and, most of all, the authority of the biological father. 'Abuse' within the family, in other words, could only be imagined once paternal power was discursively dislodged from the realm of the 'natural'.

To 'denature' paternal authority, however, was to cut across the grain of acquired juridical and cultural 'truths'. It challenged the dominant understandings of familial and gender relations that shaped the lives of French families as well as contemporary representations of the family that circulated in novels, plays, short fiction and visual images.[41] How then can Tallon's and other legislators' apparent willingness to overturn Napoleonic tradition and especially its reliance on 'nature' as a referent for the juridical ordering of the family be explained? In part, the passage of the 1874 law on children in the itinerant professions was facilitated by the fact that the penal code already contained provisions by which the courts could strip parents of their rights under certain conditions, especially when the criminal conviction of a parent resulted in the loss of all other civil rights. Ironically, then, the Napoleonic legal codes themselves provided legislators with some of the most essential tools for transforming the foundation of family law when circumstances seemed to call for a substantial reconfiguration of the relationship between government and governed, as they apparently did in the years following the 'terrible year' of 1870-71.

The intensifying wider efforts to shift the ground of the family and its rights from the realm of nature to the realm of the social may also have played a critical role in disarming the critics of the proposed law. In fact, 'nature' was becoming an increasingly untenable as a general foundation for the law of the late nineteenth century. As sociologist and legal theorist François Ewald puts it, by the end of the century 'law referred less to nature than to society ... Law became social and corrective: re-establishing destroyed balances, reducing inequalities through the redistribution of social responsibilities'.[42] In 1874, the process of moving nature to the margins was only just beginning, but even these preliminary gestures yielded surprising results. If any kind of epistemological break can be found in the late nineteenth-century reform of Napoleonic law, it may well be in this subtle but monumental shifting between these fields of reference.

The legislative turn away from nature can also be attributed to the Third Republic's enthusiasm for science. Among militant republicans in particular, Comtean positivism grounded the sense that humankind was not subject to nature, but that nature could be put to the service of humankind. To be sure, scientific and social scientific researchers in this era devoted themselves to the project of discovering the 'laws' of nature and society through empirical investigation. Nevertheless, their project was in no way identical to grounding social order in natural law. Rather, 'law' came to signify the law of empirical observation and prediction.[43]

The political disincentives for referring to nature were perhaps as powerful as the epistemological ones. In the legislative arena, accepting the authority of nature in matters of law or social policy may have seemed dangerously close to an acceptance of some kind of divine origin of natural law, a notion that would have been anathema to the anti-clerical, anti-monarchist Republicans of the 1870s and 1880s. Overall, another historian has argued, the Third Republic had little stake in finding its proper metaphysics, whether in a spiritual or a natural order.[44]

Paradoxically, however, despite their pronounced distaste for nature as referent in politics or social theory, liberal republicans continued to refer their discussions of the family, albeit at an increasingly remote level, to a notion of a natural moral order. In fact, the realm of family law, so deeply tied in the late nineteenth century to questions of reproduction, was perhaps the last to make the transition from the natural to the social grid.

The persistent but increasingly vague invocation of nature should not, however, be confused with an epistemological or discursive reliance on it. Even as they spoke of natural order, the reformers of the early Third Republic were engaged in a process of radical detachment. Indeed, it was by working the paradox of nature as social referent for the family against itself that the lawmakers began to delimit a widened terrain of child protection.

This shift, to be sure, was neither simple nor complete. Uncertain in the 1870s whether they were actually violating natural law in subordinating paternal authority to the abstract authority of the state, legislators and critics continued their ambivalent circling of nature. Invoking it, partially, critically, obliquely, and uncomfortably, they simultaneously looked for other ways of justifying their intrusion into the 'natural' order of the family.

In the debate on the law on the employment of children in itinerant performance, the challenge to the sacred or natural rights of parenthood became most tenable where legislators explicitly delineated the populations and spaces to which it would be applied. Like the laws regulating the apprenticeship and industrial employment of minors, this law also only operated beyond 'the threshold of the father's home'. The law's authors posited it in a social space constituted by a presumed breakdown of family life; the law regulated family relations only where the state could defend itself from the accusation that it had crossed the forbidden border between it and the still ideologically sacrosanct domestic life of its citizens. The abuses suffered by children in the itinerant trades, lawmakers like Tallon argued, thus sprang from the fact that they worked and lived in the unregulated spaces of public display, commodification, and the circulation of strangers.[45] In this description of the dangers of public space and the commodification of the child's body in that space, legislators also returned to the Napoleonic penal code's early provisions for regulating parental power; in this frame, all public performance could be analogized to prostitution and thus subjected to legal intervention without destabilizing prevailing understandings of parental right.

Raising questions of commodification and the public market for bodies to put to use in the creation of spectacle were not the only means of isolating a particularly problematic social space of family relations. There was also the question of itinerance itself.[46] A wide-spread and historically deep-rooted fear of transience, both geographical and social, provided lawmakers with yet another cultural validation of their desire to protect children against their own parents.[47] Because there was no paternal foyer at all, because the entire life experience of the child in the itinerant trades appeared to take place in public, the highly volatile question of state-sponsored trespass could be avoided altogether. And as the flip-side of the problem, because the parents of children employed in these professions had failed to provide them with a protected 'private' life, they were already derelict in the fulfillment of their parental role. As Tallon put it, the loss of rights was something parents called upon themselves when they 'violated the laws of nature, of affection and of duty'.[48]

Third, intervention in the 'natural' order of the family was justified through references to travelling children's overexposure to public life, its abuses and its temptations. For these children, doubly cursed by the lack of a permanent home and by premature exposure to a public world saturated with 'vice',

ideas of the right and the good, the lessons of an honest and hard-working father, the caresses of a good and loving mother, all these sacred ties which throughout his entire life bind man to the path of honour and duty, are replaced by coarse talk, perverse stimulation, the spectacle of drunkenness, of dishonesty, of debauchery, by the incessant expression of the most base sentiments and the perpetual negation of the most noble aspirations of human nature.[49]

The discussion of the physical dangers of contortionism provided legislators with a particularly concrete emblem of the 'denaturing' effects of children's performative experiences. Indeed, the emphasis in the legislative debate on a category of performance whose essences was defined as the 'unnatural' and spectacular deformation of the human body provided legislators with a archetype of demoralizing performance that gave physical form to their sense that child street performers also embodied the spectacular distortion or denaturing of their parents' natural protective sentiments.

Finally, the fact that the problem of the itinerant trades and street performance was initially cast as one imported by foreign immigrants — Italians, Bohemians or 'gypsies' — helped legislative reformers to render their distinctions between categories of families and familial labour even more plausible.[50]   The presumed alien origins of the troubling population of workers, a presumption that overlooked the growing number of French-born performers, denoted all that was unfixed, irregular and beyond the pale in the cultural imagination of the late nineteenth century. By contrast, the French labouring classes, no matter how problematic or pathological it appeared to more conservative French observers, seemed fully integrated into the social order when compared to outsiders.

By addressing the question of exploitative labour in the terms of nationality and ethnicity, French legislators perhaps felt more secure in experimenting with norms of parental responsibility and state obligation, norms that would later seem applicable to the French populace as a whole.[51]   Lawmakers in 1874 appear to have found it fairly easy to construct discursively valuable distinctions between vagrant and possibly foreign parents from 'authentic' honourable French parents. Through this lens of discursive — though not juridical — differentiation, they were able to subject both the former and the latter to severe legal sanctions without disturbing the state's avowed respect for France's own 'family men' or '*bons pères de famille*'.

Creating these patterns of particularities and generalities and these frames of inclusion and exclusion was a fundamental element in the Third Republic's approach to the legislative regulation of the family beginning in the 1870s. On the ground of the specific case, marked and contained by the limits of class, nationality, sex and the occupation of a distinctive social and moral space, lawmakers devised new measures that ultimately effaced those differences in the abstract universality of both their immediate scope and their wider implications.

The debates on 1874 law on children in the itinerant professions provided the script and the rehearsal space for future, more radical state action in the protection of children. They introduced the possibility of separating children's 'vulnerable interests' from the 'dangerous self-interest' of their parents. Even more important, perhaps, was the way in which the debates and the new law recast contemporary understandings of the corporeal and spatial dimensions of childhood. By collapsing the physical and moral 'bodies' of the child and positing the determining significance of moral environment, the 1874 law would point toward the possibility that the state might 'legitimately' attempt to protect children in the most juridically and culturally sacred of all spaces in nineteenth-century France: the interior space of family life. The modern French regime of child protection owes much of its existence — and its complexity — to these early reflections on the government of social space, the limits of adult authority and the moral status of the child's body.

Notes

1. Ian Hacking, 'The Making and Molding of Child Abuse' (1991) 17 Critical Inquiry 259.

2. *Ibid.* at 254.

3. The literature on child protection and the regulation of the family in Europe and the United States is far too vast to cite here beyond a few exemplary titles. On the United States, see Linda Gordon's *Heroes of Their Own Lives: The Politics and History of Family Violence* (Penguin Books, 1988); Joyce Antler and Stephen Antler, 'From Child Rescue to Family Protection: The Evolution of the Child Protective Movement in the United States', [1979] Children and Youth Service Review 1; and Michael Grossberg, *Governing the Hearth: Law and the Family in Nineteenth-Century America* (University of North Carolina Press, 1985). On Britain, see George K. Behlmer, *Child Abuse and Moral Reform in England, 1870-1918* (Stanford University Press, 1982); Jane Lewis, *The Politics of Motherhood: Child and Maternal Welfare in England, 1900-1939* (McGill-Queen's University Press, 1980); and Clark Nardinelli, *Child Labor and the Industrial Revolution* (Indiana University Press, 1990). On Austria, see Peter Feldbauer, *Kinderlend in Wien: Von der Armenkinderpflege zur Jugendfürsorge, 17.-19. Jahrhundert* (Gesellschaftskritik, 1980). For a comparative perspective, see Valerie Fildes *et al.* (eds.), *Women and Children First: International Maternal and Infant Welfare 1870-1945* (Routledge, 1993).

4. On the foundation of the Third Republic see Jean-Marie Mayeur, *Les débuts de la IIIe République, 1871-1898* (Editions du Seuil, 1973). For a survey of the Third Republic's efforts to protect children, see Catherine Rollet-Echalier, *La politique à l'égard de la petite enfance sous la IIIe République* (Presses Universitaires de France/INED, 1990).

5. Claudia Scheck Kselman reviews this constellation of laws in 'The Modernization of Family Law: The Politics and Ideology of Family Reform In Third Republic France', Dissertation, University of Michigan (1980). See also Sylvia Schafer,

'Children in "Moral Danger" and the Politics of Parenthood in Third Republic France, 1870-1914', Dissertation, University of California, Berkeley (1992).

6. On the history of family law in France see Jules Thabaut, *L'Evolution de la législation sur la famille depuis 1804* (Edouard Privat, 1913) and Charles Lefebvre, *La Famille en France dans le droit et dans les mœurs* (Marcel Giard, 1920).

7. Included among the labour law's provisions were limitations on the length of the workday and the work week, the establishment of minimum ages of employment, and prohibitions against employing young children for night work, work underground in the mining industry, and work in 'dangerous' industries, particularly those involving toxic chemicals. Many of these protective restrictions also applied to adult women. In addition to regulating the conditions of labour, the law also introduced minimal educational requirements for working children and held employers responsible for adjusting the children's hours according to their level of primary instruction. In focusing exclusively on large-scale industrial production, however, the law left entirely untouched minors employed in small workshops, the most common unit of manufacturing in nineteenth-century France. It also excluded from its purview the vast majority of child labourers who worked in agriculture. For more extensive discussions of child labour law and its implementation, see Lee Schai Weissbach, *Child Labor Reform in Nineteenth-Century France: Assuring the Future Harvest* (Louisiana State University, 1989) and Colin Heywood, *Childhood in Nineteenth-Century France: Work, Health and Education Among the 'Classes Populaires'* (Cambridge University Press, 1988). On state regulation of women's labour in the late-nineteenth century, see Mary Lynn Stewart's *Women, Work and the French State. Labour, Protection, and Social Patriarchy, 1879-1919* (McGill-Queen's University Press, 1989). The debates on and texts of these laws can be found in the official record of the National Assembly, *Le Journal Officiel* [hereafter *JO*].

8. On the regulation of wet nursing in the nineteenth century, see Joshua Cole, 'The Power of Large Numbers: Population and Politics in Nineteenth-Century France', Dissertation, University of California, Berkeley, (1991) and George D. Sussman, *Selling Mothers' Milk: The Wet-Nursing Business in France 1715-1914* (University of Illinois, 1982).

9. In this period, this sort of elision between morality and the body was endorsed by legitimate science as well as popular opinion. See Robert A. Nye, *Crime, Madness and Politics in Modern France: The Medical Concept of National Decline* (Princeton University Press, 1984) and Ruth Harris, *Murders and Madness: Medicine, Law, and Society in the* fin de siècle (Oxford University Press, 1989).

10. Law in pre-revolutionary France was exceptionally complex. In the north, a common law system tended to prevail, while in the south, written Roman law provided the referent for secular justice. A third set of legal doctrines and courts, those of canon law, also served as a frame for the legal life of the nation. Legal practices also seem to have varied from region to region.

11. The *Code Napoléon*'s long-term influence ranged far beyond the national boundaries of France. Among the countries that had experienced Napoleonic rule and domestic reorganization in the first decades of the century, the civil code served as one of the cornerstones of exported French 'civilization', and left permanent imprints even after Napoleon's empire crumbled. Among the European countries where Napoleon's imposition of some form of the French civil code transformed indigenous structures of domestic order were Italy (that is, the northern regions of modern Italy and the kingdom of Naples), Holland, Westphalia, and parts of Spain. Although it was not enforced with equal rigor in all parts of Napoleon's empire, historians agree that the secular legal frame of the code made an enduring impression wherever it had been imposed. See Owen Connelly, *Napoleon's Satellite Kingdoms* (The Free Press, 1965).

12. On the distinctive qualities of code-based civil justice, see John Henry Merriman, *The Civil Law Tradition: An Introduction to the Legal Systems of Western Europe and Latin America*, 2nd ed. (Stanford University Press, 1985).

13. Centuries of Roman occupation in the early part of the millennium spliced Latin visions of the family into indigenous Gallic traditions. Roman law vested an almost limitless power in the person of the family patriarch. Even after the dissolution of the empire, various regional legal traditions maintained this principle of *patria potestas* for centuries, particularly in Mediterranean and southern France. See Yvonne Knibiehler, *Les pères aussi ont une histoire* (Hachette, 1987), especially chapter one, 'La puissance paternelle'. See also André Pelletier, *La femme dans la société gallo-romaine* (Picard, 1984).

14. *Code Napoléon*, art. 373. The content of subsequent articles makes clear that French law left to fathers the domestic governance of both their children and, through a series of articles outlining the 'civil death' of women upon marriage, their wives. *Code Napoléon*, Book I, title v, chapter vi, '*Des droits et devoirs respectifs des époux*', describes the legal subordination of a woman to the authority of her husband, including the obligation to 'obey', and to reside in her husband's house. She was also denied the right to appear in court or to dispose of goods and property without her husband's permission. The use of *l'autorité parentale* and *la puissance paternelle* as synonyms introduced a curious contradiction into French civil law. The mother's appearance as a 'parent' endowed with rights, however fleeting, also brought her under the regulating

power of the law in that parental capacity. If it tended to exclude her from the legitimate exercise of parental authority, the code nonetheless provided the means for holding her legally responsible as an authoritative parent. The civil code also provided for the delegation of *la puissance paternelle* to his wife in the case of his prolonged absence. In the instance of a father's legally-declared disappearance, the code permitted the mother to exercise 'all the husband's rights in child-rearing and in the management of their [the children's] property.' *Code Napoléon*, article 141. During the Third Republic, the legal foundation of marriage underwent a series of important reforms, including the legalization of divorce. In particular, the Third Republic's reforms initiated the gradual erosion of the 'civil death' of married women. All citations for the Napoleonic law codes come from *Codes Napoléon*, 7th ed. (Auguste Durand, 1852). See also Thabaut, *L'Evolution de la législation sur la famille* and Lefebvre, *La Famille en France dans le droit*. For a useful survey of the Third Republic's reforms, see Kselman, 'The Modernization of Family Law: The Politics and Ideology of Family Reform in Third Republic France', Ph.D. Dissertation, University of Michigan, 1980.

15. *Code Napoléon*, Book I, title ix, *'De la puissance paternelle'*, articles 371-372. Book I, title x, chapter iii of the Code described the conditions for 'emancipation': minors are automatically emancipated upon their marriage, and may be voluntarily emancipated by their parents, before a justice of the peace, at the age of fifteen, even when not married. Although emancipated minors were no longer subject to their parents' authority, the code did not permit them to exercise the full rights of adulthood until majority at the age of twenty-one.

16. *Code Napoléon*, arts. 374-387.

17. The codification of French penal law was completed in 1810.

18. *Code Penal*, article 66. By the tenets of French criminal justice, minors accused but formally acquitted of crimes were still considered culpable and in danger of further moral decline. In 1850, new legislation called for the incarceration of acquitted minors in agricultural colonies where hard work, segregation from dangerous adults, and close supervision would ensure their moral rehabilitation. On the history of these colonies and the institutionalization of this notion of the moral instability of the acquitted minor, see Henri Gaillac, *Les Maisons de correction 1830-1945* (Éditions Cujas, 1971).

19. *Code Penal*, articles 334-335. These measure applied to all adults accused of prostituting minors, but cast parents as a special category of offender and imposed harsher sentences on them. On the prostitution of minors and their legal status, see Jill Harsin, *Policing Prostitution in Nineteenth-Century Paris* (Princeton University Press, 1985), especially at 28-29.

20. Harsin notes that the law, originally intended to be used in the policing of bordellos, was rarely applied. Harsin, *Policing Prostitution*, 28-29.

21. This legislative effort was also inspired in part by an Italian law of 1865 regulating children's performative labour. See Tallon's report on the bill, *JO*, 4 March 1874, 2518. On the debates in the Italian legislature about child street performers, see John E. Zucchi, *Little Slaves of the Harp: Italian Child Street Musicians in Nineteenth-Century Paris, London, and New York* (McGill University Press, 1992), 144-163.

22. On the cultural meanings of work and mendicancy in this period, see Steven Laurence Kaplan and Cynthia J. Koepp, eds., *Work in France: Representations, Meanings, Organization and Practice* (Cornell University Press, 1986). Kaplan and Koepp note in their introduction the long-standing moral opposition that pitted the virtuous work against shameless begging and vagrancy. *Work in France*, 19. Zucchi argues that the case of street performance put this opposition to the test in obscuring these essential moral distinctions between the appearance of work and the immoral spectacle of begging. See Zucchi, *Little Slaves, supra* note 21 at 7, 52.

23. *JO*, 4 March 1874, 2515.

24. *Ibid.*

25. *Ibid.* at 2514.

26. Zucchi argues for example that few child street musicians in late nineteenth-century Paris played their instruments with any facility. In the eyes of contemporaries, playing instruments served as an ineffectual screen for a form of begging. Zucchi, *Little Slaves, supra* note 21 at 54.

27. On perceptions of these child labour practices as a form of commerce, see Zucchi, *Little Slaves*, 40-41.

28. *JO*, 4 March 1874, 2514.

29. *JO*, 23 June 1874, 4260.

30. *JO*, 24 June 1874, 4283-84.

31. *JO*, 23 June 1874, 4262.

32. *JO*, 4 March 1874, 2515.

33. Tallon was here referring directly to the *Code Napoléon*, Article 203, Livre I, titre v, chapitre v, *'Des obligations qui naissent du mariage'*.

34. *JO*, 8 December, 1874, 8084.

35. On the construction and government of the social, see Giovanna Procacci's innovative study of poverty in nineteenth-century France, *Gouverner la misère: La question sociale en France 1789-1848* (Editions du Seuil, 1993).

36. *JO*, 8 December 1874, 8083.

37. *JO*, 23 June 1874, 4262.

38. The mandatory sentence called for a six-month to two-year term of imprisonment and the imposition of a fine ranging from sixteen to two-hundred francs. These penalties applied to unrelated employers, legal guardians, and parents alike.

39. *JO*, 4 March 1874, 2514-15.

40. *JO*, 4 March 1874, 2515, and 8 December 1874, 8084.

41. On paternal authority in the family, see Knibiehler, *Les pères*, *supra* note 13. On representations of the family in nineteenth-century France, see Michelle Perrot (ed.), *From the Fires of Revolution to the Great War*, trans. Arthur Goldhammer, vol. 4 of *A History of Private Life*, Phillippe Ariés and Georges Duby, eds. (Belknap Press, 1990), at 167-180 and Roddy Reid, *Death of the Family: Discourse, Fiction and Desire in France* (Stanford University Press, 1994).

42. François Ewald, *l'Etat providence* (Grasset, 1986), 19.

43. On positivism and social science in this era, see Robert A. Nye, *The Origins of Crowd Psychology: Gustave Le Bon and the Crisis of Mass Democracy in the Third Republic* (Sage, 1975).

44. See Jacques Chastenet, *La République des Républicains, 1879-1893*, volume 2 of his *Histoire de la Troisième République*, 7 volumes (Hachette, 1954), esp. chapter 1, 'La pensée française à l'avènement de la république des républicains.'

45. Catherine Gallagher's study of representations of the social body in the work of the British social observer Henry Mayhew provides a fascinating account of contemporary fears of nomadic street labourers. Gallagher argues that Mayhew was particularly disturbed by the economically liminal, constantly circulating food-provisioners because they so clearly embodied — and escaped — the workings of the competitive market. See Gallagher, 'The Body Versus the Social Body in the Works of Thomas Malthus and Henry Mayhew', Representations 14 (Spring 1986).

46. Historian Michelle Perrot writes: 'Of all solitary men and women, the homeless aroused the greatest suspicion in a society where residence was a condition of citizenship and the hobo was seen as one who rejected the prevailing morality.' Perrot, 'Roles and Characters' in *From the Fires of Revolution to the Great War*, *supra* note 41 at 302. Zucchi notes that the Paris police had long used vagrancy laws, along with anti-mendicancy and anti-sedition ordinances, against street performers, especially those of apparently foreign extraction. Zucchi, *Little Slaves*, *supra* note 21 at 42-52.

47. Many studies, particularly those by — and provoked by — Michel Foucault have centred on the anxiety about the dangers embodied in unfixed populations and those hidden in the darkness of 'obscure' social spaces. See especially Foucault's *Discipline and Punish: The Birth of the Prison*, trans. Alan Sheridan (Vintage Books, 1979); Patricia O'Brien's *The Promise of Punishment: Prisons in Nineteenth-Century France* (Princeton University Press, 1982); Michelle Perrot, ed., *l'Impossible Prison* (Seuil, 1980). See also Philippe Meyer, *L 'Enfant et la raison d'état* (Editions du seuil, 1977); Nye, *Crime, Madness and Politics*, *supra* note 9; Harris, *Murders and Madness*, *supra* note 9; and Louis Chevalier's classic discussion of the bourgeois reading of 'vagrancy' in his *Labouring Classes and Dangerous Classes in Paris During the First Half of the Nineteenth Century*, trans. Frank Jellinek (Princeton University Press, 1973).

48. *JO*, 8 December 1874, 8084.

49. *JO*, 4 March 1874, 2512.

50. On the particular status of child street musicians from Italy in nineteenth-century Paris, see Zucchi, *Little Slaves*, *supra* note at 42-75.

51. See Kselman, 'The Modernization of Family Law', *supra* note 5 at 183-4.

II

The Gendering of Social Control: Sex Delinquency and Progressive Juvenile Justice in Denver, 1901-1927

PAUL COLOMY & MARTIN KRETZMANN

THE EMERGENCE OF INSTITUTIONS AND PRACTICES to address female juvenile delinquency in the progressive era has long been neglected. Recently, however, a reasonably coherent account has begun to appear. Highlighting the profoundly conservative character of female juvenile justice, that account is organized around several key points. First, progressive reformers constituted boy and girl delinquency in radically different ways. Whereas boys were often charged with offenses that would be deemed criminal if committed by an adult, the majority of girls' alleged offenses fell under the loose heading of immorality.[1] Second, though in practice immorality covered a wide array of behaviors, including staying away from home, associating with bad company, and going to dance houses, the symbolic core of this charge revolved around sexual precocity (Schlossman and Wallach, 1978, p.72). Third, the preoccupation with sexual precocity reflected a traditional, even a reactionary, code of morality that affirmed Victorian views of a woman's social role and sexuality and the virtues celebrated in the contemporaneous social purity movement (*ibid.*). Fourth, these conventional assumptions sanctioned discriminatory practices throughout the juvenile system; though typically charged with noncriminal offenses, girls were treated more punitively, receiving probation much less often than boys and experiencing significantly higher levels of incarceration (Shelden, 1981). Finally, since reformers' sensibilities reflected a privileged class position and a waspish aversion to 'alien' customs and conduct, the daughters of working class and immigrant families were more likely to be brought before the court and, once there, more likely to receive harsher treatment (Schlossman and Wallach, *op. cit.*; Chesney-Lind, 1989).

There is considerable merit to this account, but we wish to caution against the premature crystallization of a standard or uniform history of female juvenile justice. In particular, we argue that an important strand of the early juvenile court movement did not adopt a consistently conservative posture toward female delinquency. Advanced most forcefully by Judge Ben B. Lindsey, this more genuinely progressive moment in the juvenile court movement raised serious questions about the traditional morality deployed to constitute the female delinquent, proposed laws to protect girls' interests against a society seemingly organized to contravene those interests, and engaged in practices that attempted to buffer the female delinquent, particularly those accused of sex delinquency, from the repressive responses of the girl's family, school, church, and larger community.

We address this issue, first, by outlining a model of institutional entrepreneurs and projects that helps to illuminate the ideological and substantive differences within the juvenile court movement. Next, we discuss Judge Lindsey's project, giving special attention to his constitution of the female delinquent subject, attempt to create a sympathetic court, and ambitions for wide-ranging social and legal reforms. Finally, we present a provisional analysis of quantitative data which reveals considerable consistency (as well as some significant discrepancies) between Lindsey's project and the actual operation of the Denver court.

I. ENTREPRENEURS, PROJECTS AND INSTITUTION BUILDING

WE ELUCIDATE THE DIVERSITY characteristic of the early stages of institution building, and the distinctiveness of Lindsey's project, by drawing on Eisenstadt's (1964, 1965, 1971, 1973, 1980) discussion of institutional entrepreneurs, a term designating those individuals and groups who adopt leadership roles in episodes of institution building. Critical of approaches that depict institution building as a product of evolutionary problem solving, system adaptation to environmental exigencies, or as a 'mere' reflection of class, status, or occupational interests, Eisenstadt maintains that institutional change is partially contingent on the activities of particular entrepreneurs who crystallize broad symbolic orientations in new ways, articulate specific goals, and construct novel normative, cognitive, and organizational frameworks.

The creative role of these movers and shakers is organized around a project[2] (DiMaggio, 1988, p.14; Colomy and Rhoades, 1994). The notion of an institutional project presumes that 'man [sic] is characterized above all by his going beyond a situation, and by what he succeeds in making of what he has been made ... The most rudimentary behavior must be determined both in relation to the real and present factors which condition it and in relation to a certain object, still to come, which it is trying to bring into being. This is what we call the project' (Sartre, 1968, p.91). The formulation of an innovative project and the attempt to institutionalize it carve a free space between entrepreneurs' actions and the macro environments in which they are pursued, imbuing innovators' efforts with a degree of creativity and voluntarism.

The creativity and voluntarism attendant on fashioning and advancing a new institutional program is conditioned in several ways, however. A project constitutes, phenomenologically, some macro environments that it treats as unchangeable. Consequently, most entrepreneurial projects are constrained by the material and ideational structures defined as obdurate features of social organization. The study of institutional projects, therefore, must attend not only to what entrepreneurs explicitly seek to change — i.e., to a given project's manifest contents — but also to taken-for-granted elements of the macro environment.

Substantively, institutional programs advance claims with instrumental-adaptive and symbolic dimensions. The instrumental-adaptive aspect is reflected in the identification of a problem as a pretext for structural change. Entrepreneurs attempt to enlist support for their project by infusing new and distinctive content into a technical, problem-solving frame — an institutionalized formula (Meyer and Rowan, 1977) available to innovators advancing a broad array of programs. The project asserts that a vital problem or societal need is either unduly neglected or is currently being addressed through inefficient or ineffective methods. When the postulated problem includes 'troubled persons' (Gusfield, 1981), the project also constitutes a collective subject, usually providing a classificatory scheme distinguishing subjects from others in the population and differentiating sub-types of subjects, an etiology of the typical subject, and an intervention strategy designed to transform the subject and conditions thought responsible for the subject's troubles.

Supplementing these instrumental-adaptive considerations are the dramatic, symbolic, and moral aspects of entrepreneurial claims. Existing arrangements are not simply inefficient or ineffective; they are condemned as evil, inequitable, beholden to special interests, and fundamentally unjust. In seeking legitimation and support, entrepreneurs construct an institutional myth — a complex of symbolic associations and representations — that situate the project in a broader framework of meaning. The institutional remedy is portrayed as a symbolic and moral 'contrast conception' (Shibutani, 1970) to an established, yet discredited, institutional order.

Though they contain an inventive dimension, projects are not articulated in a sociological vacuum. Each of the most significant institutional orders of Western society (e.g., the capitalist market, bureaucratic state, democracy, nuclear family, science, art, medicine, Christianity) has a central logic — a set of material practices and symbolic constructions — that constitutes its organizing principles and that is available to entrepreneurs to elaborate (Friedland and Alford, 1991). No single discourse is hegemonic, and the existence of multiple and contradictory institutional formulas constitutes a resource that entrepreneurs can use to contest a particular institutional configuration by artfully critiquing it in terms of a competing logic and/or to legitimate a proposed innovation by redeploying the complementary features of a highly regarded institutional code. Moreover, the prevailing symbols and practices associated with a specific institutional order are themselves subject to creative reinterpretation and manipulation by entrepreneurial groups. Elements of contemporaneous general social movements (e.g., progressivism, populism, feminism) also provide innovators with potent instrumental and symbolic resources that can be invoked to enhance the general appeal of their critiques and reform proposals.

The symbolic and moral components of these institutional myths are readily apparent in the narratives entrepreneurs construct to legitimate their projects. Narratives designate communicative acts that selectively appropriate past events and characters, imbue these events and characters with temporal order (i.e., with a beginning, middle, and end) and relate them to one another within an overarching structure, often a context of opposition or struggle (Ewick and Silbey, 1995). The temporal and structural ordering ensure both narrative closure and narrative causality; in other words, they explain how and why the recounted events and characters occur. Narratives also have a strategic dimension; they are told to entertain, instruct, persuade, examine, or indict. In this vein, Ewick and Silbey (*ibid.*) distinguish between hegemonic and subversive narratives. The former serve to reproduce existing structures of meaning and power, whereas subversive accounts expose and discredit those structures and, at times, politically transform the storyteller and her or his audience. Since a single narrative frequently serves both hegemonic and subversive purposes, we recommend that the distinction between hegemonic and subversive narratives be treated in an analytic rather than a concrete way.

While they may agree about the broad contours of a particular problem, different entrepreneurial groups frequently fashion distinctive instrumental remedies and symbolic appeals, ranging from incommensurate projects to idiosyncratic but complementary versions of a roughly similar program. The articulation of alternative projects and the possibility of reconciling differences between them is partially conditioned by the degree to which power and legitimate authority are centralized in the environing system. In systems marked by highly centralized decision making power, a choice or compromise between programs is probable at the early stages of institution building. However, when decision making power is decentralized, distinctive projects are more likely to be formulated and implemented in autonomous locales.

Projects can be distinguished by identifying the primary conditions they aspire to change (Turner and Killian, 1987). Personal transformative projects attempt to alter people's identities, attitudes, and behaviors. Projects concerned with societal manipulation aim at transforming a social system's culture, social structure, laws and regulations, or distribution of resources. Many projects, of course, are oriented to both personal transformation and societal manipulation.

Whether oriented primarily towards personal transformation or societal manipulation, projects also vary in terms of their respective scope. At one extreme are elaborative projects, which maintain that relatively   minor alterations of people's conduct or social conditions represent the most viable remedy to existing problems. The myths advanced by elaborative projects are narrow in scope and involve stretching established institutional logics and symbol systems or invoking moderate elements of general movements to justify incremental reforms. Entrepreneurs promoting elaborative projects resemble innovators 'with the brakes on', sponsoring change, in part, to protect traditional interests and values. Reconstructive projects, on the other hand, insist on the creation of new structures and/or the fundamental reconstitution of personalities. The mythical components of these projects are generalized, and draw on the more transformative components of general movements or the more critical strands of extant institutional logics to assail an allegedly pervasive pattern of injustice or corruption in the current system.

Their generality, in turn, supports an equally broad program of reform, and is typically associated with a potentially new source of material interest, e.g. with the construction of new positions, roles, and organizations.

The substantive section of this paper demonstrates how this model of institution building helps to explain the initially heterogeneous response to female delinquency. Specifically, we examine how the distinctive institutional project advanced by Judge Ben B. Lindsey diverges from the overwhelmingly conservative character of the juvenile courts established elsewhere.

II. JUDGE BEN B. LINDSEY
AND THE JUVENILE COURT MOVEMENT

THE JUVENILE COURT MOVEMENT EMERGED in an environment characterized by the fragmentation of political power, a cultural tradition of antipathy to control by the federal government, and local communities marked by social and economic diversity. Arising in this context, the juvenile court movement was composed of several local groups spread across the country who shared a diffuse commitment to designing new strategies for coping with wayward youth. These dispersed, localized groups were linked through personal, professional, and ideological networks; resources, information, and personnel were exchanged across these inter-group channels. But the decentralized character of the movement also lent considerable independence to each local unit, an autonomy which enabled different entrepreneurial groups to devise and implement distinctive renditions of the juvenile court. Aside from Chicago, the most widely influential rendition of the juvenile court was implemented in Denver.

Soon after his appointment as judge of Arapahoe (later Denver) County Court in 1901, Judge Ben B. Lindsey and his supporters established a de facto juvenile court organized around an informal court procedure and informal probation system. Lindsey quickly became the movement's most ardent, national entrepreneur, far outshining the efforts of Chicago advocates such as Timothy Hurley, George Stubbs, Judge Mack, and Judge Tuthill. Between 1902 and 1910 Lindsey agitated for juvenile courts throughout the nation, leading successful campaigns for juvenile court legislation in Washington, Oregon, California, Iowa, Kansas, Utah, and Nebraska, prompting an editor of *Charities* (1905, p.649) to remark that these states were all 'scalps for the belt of Judge Lindsey'.

More so than any other figure in the movement, he presented and embodied the court to the larger society in compelling representational imagery, characterizing it as a benevolent, just institution charged with redeeming basically good children whose untoward conduct constituted a natural manifestation of youthful, albeit misdirected, energy and/or deleterious circumstances over which they had little control. In Lindsey's portrayal, the court was staffed by those with a special gift for understanding the real meanings and sources of wayward behavior, intuiting the most appropriate and judicious responses to it while acting to promote both the youth's and society's best interests.

Legal scholars and social scientists alike have acknowledged Lindsey's role in galvanizing child savers and legislators in support of the juvenile court, though less attention has been given to the symbolic and legitimating functions Lindsey fulfilled on the court's behalf. More problematic, however, is that divergent features of Lindsey's project have been subordinated to a single, standardized history that omits substantive and ideological differences within the movement. This omission is particularly glaring with regard to female delinquency. To rectify that omission, we describe Lindsey's constitution of girl delinquency, giving particular attention to the reconstructive thrust of his project.

A.   Constituting the Female Delinquent

Proponents of institutional change draw on a diffuse problem solving frame to legitimate their efforts, portraying their project as an effective instrument to combat a significant social problem. When there is uncertainty concerning the causes, extent, and nature of a problem, the project will constitute these and, if the problem concerns a category of persons, the project must constitute a collective subject. Accordingly, a crucial component of that part of the juvenile court project which addressed female delinquency involved specifying the nature of the problem to which this new institution was a response.

The existing literature maintains that sexual precocity was the primary preoccupation in constituting female delinquency. Relying on traditional morality and the conventional double-standard, the early juvenile court reaffirmed a rigid moral boundary between good girls, who abided by traditional moral precepts, and bad girls who violated them. Most courts advanced essentially elaborative projects that did little more than formalize and police tradition-bound conceptions of female sexuality and a woman's proper social role (Schlossman and Wallach, *op. cit.*). Targeting primarily working-class and immigrant girls, the juvenile court subjected sexually active female adolescents, as well as those merely suspected of such activity and even those deemed likely to become sexually active sometime in the future, to status degradation ceremonies and various forms of ritual abasement. In the course of these proceedings, the sexually precocious girl's total character was impugned; she was deemed ruined, morally impure, and polluted; and she was sequestered away from the larger society.

In contrast to other child savers who deplored sexual precocity, Lindsey 'normalized it', refusing to treat its occurrence as an occasion for moral condemnation. Maintaining that sexual liaisons were much more common than most adults supposed, he reported that more than 90 per cent of youth who went to parties, attended dances, and rode together in automobiles indulged in hugging and kissing. At least one-half of that number 'indulge in other sex liberties which, by all the conventions, are outrageously improper' (Lindsey and Evans, 1925, p.59). And 'fifteen to twenty-five percent of those who begin with the hugging and kissing eventually 'go the limit''(*ibid.*, p.62). Lindsey also calculated that at least 4,000 of the girls between the ages of 14 and 17 living in Denver in 1920 engaged in sexual intercourse. This figure, he emphasized, represented a minimum and he suggested that the actual number of cases was 'far above' what his ballpark estimate indicated (*ibid.*, p.81). Lindsey's intent in presenting these figures was not to sound a traditional alarm about wanton youth but to suggest that young people were beginning to articulate a new and distinctive morality that resonated more faithfully with modern conditions.

Lindsey normalized sexual precocity not only by citing figures attesting to its frequency, but also by observing that adolescents from every social class and ethnic group engaged in sexual conduct. He explicitly rejected the view that sex delinquency was restricted to, or even more prevalent among, working-class or immigrant children. In fact, Lindsey took particular delight in presenting subversive narratives impugning the moral authority of the well-to-do. He revealed that it was the children of Denver's most respected classes and those who publicly decried youthful immorality most stridently who frequently came to the juvenile court seeking counsel about their sexual entanglements.

I recall a Denver minister, who some years ago publicly denounced me and my warped vision, and my 'libels on American youth.' His eloquence was as great as his indignation, and I don't doubt that many were convinced by his fiery words. As he spoke those words, he no doubt had in mind the vision of his own sweet and beautiful daughter. Perhaps she sat there listening to his words. How unthinkable that *she*, or that thousands of other pure young girls in Denver, could be considered in the same breath with such preposterous notions. For his premise was that to say or admit that young people make mistakes, particularly in matters of sex contact, is to say that they are 'immoral,' a view with which I strongly disagree.

Well, at the time those words uttered, in denunciation of me, that young girl was under my care, and I was having her treated for an infection by a physician on whose discretion I could rely. Her father didn't know it; and he doesn't know it to this day. He would drop dead if he did. Knowing that he must not be told, she was forced to come to me for the help, tolerance, and loving sympathy she should have been able to seek from him... What a pity his own intolerance barred her way to his confidence (*ibid.*, pp.37-8).

Rather than publicly rebuking girls accused of immorality, he frequently 'condemned the condemners', insisting that the real immorality and indecency resided not in the wayward girl's sexual precocity but rather in those who persecuted her. Lindsey's sympathies are expressed unequivocally in his account of a high school girl who had sexual relations with a male student. Having internalized society's traditional sensibilities about premarital sex, the young woman reproached herself so terribly that she sought comfort from one of her teachers, who immediately took the girl's story to another female instructor. The school authorities quickly learned of the young woman's behavior and, according to Lindsey (*ibid.*, pp. 186-187), 'called the girl on the carpet, grilled her, smacked their lips solemnly over the details of her story, and expelled her as a moral menace to other students. She was bad; she was contaminated; she was impure.' Lindsey's own conclusion reverses the target of moral indignation. Far from being ruined, the young woman had, at worst, 'simply made a mistake' (*ibid.*, p.187). Lindsey's outrage is directed at the teachers who orchestrated the status degradation ceremony against the girl. Indeed, Lindsey (*ibid.*) describes the young woman

as a very fine girl, with a moral sense about her that placed her infinitely above the two she-cats who dragged her down, and above the purblind pedagogues who finding her on the edge of the cliff kicked her over into the abyss. Those two women are active workers in one of our large Denver churches. They go to service every Sunday and are socially well-known. They deserve to be in the penitentiary.

Lindsey challenged the conventionally rigid moral boundary between putatively good and bad girls zealously reaffirmed in other courts. While defenders of the traditional order placed youth 'who don't go wrong' on the virtuous side of this moral divide, Lindsey questioned the motives, character, and sincerity of adolescents who never deviated from the straight and narrow. Among youth least likely to get into trouble, Lindsey counted those boys and girls who lacked energy, self confidence, and initiative. 'One characteristic of most of the boys and girls who get into difficulties', Lindsey wrote, 'is that they have just these qualities, and are all the more worth saving on that account. It is not always true that the boy or girl who is never willful or troublesome lacks energy and character, but it is quite likely to be so' (*ibid.*, p.94). In Lindsey's view, many who conformed to the established social code did so not because they whole-heartedly embraced its tenets, but for the more expedient consideration that they feared the consequences should they be caught violating what they often regarded as its arbitrary strictures.

B.   A Sympathetic Court

Lindsey claimed many sources — legal, scientific, and charismatic-like insight into the depths of the human soul — for the juvenile court's authority. The source he adduced most frequently, however, is the knowledge and expertise acquired from conversations with young people. His work in the juvenile court and the Juvenile Employment Agency combined with his reputation for providing wise and sympathetic advice on a variety of sensitive issues, brought him into contact with a cross section of young people in Denver and across the nation. Through these encounters he acquired 'insider' knowledge about the beliefs and conduct of contemporaneous youth, a knowledge far more accurate and extensive than that available to the teacher, principals, ministers, parents and other adults who claimed to speak authoritatively about young people.

Girls from a wide variety of backgrounds entrusted Lindsey and his staff with secrets and questions they could share with no one else. A significant proportion — for the years 1920 and 1921, Lindsey estimates that it was seventy-five percent — of the girls coming to the Denver court did so 'of their own accord' (*ibid.*, p.78). It was, he intimates, his non-judgmental stance (at least relative to other adults) and his and his staff's reputation for honesty and openness that prompted so many girls to search out the court voluntarily.[3] An unmistakably self-serving and institutionally legitimating quality infuses Lindsey's narrative accounts of many courtroom encounters: the wise, sympathetic elder dispensing sagacious advice to the initially frightened, confused, deer-frozen-in-the-headlights-like but subsequently enlightened and eternally grateful young girl. These are not the only characters presented in Lindsey's melodramatic narratives, however. In fact, Lindsey readily casts himself as the naive student instructed in the mysterious ways of the modern world by a self-possessed, knowledgeable young woman slightly impatient with the dull pupil before her. For instance, when a young woman describes the rationale for the open marriage she and her husband have agreed to, Lindsey is, initially, so overwhelmed by the woman's logic and, as he sees it, courage in challenging a hegemonic convention that he cannot speak. And by the end of this tutorial, it is Lindsey who is enlightened and 'greatly obliged' for the instruction (Lindsey and Evans 1927, pp.21-31).

Lindsey's contact with young people was not limited to those who came before the court, voluntarily or otherwise. He spent considerable time outside the courtroom, speaking to community groups, including junior high and high school students, in Denver and throughout the nation. His accounts of these meetings indicate that he learned as much as he taught, and that girls and young women often supplied the education.

In a limited way, Lindsey gave voice to girls, frequently juxtaposing their intelligence, honesty, and integrity to their parents' obtuseness and hypocrisy. By doing so, Lindsey intended to rest the court's authority and the validity of its judgments, in part, on an appreciation and first-hand knowledge of the actual life conditions, burgeoning 'modern' sex code, and changing gender roles that regulated the life of young women. To be effective, Lindsey suggests, a court must acknowledge and affirm the moral code regarded as legitimate and authoritative by those whose conduct the court is charged with correcting. Without such knowledge and affirmation the court is condemned to enforce a morality rejected as capricious by those subject to it. An institution of that nature, Lindsey avers, is inherently unjust and should not survive.

Far from subjecting girls to the status degradation ceremonies practiced in other courts, the Denver court was organized so as to protect their dignity, self-respect, and privacy. First, the large number of girls and boys of high character, poise, and unassailable reputations visiting the court for laudable ends (e.g. help in securing employment or learning how the court works) furnished 'the camouflage that protects from suspicion other young people whose relations with me [Lindsey] are of a different sort' (Lindsey and Evans 1925, p.72) and who, shielded by this camouflage, could visit the court without fear of exposure. For those whose relations with the court were 'of a different sort', Lindsey promised that no records were made or kept that would ever be used against the child.[4] Deploying a self-congratulatory analogy, Lindsey likened the Denver court to an 'impersonal oracle to which these hard-pressed children may come with the certainty that their confessions will not be betrayed, that their point of view will be understood, and that here they will always find sympathy for the sinner though not for the sin' (*ibid.*, p.73). Endeavoring to avoid even the appearance of evil, the court's conferences with girls were simultaneously private and public. The conferences were convened in Lindsey's judicial chambers behind a closed door which anybody (e.g., reporter, court official, or casual visitor) was free to open and walk through at any time, an invitation which reporters and other visitors acted on nearly every day Lindsey's court was in session. As a further precaution, Henrietta Lindsey, Judge Lindsey's co-worker and wife, had her desk in the adjacent room from which she could enter her husband's chambers through another door. In Lindsey's estimation, the protection provided by these arrangements for girls who came to the Denver court were far greater than those provided by the average physician.[5]

Rather than aligning the juvenile court with convention, Lindsey frequently depicts the court as a protective buffer between the girl and a punitive traditionalism. His account of Ellen is typical. After seducing a boy, Ellen became pregnant much to the consternation of her parents, who brought her to the court. Lindsey instructed the parents to tell the family's friends and neighbors that Ellen had travelled east for a visit. In fact, Ellen remained at home. Meanwhile, Lindsey contacted a couple wanting to adopt and told them to employ a physician friendly to the court. (Lindsey had also persuaded Ellen and her parents to hire another physician also friendly to the court.) Informed that Ellen was about to give birth, Lindsey contacted the foster parents and their physician.

Finally, it was all over, and the new baby was ready for the transfer. The two physicians met in the darkness on a street corner. Neither of them knew the other or could see the face of the other. Each carried a satchel. The one didn't know where the child was coming from, the other didn't know where it was going. They transferred the baby from one satchel to the other, and parted... Presently, Ellen's baby was in its new home (*ibid.*, p.92).

Lindsey justifies this street corner exchange as an attempt to protect Ellen

from being torn to pieces by our enlightened and moral society. I let her hide behind my judicial chair, so to speak, till the chase should go by. Then she came out into the daylight. Today she isn't 'ruined'. She is happily married, and has babies of her own, that she can keep. That is better than 'ruin', I think (*ibid.*, p.92).

C.   A Reconstructive Project

Lindsey's project was reconstructive, and he devoted a substantial part of his energies not to condemning sexually precocious girls but to indicting outmoded and repressive traditions. For Lindsey, it was not the girl but these conventions, which he invariably described as superstitious, intolerant, and hypocritical, that were the central problem. Consequently, unlike the more tradition-bound projects pursued elsewhere, the Denver court rejected key components of conventional morality as a basis for controlling the conduct of female adolescents and as a tool for punishing those who violated its precepts. Instead, Lindsey articulated a quasi-sociological conception of morality, arguing that valid ethical principles must be consistent with existing social conditions. When conditions change, he asserted, established moral precepts must be reassessed and those that diverge from new social realities should be discarded. Lindsey held that genuine morality rested on internal and voluntary restraints. Outmoded tradition, on the other hand, could be sustained only through external imposition, ignorance, and a conspiracy of silence. Much traditional morality about sexual behavior, Lindsey believed, relied not on internal and voluntary restraints but on external imposition. These repressive, outmoded ideas about sexual behavior required reevaluation; a new sexual code, one that corresponded to modern social conditions, needed to be devised. In this regard, Lindsey (*ibid.*, pp.277-278) wrote,

[O]ur sex taboos, saturated as they are with superstitions, are a trap that destroys human happiness. They are no more rational than were the Salem witch-hangings, and they work out to a perfectly logical conclusion in the occasional tar-and-feathering practices of the Ku Klux Klan when it deals with persons of whose morals it does not approve. Society applies some kind of tar and feathers to all women who violate its sex code. It is time we reappraised that code and found a more rational way to treat those whose natural impulses lead them to violate it.

Lindsey maintained that traditional gender roles were in the process of being fundamentally transformed.   He tied this transformation to the crystallization of a distinctive and, in some respects, oppositional youth subculture, on the one hand, and to significant alterations in marital relations, on the other.   Conceding the popular point that youth 'has always been rebellious', Lindsey was nevertheless convinced that the 'revolt from old standards [now] taking place....is unlike any revolt that has ever taken place before' (*ibid.*, p.54).   The then contemporary revolt of modern youth had

the whole weight of a new scientific and economic order behind it. It has come in an age of speech and science; an age when women can make their own living; an age in which the fear of Hell Fire has lost its hold. These boys and girls can do what boys and girls never were able to do in the past. They can live up to their manifesto, and nothing can prevent them. The external restraints, economic restraints that were once so potent, have gone never to return (*ibid.*, p.54).

Such innovations as the automobile, telephone, movies, and good wages, in conjunction with the changes described above, provided young women with the necessary social, economic, and psychological resources and opportunities to question traditional morality and the customary relations between men and women.   Lindsey observed that because they were brighter, mature, possessed a stronger inclination toward independent thought, and ultimately had more at stake, girls led the intellectual assault on these conventions.   Referring to a group of sixty female high school students who convened an informal round-table discussion with Lindsey during which they demanded 'some plain speech and some truthful information' (*ibid.*, p.112) about morality, sex, love, marriage, and divorce, Lindsey wrote,

[t]hose girls were not satisfied with their received traditions, they resented the attempt to muzzle me,[6] and they had a perfectly proper desire to know. They were refusing to be put off. The directness of their methods suggested an intelligence and independence of spirit of which their purblind elders would have done well to take account. The frankness of their speech showed moral health. Everything showed that they were engaged in an honest search for valid principles of conduct *for women*. They were not asking what boys should do. It was plain that they would decide all that for the boys so soon as they had decided on the proper courses for themselves.

Still another thing is evident. This active and aggressively inquiring attitude of mind on the part of girls has of late years become general rather than exceptional. Also, it is more and more unconcealed. The reason is that social and economic conditions have placed these girls more on a level with men. Many of them, when they leave school, take positions in which they make more money than the boys they go with. The result is that many a youth finds himself subject to rather contemptuous inspection by the young woman of his choice (*ibid.*, p.121).

As the last sentence implies, the changes Lindsey saw and approved were not merely intellectual or attitudinal. Many girls with whom Lindsey spoke, in the court as well as in other venues, informed him that they had 'dropped the fiction that a woman must be wooed' (*ibid.*, p.89), reversed conventional gender expectations, and seized the initiative in pursuing boys. In support of these contentions, Lindsey recounted a boy's story about how a girl stopped her automobile and asked him to 'take a ride'; a father's account about a group of girls congregating in front of his house in the evenings, whistling for his son to come outside; a girl's recollection of a pact she and five female friends, all from wealthy homes, agreed to, obliging each to 'have a sex experience sometime during the summer vacation then approaching, so that they might compare notes in the fall' (*ibid.*, p.90); and his own experience with a heartbroken young man who 'burst into tears, leaned his head on the [courtroom] table', and sobbed that his (former) girlfriend and lover "ditched me!" ' (*ibid.*, p.126).

These changes in attitude and behavior, along with increased social and economic resources and opportunities, empowered young women, enabling them to act more like free agents in their relations with boys, and to distinguish young men suitable for affairs but unfit for marriage from those who would make satisfactory husbands (*ibid.*, p.125). Lindsey saw in this altered climate unequivocal evidence of movement toward 'a woman-made code of sex morality on which women of the future will act, for their own protection and for the protection of children — and on which they will therefore require men to act' (*ibid.*, p.120).

The changes Lindsey described were not restricted to adolescents. Subtle but significant alterations were also occurring in 'the marriage contract'. The younger generation (particularly girls), in concert with many married women themselves, was largely responsible for creating more egalitarian gender relations. 'The revolt in which our younger generation is now engaged', Lindsey wrote, advances the 'ideal of marriage as a partnership composed of two independent personalities, who must first of all respect each other' (*ibid.*, p.210). This conception of marriage as an equal partnership also reflected young women's increasing experience in the work force:

[A]n increasing number of married persons are acquiring notions of justice and fair dealing, financial and economic, in the marriage relationship which they never learned in school, and which are an outcropping of the spirit of the times. The old idea that what a husband earns belongs to him, and that whatever he gives his wife and family is a gratuity provided by his lordly bounty and generosity is no longer fashionable. Women no longer tamely accept this view. Women are carrying over into marriage those practical principles of equity and common sense which they learn in business before they get married. An increasing participation in business, and in the world of affairs, has done it; and to the shame of our schools and churches it must be said that they have contributed little to this change. Once women were ignorant of these matters, and the man determined the economic basis of the marriage. Now the woman is more sophisticated, and insists *from the start* on terms similar to those of any real partnership. From the start it is made clear that her contribution in marriage is quite as valuable as money. Joint bank accounts are more common than they used to be, and the man who keeps his wife helpless simply by keeping her poor is slowly becoming a back number (*ibid.*, pp.209-210).

III. THE WORK OF THE DENVER JUVENILE COURT

THE DENVER COURT'S CONSTITUTION of the female delinquent, relatively sympathetic stance toward young people, and reconstructive thrust suggest that, rhetorically, it differed substantially from other juvenile courts. While these discursive differences are in themselves significant, it must also be determined whether the actual operation of the court was consistent with Lindsey's progressive project.

The Denver Juvenile Court's work with girl delinquents must be viewed within the context of the exceptionally broad legal jurisdiction created by Judge Lindsey, and the departments reflecting this legal framework. The Denver Juvenile Court was not established at one distinct point in time with one well-defined jurisdiction. Instead, the Court developed in an *ad hoc* fashion through successive statutory enactments authored by Judge Lindsey which encompassed all matters of child welfare. Almost from the beginning, delinquency as such constituted only a small proportion of the Denver Juvenile Court's total casework, and actually decreased over time. By the 1920s, the various 'Lindsey Laws' invested the Denver Court with an inclusive, albeit ill-defined, jurisdiction over virtually any matter affecting the welfare of minor children. Many of Judge Lindsey's statutory enactments were innovative for their time, with the majority directly addressing the welfare of mothers and young women, as well as delinquents.

The first legal basis for the Denver Juvenile Court was established under Colorado's School Law (Colorado Session Laws [hereafter CSL], 1899, Ch. 136). On an informal basis, Judge Lindsey convinced the District Attorney to file criminal charges against children as cases of 'disorderly juvenile persons' which could then be handled in his court under the provisions of the School Law. This initial legal basis was expanded by a 1903 law (CSL, 1903, Ch. 85) which gave the Court exclusive jurisdiction over all 'juvenile delinquent persons' age sixteen or under, with a similar law (CSL, 1903, Ch. 86) providing original jurisdiction over criminal cases involving minors under the age of twenty-one.

In the same year, Judge Lindsey created the first of his highly original *Contributing to Delinquency* laws (CSL, 1903, Ch. 94; 1905, Ch. 81; 1909, Ch. 157) which gave the Denver Court criminal jurisdiction over any adult 'who shall encourage, cause or contribute to the dependency, neglect or delinquency' of any child. Another early Lindsey law (CSL, 1913, Ch. 51) prohibited printed publicity in all juvenile court cases, making publication of the picture, name, or address of child or parents a crime. While this law applied equally to boy and girl cases, Judge Lindsey and his supporters made it clear that its intent was to protect the reputations of young women (e.g., Denver Juvenile Court, 1925, p.22).

In 1907, the Denver Juvenile Court was formally established as a court of record separate from the county court. The formal enactment authored by Judge Lindsey (CSL, 1907, Ch. 149, Sec. 2) delineated a virtually unlimited jurisdiction which was to have

original jurisdiction in all criminal cases or other actions or proceedings in which the disposition, custody or control of any child or minor, or any other person, may be involved under the Acts concerning delinquent, dependent or neglected children, or any other Acts, statute or law of this State now or hereafter existing concerning dependent, delinquent or neglected children, or which may in any manner concern or relate to the person, liberty, protection, correction, morality, control, adoption or disposition of any infant, child or minor, or the duties to, or responsibility for such infant, child or minor, of any parent, guardian or of any other person, corporation or institution whatsoever.

This remarkably expansive conception of the Denver Juvenile Court led to jurisdictional challenges from County and District Courts but, despite this, the jurisdiction of the Denver court was usually upheld and was reaffirmed in 1923 (CSL, 1923, Ch. 78).

Giving substance to this greatly expanded jurisdiction over child welfare, Judge Lindsey created Colorado's first *Mother's Compensation Act* (CSL, 1907 Ch. 168; amended 1913, 1919) which provided for the financial support of children in homes where the father had deserted or was deceased. The financial support of single mothers was supplemented by another law (CSL, 1911, Ch. 179) making non-support on the part of the fathers of both legitimate and illegitimate children a felony offense. This was accompanied by unsuccessful attempts to guarantee the employment of fathers in prison to provide financial support for their dependent children. Later, the *Mother's Compensation* law was supplemented by the *Maternity Fund Act* (or Maternity Law) (CSL, 1923, Ch. 77) which provided for the support of unborn children from the time of their conception.

Underlying much of this child support legislation was a desire to reduce the number of illegal abortions in Denver among young unmarried women. In Judge Lindsey's experience, the true causes of these abortions were

largely because women were the victims of poverty, fear and the inability to make the man do his part in the support of the unborn child by aid to the mother during the time that she was unable to provide aid for herself. Hundreds of children have been saved from the abortionists and hundreds of girls and women have come voluntarily to the Juvenile Court in the secret confidences of its administrative work for these unborn innocents (Denver Juvenile Court, 1925, p.52).

Another law directed primarily to the welfare of young women included a law (CSL, 1909, Ch. 158) which allowed the judge to appoint a 'referee' or assistant judge with the powers of a court clerk to hear cases and make recommendations to the judge. In practice, this formally established a separate girls' department in 1909 within the Denver Juvenile Court under a woman referee, though in fact Ida Gregory had already been serving as assistant judge in girls' cases since 1903.

Whenever the work of the court suggested the need for a law, Judge Lindsey created it and, in effect, Lindsey's court did not serve the law; the law was created to uphold the work of the court. Through this profusion of Lindsey Laws, the Denver Juvenile Court acquired multiple jurisdictions which were roughly divided among several departments. Delinquency complaints were generally handled by the Girls' and Boys' Departments of the court. Under its criminal jurisdiction, the court heard cases against adults who contributed to delinquency or dependency, as well as criminal cases against minors under the age of twenty-one. In effect, the contributory laws and Section 2 of the 1907 law established a criminal jurisdiction within the court over any adult who in any way harmed or endangered the morals of any minor. This included many cases of a sexual nature, including incest and rape cases involving young women 18 years old or younger. Judge Lindsey believed that such cases could be handled most effectively in the juvenile court, as in the criminal courts defendants were typically acquitted by all-male juries.

The greatest share of the court's workload, however, was handled by the Domestic Relations Department, formally established in 1920 with Harry Ruffner as its director. This department investigated and administered cases of non-support and dependency, mother's compensation petitions, marriage annulments, coordinated adoptions and home placements for dependent children, and in general, acted as a clearinghouse for family disputes.

A. Girl Delinquency in the Court[7]

The juvenile court and its methods were broadly conceived as a response to the problem of boy delinquency, and this was reflected in the relatively small proportion of girl delinquents handled in most early juvenile courts. Overall, girl delinquency ranged between ten to twenty-five per cent of all juvenile court casework. While the first few years of the Denver Court were dominated by work with boy delinquents, the proportion of girls grew steadily, along with a separate Girl's Department. In 1909, for example, girls represented only 13.4 per cent of the court's work; by 1921, the proportion of girls rose to 23 per cent of all complaints handled by the Denver Juvenile Court.

Girl delinquency was handled rather differently than boy delinquency in the early juvenile courts. For example, while probation was a central element of the juvenile court concept, it was used less often for girls, who were more frequently committed to juvenile institutions. The general pattern was for girls to be committed at roughly twice the rate of boys and to receive probation half as often. While Denver and Chicago are comparable with respect to this tendency to institutionalize girls more often than boys, the work of these two courts also reveals substantial differences.

A distinctive feature of the Denver court was its practice of deflecting more than half of all complaints of delinquency against children from formal action by the court. This informal work of the court was handled in several ways. If initial investigation of a complaint by the judge or one of his staff showed that mediation between the parties or a warning could resolve the complaint, the record was denoted 'SOC' — settled out of court. In other cases where the complaint lacked merit, the court declined to file the complaint or persuaded the complainant to drop the complaint. Judge Lindsey's practice of settling cases out of court expanded each year. In 1909, about 52 per cent of all complaints were SOC. By 1924, Lindsey reported that his court received approximately 2300 complaints against alleged delinquents, of which 2020 cases (nearly 88 per cent) were settled out of court (Denver Juvenile Court, 1926, p.49). This practice was established at the very beginning of the Denver court, while in the Chicago Juvenile Court virtually every complaint was filed as a formal case.

Yearly reports from the Denver Juvenile Court indicate the overall magnitude of its informal work with girls. Total figures for girls' cases handled by the Girl's Department alone in four years clearly show that a great majority of girls' cases were resolved informally.[8] Of 1932 complaints made against girls, 1630 (84 per cent) were settled out of court or dropped, with only 302 filed as formal cases. Equally significant are an additional 3587 girls where there was no complainant and yet whose situations may well have resulted in a complaint. These strictly informal cases, listed in the reports as 'visits' to homes and schools, nearly double the total number of girls in contact with the court. They included many who for various reasons came to the attention of the court, and others who came to the court on their own initiative, often to see Judge Lindsey himself.

While the figures above reflect casework that was handled by the Girls' Department under the delinquency jurisdiction of the court, equally large numbers of children, from the unborn to young adults, were handled by the Domestic Relations Department of the Denver juvenile Court established in 1920 with H. Ruffner as director. In three consecutive fiscal years the Domestic Relations annual reports[9] list cases involving over 4600 children, both male and female. While the bulk of this casework involved mother's compensation, dependency and adoptions, Domestic Relations also assumed jurisdiction over many criminal cases against adult males charged with contributing to delinquency, sexual abuse and rape. Just as in the Girl's Department, the Domestic Relations staff dealt with large numbers of purely informal cases, referred to as 'outside work', the numbers of which were not recorded due to a lack of clerical staff.

These data raise the possibility that once the Denver juvenile court was established, it, like the Los Angeles juvenile court described by Odem (1991; Odem and Schlossman, 1991), was perceived by many young people and their parents as a relatively 'sympathetic institution'. But the operations of the Denver Juvenile Court also suggest a tentative extension of Odem's characterization. In view of the large number of cases handled informally by the Denver court, there is anecdotal evidence to indicate that a significant percentage of the boys and girls who came to Judge Lindsey's court found their way there via self- or peer-referral. That is, a large number of children voluntarily sought Judge Lindsey's assistance and counsel.

Even after Lindsey was removed from the juvenile court in 1927, parents and troubled young people trooped to his house seeking solace and advice. In an article entitled 'Lindsey's Juvenile Court Still Lives', the Denver Morning News (12 July, 1927) quoted Mrs. Lindsey as saying, 'The telephone rings constantly, and all day long people in trouble wait in the room of my house. Two-thirds of the work of the juvenile court was administrative and not judicial. People know that even if the judge is no longer in his court he can help them.' The story goes on to recount the saga of an unmarried mother of 17 who requested that Lindsey speak to her lover, as well as to her parents who did not know her secret.

These data on the informal work of the Denver Court provide some support for Judge Lindsey's claims that large numbers of children came to his court voluntarily, very often viewing it as a relatively sympathetic institution that would assist rather than punish them. Rhetorically, Lindsey presented the juvenile court as a buffer between the child and a hypocritical society (which he viewed as the true cause of delinquency), and eschewed formal court procedures as inappropriate or even harmful in the majority of cases. Lindsey found this to be especially true in many cases of girl delinquency. Though the nature of girl delinquency was viewed by the Denver Court as more difficult to resolve than boy delinquency, complaints brought against girls were only somewhat less likely (about 5 per cent lower on average) to be SOC. The additional number of girls who came to the court as voluntary delinquents may never be known with certainty as the court records for these cases are largely lost, the majority destroyed by Judge Lindsey to protect their identities.

That the problem of girl delinquency was of a different order from that of boys is clear from the types of complaint which brought them to the juvenile court.

TABLE 1: Twelve Most Frequent Complaints From 2356 Total Complaints Charged Against 1455 Juveniles Filed In Denver Juvenile Court, 1916-1921, By Sex And Percentage.

Complaints	All (%)	Female (%)	Male (%)
1. Taking Things	412 (17.5)	23 (3.0)	389 (24.4)
2. Running or Staying Away from Home	238 (10.1)	103 (13.5)	135 (8.5)
3. Truancy	210 (8.9)	27 (3.5)	183 (11.5)
4. Breaking in and Taking Things	185 (7.8)	0 (–)	185 (11.6)
5. Out Late at Night or Loitering	176 (7.5)	109 (14.3)	67 (4.2)
6. Immoral Conduct or Indecent Liberties	158 (6.7)	115 (15.1)	43 (2.7)
7. Malicious Mischief	103 (4.4)	0 (–)	103 (6.5)
8. Taking Automobile	86 (3.6)	1 (0.1)	85 (5.3)
9. Beyond the Control of Parents or Guardian	76 (3.2)	62 (8.1)	14 (0.9)
10. Disobedient	52 (2.2)	45 (5.9)	7 (0.4)
11. Assault	39 (1.7)	2 (0.3)	37 (2.3)
12. Frequenting Immoral Places or Persons	36 (1.5)	35 (4.6)	1 (0.1)
13. Other Complaints*	585 (24.8)	240 (31.5)	345 (21.6)
Total Complaints	2356 (99.9)	762 (99.9)	1594 (100)

* Other complaints represent 26 infrequent delinquencies, including the standard complaint of 'incorrigibility', which are not discussed in the present analysis.

Table One presents the twelve most common complaints filed against 1455 juveniles in the Denver court between 1916 and 1921, with separate figures for male and female delinquents. As children with formal petitions filed against them were often charged with two or more separate offenses, the total complaints in this table exceed the total number of delinquents. Each of these twelve complaints underscore a sharp contrast between girl and boy delinquency. While minor criminal offenses, 'malicious mischief' (vandalism), and the status offense of truancy were predominant complaints against boys, these complaints were far less frequent among girls. Instead, 'immoral conduct', 'out late nights', and 'running away' were the most frequent complaints brought against girls.

Like virtually all juvenile court observers, Judge Lindsey believed that girl delinquency was primarily a sexual problem. The complaint of 'immoral conduct', which normally denoted underage sexual activity, was over five times more likely to be a complaint against girls. Moreover, in cases where a boy was charged with sexual activity, the (double-standard) term of 'indecent liberties' was usually substituted. The complaints of 'frequenting immoral places' (including 'associating with immoral persons') and staying 'out late at night' were also far more frequently charged against girls. These complaints often reflected a parent's suspicions that a girl was, or was in danger of, engaging in sexual activity by virtue of overall social behavior.

In addition, the ambiguous complaint of 'incorrigibility' (not included in Table One) was in some cases used by the court to mask offenses of a sexual nature in order to protect a girl's reputation. Although Judge Lindsey destroyed his own records of informal work with girls, he made it clear that the bulk of the court's work with girls was designed to protect them from public censure. Rather than enforcing middle class standards of chastity by punishing sexual indiscretions, a large number, and perhaps the majority, of sexual complaints against girls were kept off the record. In the context of moral standards which he condemned as outdated and unrealistic, Judge Lindsey conspired to help many girls remain what Becker (1963, p. 20) termed 'secret deviants'.

In *The Revolt of Modern Youth* (Lindsey and Evans, 1925, pp.64,78) Lindsey reports that during the biennial period of 1920 and 1921 the Denver Juvenile Court dealt with 769 delinquent girls between the ages of 14 and 17. According to Lindsey, 'three-fourths of these girls came to me of their own accord'. For these young women, Lindsey's practice was to convince the man involved to voluntarily come to his court to resolve the matter. 'In many such "voluntary" appearances no formal case is filed or court record made' (Denver Juvenile Court, 1925, p.40).

In addition to sexual activity, another frequent concern revolved around the issue of girls who resisted or lacked parental control. At the time it was generally believed that girls were particularly vulnerable to the attractions and moral dangers of urban life. As Table One shows, complaints of running or staying away from home and simple disobedience were far more frequently made against girls. Though many filed complaints of incorrigibility masked immoral conduct, incorrigibility also often indicated a simple lack of parental control in the home. Indeed, comparing the home and school situations for all filed cases between 1916 and 1921 suggests that these basic institutions had a somewhat weaker hold over girls: while 50 per cent of boys were living with both natural parents at the time of the complaint and 85 per cent were in school, only 25.5 per cent of girls lived with both parents and 47 per cent were in school.

Our review of case file materials reveals that the majority of girl delinquents came from families which in various ways were disrupted by the death of a parent, divorce, separation, or desertion. Three out of four girls did not live with both natural parents at the time of the complaint. Even in cases where both natural parents were together, many of them were living with other relatives, friends, or an employer. In many cases, there were conflicts with step-parents. Many of these girls ran away, some had been physically or sexually abused, and others lied about their age and married without parental consent. In view of this, it is not surprising that of the 155 girls committed to the State Industrial School between 1916 and 1921, 10 per cent had previously been committed to an institution and another 3 per cent had been in two or even three institutions prior to being sent to the Industrial School for Girls. Overall, then, the data in Table One suggest that, while complaints against boys reflected minor criminal offenses, sexual activity and/or a lack of control in the home were the most salient concerns of complainants with respect to girl delinquency.

Another factor highlighting the alternative conception of girl delinquency is the person or agency initiating complaints of delinquency. Table Two presents the source of complaints for the 1455 delinquents arranged in the categories of family, public control agents, private control agents, private charities, and other persons. Consistent with the nature of the complaints discussed above, Table Two shows that in each category of complainant there are clear gender differences. While roughly 55 per cent of the complaints against girl delinquents originated with family members, 45 per cent of the complainants against boys were public control agents — primarily police and schools.

TABLE 2: SOURCE OF COMPLAINTS FILED AGAINST 1455 JUVENILES IN DENVER JUVENILE COURT, 1916-1921, BY SEX AND PERCENTAGE.

COMPLAINANT	TOTAL (%)	FEMALE (%)	MALE (%)
FAMILY			
Mother Only	203	107	96
Father Only	87	52	35
Both Parents	12	5	7
Step/Foster Parents	16	9	7
Other Family/Guardian	75	42	33
(Total)	393 (27.0)	215 (55.4)	178 (16.7)
PUBLIC CONTROL AGENTS			
Police or Fire	323	33	290
School Officer	160	27	133
Juvenile Court	77	19	58
(Total)	560 (38.5)	79 (20.4)	481 (45.1)
PRIVATE CONTROL AGENTS			
Railroad Agent	59	1	58
Store Detective	77	7	70
(Total)	136 (9.3)	8 (2.1)	128 (12.0)
PRIVATE CHARITIES			
(Total)	70 (4.8)	34 (8.8)	36 (3.4)
OTHER PERSONS			
Citizen	196	22	174
Employer	6	1	5
(Total)	202 (13.9)	23 (5.9)	179 (16.8)
MISSING			
(Total)	146 (10.0)	29 (7.5)	117 (11.0)
TOTAL	1455 (100)	388 (100)	1067 (100)

Table Two also indicates that, at least in Denver, girl delinquency was a more salient concern to private child-saving groups than boy delinquency. However, other persons outside of a girl's family, such as an employer, were much less likely to initiate a complaint against a girl. These data and the nature of the complaints against girls suggest that girl delinquency was perceived in terms of two related problems: girls who either lacked the controlling authority of home and school, or were defying that authority by engaging in premarital sex, or both. In the early years of the juvenile court movement, sexuality was clearly the most salient issue in girl delinquency. In their study of the early Chicago Juvenile Court, Breckinridge and Abbott (1912, pp.37-8) claim that 'more than 80 per cent of the delinquent girls are brought to court because their virtue is in peril, if it has not already been lost'. Judge Lindsey's writings suggest a similar proportion in Denver. The question we address here is the response of the Denver Court to this sex delinquency.

How the Denver court responded to the problem of precocious sexuality can be tentatively deduced from our data. Based on Table One, the complaints of 'immoral conduct' and 'frequenting immoral places' are taken on face validity as sex delinquency. Similarly, the complaints of 'running away', 'out late nights', 'beyond the control of parents', and 'disobedience' are taken on face validity as indicators of a lack of control. Based on all complaints filed against the 388 girls in our data, we placed each of these cases into one of four categories: (1) one or more control complaints with no sexual complaint, (2) one or more sexual complaints with no control complaint, (3) one or more control and sexual complaints combined, and (4) complaints other than control and sexual. The relative proportions for each category are presented in the far right column of Table Three.

The 388 girl cases filed between 1916 and 1921 indicate that the predominant concern was control: over 45 per cent of the girls in Table Three fall into the category of control alone. This compares with 17.5 per cent for cases with one or more sexual complaints and no control complaint, and 18.3 per cent for those with both control and sexual complaints. Combining the second and third categories gives a total figure of 35.8 per cent of girls with at least one sexual complaint filed, which is still smaller than cases of control alone.

Assuming that complaints of a sexual nature against girls would have been equally as frequent in Denver as in Chicago (in the range of 80 per cent), it appears that more than half of all sexual complaints against girls were resolved by the Denver Court without formal action being taken. This informal screening would explain the greater proportion of filed complaints relating to control alone, and seems to be consistent with Judge Lindsey's accounts of his court's relatively sympathetic response to sex delinquency. How, then, did the court respond to cases of girl delinquency that were formally filed in the court? To address this question, Table Three presents the court's ruling for all girls' cases. Case dispositions at first hearing are coded as dismissed (including 'released to parent' and 'continued indefinitely'), given probation, or committed to an institution.

TABLE 3: NATURE OF COMPLAINTS BY DISPOSITION AND PERCENTAGES BASED ON 388 FEMALE DELINQUENTS FILED IN DENVER JUVENILE COURT, 1916-1921.

NATURE OF COMPLAINTS	DISPOSITION				TOTAL COMPLAINTS
	DISMISSED	PROBATION	COMMITTED	MISSING	
CONTROL ONLY*	37 (21.0)	56 (31.8)	81 (46.0)	2 (1.1)	176 (99.9) (45.4)
SEX ONLY**	18 (26.5)	10 (14.7)	39 (57.3)	1 (1.5)	68 (100) (17.5)
CONTROL & SEX	19 (26.8)	16 (22.5)	36 (50.7)	0 (0)	71 (100) (18.3)
OTHER***	17 (23.3)	25 (34.2)	26 (35.6)	5 (6.8)	73 (99.9) (18.8)
TOTAL DISPOSITION	91 (23.4)	107 (27.6)	182 (46.9)	8 (2.1)	388 (100)

*   'Beyond Control of Parent', 'Disobedient', 'Out Late Nights', and 'Running or Staying Away'.
**   'Immoral Conduct', 'Indecent Liberties', or 'Frequenting Immoral Places'.
***   'Other' includes cases with no explicit charges off either sexual activity or lack of parental control. This includes 'incorrigibility' that could denote either type of delinquency.

Comparisons of case disposition with the nature of complaints provide a mixed picture of how the Denver Court responded to girl delinquency. With respect to all cases dismissed by the Denver Court, dismissal rates were highest (and roughly equal) for sexual complaints both alone or sexual and control complaints together. These differences, though relatively small, appear to suggest a comparatively progressive stance toward sexual cases. Looking at rates of commitment, however, the court appears much more conservative toward sex delinquency as the commitment rate for sexual cases alone, 57.3 per cent, is the highest among all categories, followed by mixed sexual and control cases at 50.7 per cent.

The conclusion that the Denver Court treated sex delinquency more harshly than other types should be qualified by two considerations. First, as noted earlier, we suspect that the informal work of the court initially screened out a large proportion of sex cases. If this is true, the result would be a smaller 'hard core' of sex cases less amenable to lenient responses of dismissal or probation. Second, a large number of these cases of sexual complaints were sent to the Florence Crittenton Home rather than reform schools. Of the 39 sex-only cases who were committed, 16 were committed to Crittenton, and of the sex plus control cases, of the 36 who were committed, eight were sent to Crittenton. As Crittenton Homes dealt almost exclusively with pregnant girls, and considering that the complaints against these girls came primarily from single parents who either wished to be rid of their daughter or could not support them, the court was left with little discretion in the disposition of those girls known to be pregnant. In addition, commitments to Crittenton Home help explain the very low probation rate for sex cases in Table Three. In view of these complicating factors, and the tendency to dismiss sex cases outright, we suspect that within these constraints, the response of the Denver Court to sex delinquency cases was substantially more liberal than other early juvenile courts described in the existing literature.

Though there is some evidence to support the contention that many parents and their daughters found the Denver court to be a relatively sympathetic institution and benefited from its informal methods, it is possible that the Denver court was less sympathetic to racial and ethnic minorities. Our data reveal that 60 per cent of the 388 girls filed in the Denver Court between 1916 and 1921 had native-born American parents, including African-Americans. This is comparable to the U.S. Census of 1920, which gives 58.8 per cent as the net figure for Denver. Ethnic girls — those with one or both parents foreign-born — represented 27.6 per cent of all filed cases, compared with 41 per cent of Denver's population.

On the other hand, the 49 African-American girls in our data — 12.6 per cent of the Denver Court's girl's cases — compares with the 1920 Census figure of only 2.4 per cent. This over-representation of African-Americans may be due to the pervasive racial discrimination of the times, manifest in terms of their receiving less benefit from the court's informal work. At the same time, this societal and institutional racism must also be considered in concert with the fact that, within the Girl's Department of the Denver Court, an African-American woman handled the majority of these girls. In addition to race discrimination, other variables such as the family situation of these girls could partly account for the over-representation of African-American girls. Only seven (14.3 per cent) of the 49 African-American girls were living with both parents at the time a complaint was filed compared to 25.5 per cent overall. As discussed above, a lack of parental control was highly likely to result in a filed complaint, and family situation may partially account for this over-representation of African-Americans in the Denver Court. Excepting African-Americans, the girl delinquents filed in the Denver court reflected the white native-born majority in Denver at that time, and actually under-represented ethnic minorities. These figures are consistent with Lindsey's inclusive conception of delinquency, and his emphatic conviction that delinquency 'pertains to *all* children, for all children are delinquent at some time or other' (Lindsey, 1908, p.x, emphasis in original).

Our general conclusion is that the early Denver court's constitution and treatment of female delinquents departs in important ways from the existing literature's characterization of the juvenile court. In Denver, the majority of delinquents, including sex delinquents, were handled extra-legally without any official action by the court. Rather than embracing Victorian standards of sexual morality, the Denver juvenile court consistently questioned these standards. Committing a child to an institution appears to have been a last resort, one especially likely to be used in cases where delinquent complaints had been precipitated by family conflict, the child was unwanted by the family, or the court viewed placement in an institution as preferable to the home.

IV. CONCLUSION

CURRENT ACCOUNTS OF PROGRESSIVE-ERA female juvenile justice suggest that sexual precocity was its foremost preoccupation, and that the early juvenile court reflected and enforced a traditional code of morality. Our data suggest a reexamination of this thesis. While sexual precocity was in all likelihood a dominant concern in the larger society as well as among those initiating delinquency petitions against girls, this did not automatically dictate the position of the juvenile court itself. In particular, the Denver court advanced a relatively more progressive constitution of the female delinquent, and this more sympathetic perspective informed the court's actual operations.

For example, we noted that Lindsey frequently deflected many complaints against girls involved in sexual precocity by informal means, resolving them in an informal manner. Concern over a lack of parental control (or resistance to it) was another predominant reason girls were brought to the Denver Juvenile Court. The evidence assembled here indicates that the high proportion of cases involving issues of parental control is partially due to the large number of sexual delinquency cases that were informally diverted from the juvenile justice system.

Overall, our paper suggests that there was significant variation among the early juvenile courts' responses to female delinquency, and that many parents and their daughters, in some communities at least, viewed it as a relatively sympathetic institution. More generally, these data and Lindsey's reconstruct-ive project suggest a partial refinement of Rose's (1990, p.121) contention that the juvenile court was part of a moralizing and normalizing project that has made childhood 'the most intensively governed sector of personal existence'. Without question, Lindsey's program combined science and benevolence to discursively constitute a normal child, stipulate correct child rearing practices, and bring 'new powers of judgment and scrutiny' to 'bear upon the families of troubled and troublesome children' (*ibid.*, p.129).

Though this characterization is in many respects accurate, it cannot suffice as a comprehensive description of Lindsey's project. Specifically, Lindsey's program cannot be reduced, as Rose's global assessment of the juvenile court intimates, to an attempt to compel working class parents and girls to embrace conventional bourgeois family life, a form that Lindsey consistently assailed as hypocritical and repressive. Further, the unmistakably professionalizing component in Lindsey's project did not prevent him from recognizing and explicitly supporting modern youth's revolt against traditional family life and gender relations. In brief, Lindsey's court cannot be accurately described as a unilateral imposition of a moralizing and normalizing project from above. For Lindsey, the conception of childhood and morality around which the juvenile court is structured must be partially informed by and responsive to the knowledge and morality that young people themselves articulate.

Notes

1. Chesney-Lind, 1989.

2. This discussion of entrepreneurial projects is adapted from the authors' earlier and more extensive discussion (Colomy and Kretzmann, 1995).

3. Though a large number of girls sought the court's assistance, Lindsey appears to have had a rather exaggerated notion of what it meant to come to the court voluntarily. There is some evidence to suggest that Lindsey actively solicited visits from young people, through peers or 'encouragement' from officers or friends of the court. We will return to this point.

4. In fact, Lindsey kept fairly detailed notes about many young people who came to the court. But we have uncovered no evidence that these notes were used against them, a point we will return to later.

5. In addition to whatever benefits these precautions provided girls, such measures were also designed to protect Lindsey and the reputation of the Denver court. Though small in number, Lindsey's enemies were well-organized and vocal, distributing dozens of broadsides aimed at discrediting Lindsey by questioning the propriety of his relations with the girls who visited the court. One objective of Lindsey's open door policy was to assure his supporters that his conduct, and the court itself, were beyond reproach.

6. Prior to the round-table discussion, Lindsey had given a speech to the entire high school. A few days before the scheduled speech, the school superintendent called and, at the behest of the local Board of Education, requested that Lindsey 'not touch on questions of sex, marriage, divorce, and similar topics' (*ibid.*, p.111). Much to the dismay of many students, particularly female students, Lindsey honored that request.

7. The early Denver Juvenile Court's reports and records are not complete, many having been destroyed or lost over the years. Case file records from 1916 through the first half of 1921 (located in the Colorado State Archives, Denver, CO), however, are largely complete, and provide a reasonably accurate picture of the court's work. The following quantitative analysis and discussion is based upon Denver Juvenile Court reports and case file materials from 1455 delinquency cases filed in the court between 1 January, 1916 and 1 July, 1921. The authors have supplemented these data for delinquent girls with additional case records from the Colorado State Industrial School for Girls for the period of Judge Lindsey's tenure on the Denver Juvenile Court (1901-1927). All records were examined by the

authors with permission from the Denver Juvenile Court.

8.   Denver Juvenile Court Reports were based on a fiscal year beginning 1 July. The figures used here are from the 1918-19, 1919-20, 1920-21 and 1922-23 reports, which included 'supplementary delinquency reports' on informal cases. Lindsey Papers, Library of Congress, Manuscript Division

9.   Annual Reports of the Department of Domestic Relations, Juvenile Court, City and County of Denver; 1922-23, 1923-24, 1924-25. Unfortunately, these reports do not indicate the sex of these children. Lindsey Papers, Library of Congress, Manuscript Division.

References

Becker, H. (1963), *Outsiders* (Free Press).

Breckinridge, S. and Abbott, E. (1912), *The Delinquent Child and the Home* (Charities Publications Committee).

Chesney-Lind, M. (1989), 'Girl's Crime and Woman's Place: Toward a Feminist Model of Female Delinquency' 35 Crime and Delinquency 5.

Colomy, P. and Kretzmann, M. (1995), 'Projects and Institution Building: Judge Ben B. Lindsey and the Juvenile Court Movement' 42 Social Problems 191.

Colomy, P. and Rhoades, G. (1994), 'Towards a Micro Corrective of Structural Differentiation Theory' 37 Sociological Perspectives 547.

Denver Juvenile Court (1925), *Twenty-five Years of the Juvenile and Family Court of Denver* (publisher unknown).

DiMaggio, P.J. (1988), 'Interest and Agency in Institutional Theory' in L.G. Zucker (ed.), *Institutional Patterns and Organization* (Ballinger) 3.

Eisenstadt, S.N. (1964), 'Social Change, Differentiation, and Evolution' 29 American Sociological Review 235.

_____. (1965), *Essays on Comparative Institutions* (John Wiley).

_____. (1971), *Social Differentiation and Stratification* (Scott, Foresman).

_____. (1973), *Tradition, Change, and Modernity* (John Wiley).

_____. (1980), 'Cultural Orientations, Institutional Entrepreneurs, and Social Change: Comparative Analyses of Traditional Civilizations' 85 American Journal of Sociology 840.

Ewick, P. and Silbey, S. (1995), 'Subversive Stories and Hegemonic Tales: Toward a Sociology of Narrative' 29 Law & Society Review 197.

Friedland, R. and Alford, R.A. (1991), 'Bringing Society Back In: Symbols, Practices, and Institutional Contradictions' in W. Powell and P. DiMaggio (eds.), *The New Institutionalism in Organizational Analysis* (University of Chicago Press) 232.

Gusfield, J. (1981), *The Culture of Public Problems* (University of Chicago Press).

Lindsey, B.B. (1908), 'Introduction' in T. Travis, *The Young Malefactor* (Crowell and Co.) 9.

Lindsey, B.B. and Evans, W. (1925), *The Revolt of Modern Youth* (Boni and Liverwright).

_____. (1927), *The Companionate Marriage*, (Boni and Liverwright).

Meyer, J.W. and Rowan, B. (1977), 'Institutionalized Organizations: Formal Structure as Myth and Ceremony' 83 American Journal of Sociology 340.

Odem, M. (1991), 'Single Mothers, Delinquent Daughters, and the Juvenile Court in Early Twentieth-Century Los Angeles' 25 Journal of Social History 27.

Odem, M. and Schlossman, S. (1991), 'Guardians of Virtue: The Juvenile Court and Female Delinquency in Early Twentieth-Century Los Angeles' 37 Crime and Delinquency 186.

Rose, N. (1990), *Governing the Soul* (Routledge).

Sartre, J.P. (1968), *Search for a Method* (Alfred Knopf).

Schlossman, S. and Wallach, S. (1978), 'The Crime of Precocious Sexuality: Female Juvenile Delinquency in the Progressive Era' 48 Harvard Educational Review 65.

Shelden, R.G. (1981), 'Sex Discrimination in the Juvenile Justice System, Memphis, Tennessee, 1900-1917', in M.Q. Warren (ed.), *Comparing Female and Male Offenders* (Sage) 55.

Shibutani, T. (1970), 'On the Personification of Adversaries', in T. Shibutani (ed.), *Human Nature and Collective Behavior* (Transaction) 223.

Turner, R. and Killian, L. (1987), *Collective Behavior*, 3rd ed. (Prentice-Hall).

III

Achieving the Promise of Justice for Juveniles: A Call for the Abolition of Juvenile Court

JANET AINSWORTH[*]

I. INTRODUCTION: DISILLUSIONMENT WITH THE INSTITUTION OF THE JUVENILE COURT

THE JUVENILE COURT has been a part of the American institutional landscape for nearly a century.[1] Born of the redemptive ideology of Progressivism, the juvenile justice system promised to divert youthful offenders from the rigors of the criminal justice system, both at adjudication and for disposition, and its advocates claimed that in doing so, the juvenile justice system would be able to rehabilitate young lawbreakers and derail their incipient criminal careers. As it reaches its hundredth birthday, however, the juvenile court has come under serious attack. Even its staunchest supporters acknowledge that, as it currently functions, the juvenile justice system is deeply flawed.[2]

The unhappy truth is that contemporary American society does not particularly value young people,[3] and inequities in the current juvenile justice system betray that lack of regard. In exchange for being spared from formal criminal prosecution, juveniles accused of law violations receive procedurally and substantively inferior adjudication in comparison to that accorded to adult defendants. Notwithstanding the efforts of a handful of exemplary public defender offices who strive to zealously represent their juvenile clients,[4] most of the advocacy on behalf of juvenile defendants is only a pale shadow of that received by adults charged with crimes. Indigent juvenile defendants are frequently represented by lawyers who are less experienced and who carry heavier caseloads than their counterparts who represent adult defendants.[5] Even those lawyers willing and able to provide vigorous advocacy for their clients are hamstrung in their ability to do so because, in most jurisdictions by law and in the rest by practice, juvenile defendants are deprived of jury trials.[6] The trials that juveniles accused of crime do receive are all too often perfunctory and barely contested.[7]

The traditional rationale for a separate and unequal juvenile court system justified its procedural inadequacies on the grounds that juveniles receive in exchange the benefit of non-punitive, individualized dispositions in place of the criminal sanctions that would otherwise be imposed. Whatever euphemistic label is applied to institutions of incarceration for juveniles, however, being ordered to undergo such incarceration is unmistakably experienced as punishment.[8] Furthermore, the promise of individualized dispositions crafted with attention to the social needs of the juvenile offender can only be described as a cruel hoax. Despite the earnest endeavors of many well-intentioned and hard-working juvenile court judges and lawyers, young offenders do not and, in many jurisdictions now, can not receive dispositions tailored to address their social needs.[9] Never has the juvenile justice system been accorded the resources necessary to supply the kind of social services that might provide meaningful intervention in the lives of young offenders. Given this depressing assessment, should the juvenile court survive beyond its centenary? The severe shortcomings of the juvenile justice system and its intractability to meaningful reform[10] have led a number of commentators to press for its total abolition, replacing it with a unified criminal justice system.[11]

A counter-attack upon the advocates of a unified court system has not been long in coming.[12] Although the defenders of the separate juvenile justice system acknowledge the existence of the procedural and substantive deficiencies of the juvenile court system and agree with the abolitionists that the juvenile court has failed to live up to its institutional mandate,[13] they nevertheless advocate the continuation of the two-tiered juvenile-adult criminal justice system. Supporters of the juvenile court accuse abolitionists of having an unrealistically romanticized perception of the procedural protections of the adult criminal justice system. Juvenile court supporters maintain that theoretically desirable features of the criminal process such as trial by jury are in reality relatively unimportant in the actual day-to-day workings of the adult criminal courts.[14]

The emotional heart of the argument against abolition of the juvenile court, however, is that the existence of the juvenile court system shields at least some younger offenders from the draconian penalties of the criminal justice system.[15] This justification for the continued existence of a separate juvenile court must be given serious consideration. In recent years, both state and federal lawmakers have enacted legislation dramatically increasing the severity of criminal sanctions,[16] including statutes requiring mandatory incarceration and mandatory minimum terms for a variety of offenses.[17] As a result, the United States now has the dubious distinction of having the highest rate of incarceration in the world,[18] and has seen its prison population nearly quadruple since 1976.[19] With no end in sight to the clamor for harsher criminal penalties, it is tempting for those who are appalled at the cruelty and waste in such policies to join with those who gloss over the shortcomings of the juvenile court system and to recommend the continued existence of a two-tiered criminal justice system as the only politically practical way to spare some young offenders from the full impact of America's current inhumane sentencing policies.

As tempting as that option may be, however, a unified criminal justice system is nevertheless preferable to our present two-tiered adult-juvenile court system. Indeed, the cultural and ideological assumptions that underpin the current two-tiered justice system not only engender many of the serious shortcomings of the juvenile justice system but also serve to exacerbate the very policies and practices of the adult criminal justice system that make it so abhorrent to defenders of the juvenile court. Critics of juvenile court abolition thus miss the point when they argue that juveniles would be worse off than they are at present if they were to be tried as adults in 'adult court'.[20] Advocates of the abolition of juvenile court are, in fact, necessarily arguing for the abolition of 'adult court' with all the assumptions entailed by its necessary contrast with juvenile court. In proposing the abolition of a separate juvenile court and its replacement with a unified criminal court system, abolitionists plead for a radical rethinking of the entire criminal justice system, making it more responsive to the characteristics of all those it touches, regardless of age.

II. THE IMPACT OF ESSENTIALISM
ON THE JUVENILE COURT

IN ORDER TO UNDERSTAND the problems of today's two-tiered justice system, it is necessary first to understand how it came into existence.[21] The juvenile court was the product of larger social and cultural forces at work in the late nineteenth century and early twentieth century.[22] Although the social and cultural landscape of contemporary America has changed markedly since then, the ideological assumptions that made the concept of the juvenile court appear so attractive at the turn of the century still live on today in both the juvenile court and in the 'adult' criminal justice system, and these assumptions help to reinforce many of the most deleterious aspects of both halves of the two-tiered criminal justice system.

A. The Historical Context of the Creation of the Juvenile Court

The turn of the century was marked by sweeping sociological changes in the American way of life, as an America predominantly made up of rural and agrarian communities gave way to an urban, industrialized America with changing demands on its labor force. As small-scale farming and handicraft production were overtaken in the labor economy by industrial mass production, fewer and fewer jobs could be efficiently performed by the young, who lacked the skills and strength of older workers. In addition, the potential labor pool included a large proportion of recent immigrants from southern and eastern Europe, who were believed to be resistant to the cultural assimilation necessary for their incorporation into the industrial labor force. These factors combined to make it both possible and desirable to delay the entry of teenagers into the work force and to impose instead a longer period of formal education and cultural socialization. The Progressive Era heralded the enactment of a multitude of laws to facilitate the changing needs of an industrial society, including laws requiring compulsory school attendance, limiting the hours and conditions of youth employment, and raising the legal age of marriage.[23] Thus, one byproduct of the industrial metamorphosis of American life was the prolongation of the period of economic dependency of young people and a consequent postponement of their attainment of full personhood within society.

At the same time that economic and social factors provided the impetus for a legally-enforced prolongation of pre-adulthood and dependency, the cultural understanding of what it meant to be a child was undergoing an equally dramatic change. The socially-shared meaning of childhood — both who is classified as a child and what are assumed to be the essential attributes of the child — have changed radically throughout history.[24] Although the medieval world barely recognized childhood as a significant phase of human development,[25] in later centuries, the stage of life between infancy and sexual maturity came to be invested with a set of specific qualities that served to distinguish children from adults.[26] Children were seen as dependent and vulnerable creatures, lacking the capacity to appreciate the future consequences of their actions or to control their behavior. Children's characters were thought to be not yet fixed, but rather were malleable, necessitating close adult training, supervision, and control in order to become competent and virtuous adults. Because the attributes of children were considered to be biologically rooted, and thus intrinsic and invariant, these essential characteristics of children justified, indeed demanded, that as a class they be treated differently from adults in almost every aspect of their lives.[27]

The historical trend toward greater and greater age segregation and age-specific treatment of the young reached its zenith during the period between 1850 and 1950, which has been called 'the high watermark of childhood' as a separate, cognizable stage of life.[28] Moreover, by the turn of the century, the perceived attributes of childhood were being applied to young people who would have been classified as adults in an earlier era, but who were now considered as a new subclass of child — the adolescent.[29] Given the social construction of childhood prevalent during the Progressive Era, it is unsurprising that the legal status and treatment of young people in this period reflected these assumptions about their inherent characteristics.[30]

B. The Cultural Construction of the Child and Juvenile Court Jurisdiction

This, then, was the cultural context in which the juvenile court was created and flourished.[31] Juveniles were thought to be so intrinsically different from adults as to inescapably compel the creation for them of an entirely separate and independent justice system. The juvenile court was distinguished from the criminal justice system by its refusal to confine its jurisdiction to the adjudication and punishment of violations of the criminal code. Rather, the juvenile court used the occasion of an allegation of criminal behavior as an opportunity to impose on the young offender a rehabilitative program designed to correct the socially deviant tendencies that caused the particular law violation.[32]

In contrast to the criminal court, juvenile court jurisdiction and sanctioning power could be validly triggered by any kind of behavior considered to be anti-social or inappropriate, regardless of whether it involved the violation of a criminal law. Young people who smoked, cursed, stayed away from school, or whose parents found them insufficiently controllable, were as subject to the full coercive authority of the juvenile court as were those accused of crime.[33] Violating the criminal law was seen as just another item in the catalog of socially deviant behaviors that warranted coercive correction. In fact, advocates of the juvenile court system insisted that young people were literally incapable of committing crimes in that they lacked the moral and cognitive capacity necessary for criminal liability.[34] To that end, juvenile judges did not preside over criminal trials in which defendants were found guilty and sentenced to prison; rather they held 'adjudicatory hearings' at which 'respondents' were found 'delinquent', resulting in a 'disposition' that sent them to 'training school'. Today, such terms may strike us as mere euphemisms, but in the cultural and ideological context of the world that spawned the juvenile court, such language exposed the central role in Progressive ideology of the essential otherness of the young.

C.   Changing Conceptions of Childhood

The world of late twentieth century America is as different from that of the Progressives as theirs was from the agrarian society of the early American republic. Just as the social, economic, and technological conditions of the Progressive era created the turn of the century concept of childhood, so, too, the post-industrial era has in turn created a different concept of the nature of childhood.[35] As many sociologists and historians have noted, the contemporary understanding of childhood views that stage of life as far less intrinsically different from adulthood than did those holding the prevalent beliefs of the turn of the century.[36] Children seem to us to grow up faster these days, adopting adult mannerisms, perspectives, and activities at an early age.[37] At the same time, adults indulge in styles and behaviors that would once have earned them ridicule for aping the young. The strict demarcation between childhood and adulthood has blurred in contemporary culture.

Despite the changes in the social construction of childhood in contemporary America that have softened the dichotomy between child and adult, the American legal system nevertheless maintains a two-tiered justice system of juvenile and adult criminal courts. The contemporary juvenile court, however, would be unrecognizable to the Progressive architects of the juvenile justice system. The Progressive juvenile court shrugged off due process concerns as irrelevant to the primary mission of the court, which was not the fair adjudication of guilt or innocence, but rather the crafting of dispositions to address the social needs of the offending youth.[38] The contemporary juvenile court, by contrast, has been forced to curtail its former freewheeling informality of process as a result of Supreme Court decisions according certain fundamental due process rights to juveniles accused of criminal conduct.[39] Moreover, the basic concept that the juvenile court was not punitive but rehabilitative, premised on the idea that punishment was inappropriate for children who were inherently incapable of criminal wrongdoing, has been increasingly rejected. More and more jurisdictions are adopting frankly retributive juvenile justice systems, emphasizing punishment and accountability as the basis for juvenile court sanctions.[40] Given the increased procedural formality and punitive sanctioning of the current juvenile court system, the traditional distinctions between the juvenile and criminal justice systems no longer hold. The continued existence of a separate juvenile court system would be difficult, perhaps impossible, to sustain absent an essentialist ideology about the nature of childhood that justified the system from its inception. Despite the changes in our society and culture that have altered our current cultural construction of childhood from that held by the Progressives, the juvenile justice system has nevertheless clung to the view that young people are so essentially different from adults as to necessitate a separate justice system.

D. Essentialism as Ideology

As a philosophical stance, essentialism can be defined as the belief that a type of person or thing has a true, intrinsic, and invariant nature, a nature that is constant over time and across cultures, and that consequently defines and constitutes it.[41] Essentialism is thus ahistorical and culturally universalistic in its insistence that essences precede cultural and historical interpretation.[42] In looking at classes of persons, essentialism often credits biology as the source of the natural essences in question. An essentialist view of the child, then, posits the existence of innate and uniquely differentiating characteristics of children which invariably distinguish them from adults. This essentialism accords primacy to that aspect of identity that it calls 'child', and in highlighting those attributes, it necessarily shrouds other aspects of identity that are at least equally constitutive of identity,[43] such as race,[44] gender,[45] and class.[46] Since essentialism maintains that the unique essence of the child exists universally, then this intrinsic nature of the child must by necessity constrain humanly-created social institutions dealing with the young.

Examples of this lingering essentialism can be found in language used by children's advocates. For example, a recent law review article by Professor Wendy Anton Fitzgerald[47] relies heavily on the assumption that children are so unlike adults that adults can never achieve an understanding of what she calls the 'mystery that is childhood'.[48] She maintains that 'a deep gulf divide[s] [adults] from children and childhood ... Children and childhood appear across the divide, not as comprehensible lesser versions of adults, but as mysteriously different from us'.[49] Because this difference is incommensurate with adult understanding, she exhorts us to 'craft legal personhood and the law ... to accept and even admire the mysteries of childhood forever beyond our adult apprehension'.[50] Although Professor Fitzgerald is not primarily addressing the juvenile justice system in this article,[51] such assumptions about the inherent nature of childhood typify the essentialism that still guides the advocates of a separate juvenile court system.[52]

E.   Essentialism as Justification of the Juvenile Justice System

The appeal of essentialism to advocates of a separate juvenile justice system is obvious, for it provides an ideological justification for disparate treatment of young persons accused of criminal violations. Essentialism, however, does more than merely rationalize a two-tiered justice system. Conceiving of young offenders as essentially different from adult offenders supports certain attitudes and practices within the juvenile justice system that constitute some of its most criticized aspects. The deleterious impact of essentialist ideology is compounded in this case by the categorization of older adolescents, who make up the vast majority of juvenile offenders, as children. In considering the sixteen-year-old juvenile as more like a ten-year-old than a twenty-two-year-old, the essential attributes ascribed to the child are imposed upon the adolescent, whether they truly fit or not. Is it any wonder that the juvenile court, an institution consciously shaped to fit the perceived essential attributes of the child, seems so ill-suited to the actual characteristics of those most often subject to its jurisdiction?[53]

That juvenile court's essentialist ideology classifies adolescents as a sub-

class of child rather than as a sub-class of adult has far-reaching consequences, as can be seen by considering psycholinguistic research on how the
creation and use of categories structures human thought and engenders
inferences.[54]   George Lakoff, a linguist who incorporates the findings of
cognitive research in his work on semantics, found that this psychological
research supports the conclusion that certain categories, which he calls basic-
level idealized cognitive models (ICM), are more basic to human thought than
others.[55] These ICM categories serve as templates for thought, influencing the
inferences that we draw when we include something as a member of the
category in question.[56] Lakoff noted that researchers have observed certain
'prototype effects' in the use of categories, in which some members of a
category are thought of as better representatives of that category than other
members. For instance, people rank robins and sparrows as better examples
of the 'bird' ICM than owls and eagles, who likewise are thought of as better
examples than emus or penguins. Even though all of these examples in fact
fully qualify as members of the 'bird' ICM, the category has within it an
internal logic that makes some of its members seem to us more 'bird-ish' than
others.[57] Moreover, this psycholinguistic research shows that when we make
use of an ICM category, we tend to take attributes characteristic of the
'prototype' members of the category and by extrapolation apply them to other,
non-'prototype' category members.[58] This means that 'new information about
a representative category member is more likely to be generalized to
nonrepresentative members than the reverse'.[59] Thus, information learned
about 'prototype' birds like robins is more likely to be inferred as true about
less 'prototype' birds such as ducks, while information about ducks is less
likely to be attributed to robins.[60]

The category 'child' functions as a basic-level idealized cognitive model,
and prototype effects can be seen in its usage. That is, if someone were to
say, 'Look at those children', without any additional qualifying information,
the image conjured up is not of a group of infants or teenagers, but of pre-
adolescents. Even though babies, toddlers, elementary school-aged students,
teenagers, and adult offspring are all members of the ICM 'child', the most
'child-ish' prototypical members are those who are post-infancy and pre-
puberty. Since these children represent the prototype 'child', then the
classification of the adolescent as a member of the ICM 'child' results in
unconsciously adopted inferences derived from our knowledge and beliefs
about the prototype 'child' being applied to adolescents. In other words, by
calling adolescents 'children', our perceptions of specific adolescents will be

affected by what we expect and know is true of prototypical 'children'. Characteristics of the prototype 'child' thus are exaggerated in our percep-tions of the adolescent, and characteristics that are inconsistent with the prototype 'child' are minimized, trivialized, or even completely denied.

In this way, the impact of the essentialist ideology of the juvenile court is compounded by the prototype effect involved in classifying its adolescent subjects as 'children'. Those in the juvenile justice system who give credence to this ideology expect to see — and so will tend to see — in adolescents the prototypical child-like qualities of dependency, vulnerability, and malleability. Similarly, because prototypical children are said to lack the judgment and experience to understand the future consequences of their actions and to make wise decisions in important matters, adolescents will be assumed to share these deficiencies as well. Having defined the subject of the juvenile justice system as the 'child', juvenile court ideology constructs the juvenile accused as 'child-like'.

F.   The Consequences of Essentialism for Juvenile Defendants

Many of the most criticized aspects of juvenile court — the frequency of grossly ineffective assistance of defense counsel[61] and general procedural inferiority to the criminal justice system[62] — are directly related to the construction of young offenders as 'children'. Because 'children' are incapable of understanding what is in their best interests, many defense lawyers in the juvenile justice system come to think that they need not listen to the voice of the juvenile accused when he attempts to articulate what he wants to happen in his case. Instead defense counsel is encouraged to adopt a guardian ad litem-like role,[63] in which rigorous case preparation and zealous defense advocacy can be eschewed in favor of collaborating with the state in imposing a corrective disposition. In fact, defense counsel who buy into the essentialist ideology of the juvenile court may be persuaded that vigorous defense would be counter-productive to the juvenile's true best interests,[64] which can only be realized with the help of the coercive supervision of the state.[65]

Indeed, the very concept that juvenile offenders possess and can effectively exercise rights becomes problematic given the essentialist ideology of the juvenile court. American rights jurisprudence is based upon the premise that to be a legitimate rights-bearer, one must be an autonomous individual.[66]

Because 'children' are dependent and not autonomous, actors in the juvenile justice system can ignore the possibility of the effective agency of accused juveniles in exercising their legal rights.[67] Therefore, we need not trouble ourselves over procedural deficiencies in the juvenile justice system that would be intolerable if its subjects were deemed to be rights-bearing actors with true agency.

G.   The Injustice of Denying Juveniles Jury Trials

Without question, the single most serious procedural infirmity of the juvenile court in comparison with the adult criminal court is the near-total absence of jury trials.[68] Using juries as fact-finders provides a host of advantages to anyone, adult or juvenile, accused of crime.[69] For example, juries serve as a buffer for over-zealous prosecutors and a check on the rogue judge who is biased or capricious.[70] Juries also protect defendants from the more commonly found juvenile court judge whose fact-finding sensibilities are blunted from the hundreds, if not thousands, of cases that she hears every year.   Research comparing juror fact-finding with judicial fact-finding demonstrates that a defendant is far more likely to be convicted if a judge hears the case than if one has a jury trial.[71] This is the likely reason why researchers have found that, after controlling for the seriousness of charged offenses, juveniles are more likely to be convicted in juvenile court than adults charged with comparable offenses in criminal court.[72]

Why would judges convict more frequently than juries? There are several compelling explanations that analyze the ways in which judicial decision making differs from that of juries. One obvious difference is that juvenile court judges routinely hear hundreds, if not thousands, of cases every year. The same police officers and probation officers testify over and over again, often regarding juveniles with whom the judge is already familiar from earlier charges involving the accuseds or their siblings. It would be a rare judge capable of hearing and assessing the evidence in each case with the fresh ears of the average juror.

Even when the juvenile court judge is not predisposed to finding the juvenile guilty before the first witness is sworn, the very nature of fact-finding by a single person is radically different from the group decision-making of a jury. Before the jury can return a verdict, the jurors must discuss the evidence and the law amongst themselves. During the back-and forth of this deliberation, jurors have an opportunity to reconsider their positions in light of the arguments and observations of their fellow jurors. Other jurors can draw attention to facts that may otherwise go unnoticed or unappreciated and can point out logical flaws in reasoning that may cause a juror to change his or her first impression as to the correct verdict. Judges, on the other hand, do not have the benefit of anyone else's recollections of the evidence or evaluations of the case.

Judicial decision-making also differs from that by jurors because all fact-finders' life experiences inevitably color their fact-finding, both in assessing witness credibility and in judging the inherent plausibility of each side's version of the facts. Despite a growing appreciation of the need for diversity in the judiciary, judges as a group are still less diverse in economic status, racial and ethnic background, gender, and social class than the average jury pool. The typical jury is thus far richer in various dimensions of diversity than any one judge can possibly embody, better able to reflect the interplay of competing community values. Given all of these fundamental differences between judicial decision-making and jury decision-making, it should not be surprising that juries tend to acquit far more frequently than do judges.

In addition to this greater likelihood of acquittal, those who have jury trials receive more meaningful appellate review than those who are tried in bench trials, as trial by judge is called. Judges presiding over jury trials must articulate the law governing the case in jury instructions, which are later subject to appellate review to correct errors of law that have worked to the defendant's detriment. In the bench trials that the vast majority of juveniles must receive, on the other hand, prejudicial errors of law can easily go undetected because they are not articulated. Thus: '[J]uveniles denied a jury trial lose out twice. They are more likely to be convicted in the first place, and are less likely to be able to prove an error of law which would allow them to prevail on appeal.'[73]

Despite the evidence of the great advantages to an accused of having the right to jury trial, defenders of the juvenile court downplay the significance of depriving juveniles of this fundamental right. One of the most articulate opponents of the abolition of juvenile courts, Professor Irene Rosenberg, acknowledges that deprivation of the right to jury trial in juvenile court is 'significant', but not in her view 'catastrophic'.[74] She considers the right to jury trial to be of little practical importance, as evidenced by the fact that so few adult defendants avail themselves of it, instead pleading guilty.[75] The importance of the denial to juveniles of the right to jury trial, however, cannot be shrugged off as insignificant merely because the majority of adult defendants do not directly exercise the right to trial by jury. The criminal justice system operates in the shadow of the jury trial, so that the potential invocation of that right affects the charging decision and plea negotiation even in cases that eventually culminate in guilty pleas. Professor Rosenberg concedes that the possibility that a defendant could demand a jury trial operates as 'a chip to be used in the poker game of plea bargaining';[76] but it is often not just *a* chip, but the *only* chip that a criminal accused possesses as leverage.

Moreover, notwithstanding the fact that the 'sentencing stakes' for adult offenses are generally higher than for most juvenile offenses, the jury trial 'chip' is not thereby limited in usefulness to adult felony prosecutions as Professor Rosenberg claims.[77] Indeed, recent experience in the state of Washington demonstrates the transformative power of the right to jury trial even in courts with limited sanctioning authority. Until relatively recently, adults charged in Washington with misdemeanor offenses had no right to trial by jury. In 1982, the Washington Supreme Court held that the state constitution guaranteed jury trials in those prosecutions.[78] Even though misdemeanor sentences are statutorily limited to one year in length and are generally considerably shorter than that in practice, the newly created right to jury trials for misdemeanor defendants nevertheless completely changed the dynamics of practice in the municipal and district courts. Defense lawyers who practiced before and after the advent of jury trials in municipal court observed that the resulting change in misdemeanor practice was dramatic, and for the better. Overcharging offenses became less common, as prosecutors have become more realistic in their assessment of what charges are appropriate to file and of which cases present proof problems that jurors are unlikely to overlook. Even though municipal court sentences are far shorter than those authorized in felony cases, plea negotiations over sentencing recommendations still take place regularly in the misdemeanor courts, and the jury trial 'chip' has proven to be as useful there as in superior court.[79] Since sentences of juvenile confinement frequently exceed the sentences meted out to adult misdemeanants in municipal court, there is every reason to expect that granting jury trials in juvenile court would have at least as great an ameliorative effect there as has been the case in the municipal courts of Washington.

III. THE IMPACT OF ESSENTIALISM ON THE 'ADULT' CRIMINAL JUSTICE SYSTEM

AS DISCUSSED ABOVE, the essentialist ideology that supports the juvenile justice system entails a variety of detrimental consequences for accused juveniles. The consequences of this ideology, however, are not limited to the effects on those tried in juvenile court. In constructing the 'child' with its attributes, essentialism also simultaneously constructs its inverse, the 'adult'. Just as the 'child' construct shapes the practices of the juvenile court, so, too, its necessary counterpart, the 'adult' construct, shapes the practices of the 'adult' criminal court.

The dichotomous relationship between the constructs of 'child' and 'adult' can be seen as a specific example of the more general role which binary oppositions assume in contemporary Western culture. The adult/child dichotomy represents the kind of fundamental binary opposition — man/woman, rational/irrational, nature/culture, public/private — that characterizes post-Enlightenment Western thought and language.[80] Structuralist theory explored what it interpreted as the fundamental role of binary oppositions in the production of social meaning, with one of the paired terms serving as the preferred, primary term and the other as its subordinate negation or inverse, derivative of and dependent upon it for its meaning. Later, post-structuralists such as Jacques Derrida showed that this hierarchical relationship between the terms of a binary opposition could be reversed, with the supposed secondary, subordinate term actually serving to generate and define the ostensibly primary, privileged term.[81]

The existence of our present two-tiered justice system, with juvenile court separate from 'adult' criminal court, is predicated on the adult/child binary opposition. Because being a child is seen as essentially different from being an adult, the logic and legitimacy of separate justice institutions is maintained. Once the criminal court is transformed into the 'adult' court by the creation of a separate juvenile court, however, the 'adult' construct that informs the practices in that institution must be given shape and content. As in other binary oppositions, the meaning of the primary term 'adult' is defined as being the inverse of the 'child' construct. That is, what it means to be an adult is by necessity the opposite of what it means to be a child.[82] Thus, because the 'child' is seen as dependent, the 'adult' must be independent; if the 'child' has a malleable character, then the 'adult' must have a fixed character; if the 'child' is not morally responsible for his actions, then the 'adult' must be fully morally responsible for her actions. In this way, the essentialism that constructs the child by necessity concomitantly constructs the adult as well.

Just as the 'child' construct serves to define the 'adult', so, too, the juvenile justice system defines the criminal justice system to be its complementary inverse. In fact, the criminal justice system is often referred to in this context as the 'adult' court.[83] Having become the 'adult' court, the criminal justice system is seen as the inversion of the juvenile court in its characteristic goals and practices. Because the juvenile court is intended to rehabilitate malleable youths, then it seems natural for the adult criminal court to eschew rehabilitation for its non-malleable adults.[84]

Similarly, since juvenile court adjudication is intended for those who, due to cognitive immaturity, are not fully responsible for the consequences of their actions, then, of necessity, adult court becomes the forum for adjudication for those who are fully responsible for their behavior. As a result, the adult criminal justice system does poorly by those past the age of majority who do not measure up to the adult paradigm, with its presumption of full cognitive abilities. Mentally retarded individuals often have developmental disabilities that render their ability to understand the consequences of their actions at least as problematic as does the cognitive immaturity imputed to young people.[85] But whereas the cognitive immaturity of those under the age of eighteen is recognized in law by the existence of the juvenile courts, the cognitive disabilities of mentally retarded offenders receive no such dispensation. After all, they are 'adults', not 'children', with all that these categories imply. Thus, the mentally retarded offender is liable to suffer the full measure of retributive punishment appropriate to the 'adult' offender, even up to the ultimate sanction of the death penalty.[86]

Nor are the mentally retarded the only individuals under the jurisdiction of the adult criminal justice system whose classification and sentencing as 'adults' ought to give us pause. Ironically, a growing number of young people under the age of eighteen now find themselves tried in criminal court as adults. Juvenile courts have always had the authority to transfer a juvenile into the criminal justice system if it was determined that the offender was not amenable to the rehabilitation of juvenile sanctions.[87] In recent years, however, greater and greater numbers of young people are being transferred into the adult criminal justice system, some through mandatory waiver provisions[88] and some through more frequent resort to discretionary waiver procedures by prosecutors and juvenile court judges.[89] Which juvenile offenders do judges and prosecutors find so unlike the prototype 'child' that it justifies classifying them as 'adults' and expelling from the juvenile justice system? Overwhelmingly, they are the offspring of the underclass and racial minorities — juveniles whose demeanor and behavior seem to middle-class eyes to be utterly unlike the vulnerable, dependent prototypical 'child'.[90] Once waived into the criminal courts, the juvenile is transformed into an 'adult', with all that the designation entails. No longer deemed a vulnerable and salvageable 'child', the juvenile tried as an adult is written off for rehabilitation. Instead, the criminal justice system mechanically metes out punishment for the crime in full measure, commensurate with the full moral responsibility of the 'adult'. Is it any wonder, then, that advocates for juveniles find abhorrent the idea of trying and sentencing young offenders within the adult criminal justice system?

IV. TOWARD A UNIFIED CRIMINAL JUSTICE SYSTEM

THE PROBLEMS WITH THE CURRENT JUVENILE JUSTICE SYSTEM that its detractors decry and its supporters acknowledge represent the logical outcome of its essentialist ideology, and the consequences of having to categorize each offender as either a 'child' or an 'adult'.[91] The choice is all or nothing; one is either a child, subject to the jurisdiction and sentencing practices of the juvenile justice system, or one is an adult, fully subject to the jurisdiction and sentencing practices of the criminal justice system. The current system admits of no middle ground, no sliding scale of responsibility and redeemability.

In reality, the characteristics and behavior of young people do not change on the eve of their eighteenth birthdays, or at any other arbitrary point. True, very young children start out life helpless, vulnerable, and utterly dependent upon the adults in their world, without the ability to understand the consequences of their actions or conform their behavior to the expectations of others; over time, they become adults with more mature cognitive abilities and moral characters. But they don't magically achieve adult competence and responsibility all at once, and still less on a predictable time-table that justifies a uniform age upon which full criminal responsibility should be imputed. Neither is it accurate to think of everyone over the age of eighteen as fully 'adult', if by that we mean an independent, autonomous actor with a fixed, immutable character, acting in conscious regard for the consequences of her actions and thus fully responsible for those actions. Rather, there is a continuum of these characteristics and behaviors, both for juveniles and for adults. The two-tiered justice system, in forcing us to categorize offenders as either children or adults, exaggerates their differences and obscures their similarities.[92] Children are neither as dependent and incompetent, nor adults as autonomous and competent, as the essentialist ideology of the two-tiered justice system pretends.[93]

The faults inherent in the two-tiered justice system are a prime example of what Martha Minow has called the 'dilemma of difference', in which 'problems of inequality can be exacerbated both by treating members of minority groups the same as members of the majority and by treating the two groups differently. The dilemma of difference may be posed as a choice between ... similar treatment and special treatment, or as a choice between neutrality and accommodation.'[94] In this case, the 'special treatment' of trying juvenile offenders as 'children' results in giving them the second-class justice that their status as 'children' logically entails, but the 'similar treatment' of trying them as 'adults' is equally disastrous, given our assumptions about the full criminal responsibility of 'adults'. Minow wisely suggests that the law should place less emphasis on the differences said to exist between children and adults,[95] and instead consider broadening the concepts embedded in our legal norms to better accommodate the actual characteristics of everyone, be they under or over the age of majority.[96]

Only a unified justice system, rejecting arbitrary all-or-nothing categorization, is capable of recognizing the continuum of our actual attributes and accounting for it in devising appropriate and fair sanctions for any individual's criminal law violations. Because there would be no necessity to decide whether individual offenders were 'children' or 'adults', a unified court system could be more responsive to the actual characteristics of individual actors. Freed of the requirement that an all-or-nothing determination be made, judges could recognize fine gradations in dependency, malleability, and responsibility as mitigating factors in sentencing.[97] There might well be presumptions about the characteristics of an accused based on age, but any such presumptions would always be rebuttable. A unified criminal justice system would contribute to easing the grip of essentialism on criminal justice policies by erasing the indelible line between the status of adult and child, and replacing it with a nuanced continuum.

There are, of course, other legal contexts in which a strict bright line is maintained distinguishing between the legal statuses of the adult and the child. Certain rights and privileges — voting, driving an automobile, purchasing and consuming alcohol and tobacco products, and the like — are granted only when an individual reaches a specified age. Although such rules defining adult status are admittedly arbitrary, the transaction costs inherent in case-by-case determinations of maturity render any approach other than the bright line rule impractical in such legal contexts where the consequences of a mismatch in categorization are less drastic for the youth and for society than in the context of the criminal justice system. That is, it is certainly true that some persons under the age of eighteen would be thoughtful, reflective voters, and that others over the age of eighteen exercise their franchise in an irresponsible manner. The personal and social consequences of such underinclusion and overinclusion in the voting age demarcation, however, hardly rise to the levels of injustice present in the two-tiered criminal justice system. It is the magnitude of that injustice that makes imperative the abolition of the separate juvenile court and its replacement with a single, unified criminal justice system.

Opponents of abolition of a separate juvenile court maintain that one cannot talk about abolishing the juvenile court without considering the nature of the criminal justice system,[98] and they are surely correct. They point out that, notwithstanding the conceded failings of the juvenile justice system, the criminal justice system is itself not without serious flaws.[99] Again, they are correct. The shortcomings of the juvenile justice system cannot be overcome without addressing the critical failings of the larger American criminal justice agenda. Imagination and courage must be shown in considering alternatives to a failed criminal justice system that has brought America obscene levels of imprisonment and executions without making the streets feel safer.[100] Where both supporters and opponents of the abolition of the juvenile court can agree is that the only criminal justice system worthy of support is one which is capable of achieving justice for every individual entangled within it.

Notes

* This chapter is adapted from *Youth Justice in a Unified Court: A Response to Critics of Juvenile Court Abolition*, 36 Boston College Law Review (September 1995)..

1. Illinois is credited with founding the first juvenile court in the United States through its Juvenile Court Act of 1899. 1899 Ill. Laws 131 *et seq.*

2. These commentators agree that the current juvenile justice system deserves criticism, although they differ as to specifics of their objections to the system. See, for example, Irene Merker Rosenberg, 'Leaving Bad Enough Alone: A Response to the Juvenile Court Abolitionists' 1993 Wisc. L. Rev. 163 (1993) condemning juvenile courts for providing neither adequate procedural protections nor appropriate dispositional programs to juvenile accuseds; Mark I. Soler, 'Reimagining the Juvenile Court' in Child, Parent, and State 561 (S. Randall Humm *et al.*, eds. 1994), criticizing juvenile courts for offering inadequate and uncoordinated social services to juveniles in their jurisdiction; Charles E. Springer, 'Rehabilitating the Juvenile Court' 5 Notre Dame J. L. Ethics & Pub. Pol'y 397 (1991), arguing that the presence of lawyers and emphasis on due process of law has a negative impact on juvenile justice system; Travis Hirschi & Michael Gottfredson, 'Rethinking the Juvenile Justice System' 39 Crime & Delinq. 262 (1993), arguing that the juvenile justice system is based on false premises regarding young offenders' malleability and criminal responsibility.

3. Although American public rhetoric may suggest that we cherish the young, the miniscule amount of government resources dedicated to programs dealing with children's issues demonstrates that the problems of the young are a low social priority. Americans may deplore child abuse, child poverty, and high rates of infant mortality, but we are unwilling to pay for programs to effectively combat these problems, and the meagerly-funded programs that do exist are among the first targets for budget cuts. See Bob Herbert, 'In America: What Special Interest?' New York Times Section A, p. 19, 22 March, 1995, deploring congressional proposals to slash funding for children's needs, proposals that would 'throw poor children off the welfare rolls, ... eliminate Federal nutritional standards for school meals, ... cut benefits for handicapped children, ...[and] reduce protection for abused and neglected children.' Legal doctrine has been no more attentive to children's needs than have government bureaucrats. See Wendy Anton Fitzgerald, 'Maturity, Difference, and Mystery: Children's Perspectives and the Law' 36 Ariz. L. Rev. 11 (1994), demonstrating that child support provisions and child custody law are more responsive to the interests of adults and legal institutions than to the needs of the children involved.

4.   In addition, there are an even smaller number of private and public interest lawyers who specialize in defending juveniles and who vigorously and effectively represent their clients. Such lawyers are, unfortunately, very much the exception rather than the rule.

5.   Janet E. Ainsworth, 'Re-imagining Childhood and Reconstructing the Legal Order: The Case for Abolishing the Juvenile Court' 69 N. Car. L. Rev. 1083 at 1128 (1991).

6.   Ainsworth, *supra* note 5 at 1121-22.

7.   Ainsworth, *supra* note 5 at 1127-29.

8.   This fact was recognized by the Supreme Court in its landmark case *In re Gault*, 387 U.S. 1 (1967) when the Court affirmatively acknowledged for the first time that forcible detention of juveniles in state institutions constituted incarceration (p. 27).

9.   A growing number of states have adopted explicitly punitive juvenile court sentencing policies that prohibit taking the social needs of the young offender into account in disposition. For example, Washington's *Juvenile Justice Act* forbids prosecutors from considering the social needs of the offender in making the charging decision and forbids judges from doing so in sentencing. *Wash. Rev. Code* §§ 13.40.070 (3), 13.40.070 (7), 13.40.150 (4)(e).

10.   Professor Barry Feld, who has written extensively on nearly every aspect of the contemporary juvenile justice system, concluded recently that, 'After more than two decades of constitutional and legislative reform, juvenile courts continue to deflect, co-opt, ignore, or absorb ameliorative tinkering with minimal institutional change ... remain[ing] essentially unreformed.'   Barry C. Feld, 'The Transformation of the Juvenile Court' 75 Minn. L. Rev. 691 at 723 (1991).

11.   *Supra* note 5; Feld, *supra* note 10; Katherine H. Federle, 'The Abolition of the Juvenile Court: A Proposal for the Preservation of Children's Legal Rights' 16 J. Contemp. L. 23 (1990).

12.   See, e.g., Rosenberg, *supra* note 2; Soler, *supra* note 2.

13.   Rosenberg, *supra* note 2 at 165.

14.   *Ibid.* at 171-74. For a response to this argument, see *infra* notes 68-81 and accompanying text.

15.   Professor Rosenberg considers shorter sentences one of the primary virtues of the current juvenile justice system (p. 184). She expresses skepticism that, if juvenile court were abolished, state legislatures would be 'less Draconian' in sentencing juveniles than they have been in sentencing adult offenders (p. 182).

16.   As a result, the average length of incarceration upon conviction of a violent crime tripled between 1975 and 1989. Michael Tonry, *Malign Neglect: Race, Crime, and Punishment in America* at 174 (1995). By international standards, 'American punishments are all but incomparably harsher than those in other countries' (p.196).

17.   For an excellent analysis of these recent trends in sentencing, see Gary T. Lowenthal, 'Mandatory Sentencing Laws: Undermining the Effectiveness of Determinate Sentencing Reform' 81 Calif. L. Rev. 61 (1993), discussing recently enacted state and federal sentencing statutes requiring mandatory incarceration, mandatory sentence enhancements, and mandatory minimum terms.

18.   As of 1989, the rate of incarceration in the United States stood at 426 per 100,000 persons. Marc Mauer, *The Sentencing Project, America Behind Bars: A Comparison of International Rates of Incarceration* at 3, 17 (1991). In comparison, the next highest rates were in pre-majority rule South Africa, which incarcerated 333 per 100,000, and in the Soviet Union, with an incarceration rate of 260 per 100,000. *Ibid.* at 3, 17-18. No other nations for which statistics are available comes even close to matching this rate; incarceration rates in Western Europe range from 35 to 100 per 100,000, and Asian rates run from 21 to 140 per 100,000 (at 6).

19.   Tonry, *supra* note 16 at 173-74. The escalating increase in per capita rates of incarceration in the United States is unprecedented. Historically, rates of incarceration remained relatively stable from the 1920s to the mid 1970s. Alfred Blumstein, 'Racial Disproportionality of U.S. Prison Populations Revisited' 64 U. Colo. L. Rev. 743 at 744-45 (1993).

20.   Rosenberg, *supra* note 2 at 166.

21.   Much has been written analyzing the historical development of the juvenile court in the context of the Progressive movement of the early part of this century. See, e.g., Anthony M. Platt, *The Child Savers: The Invention of Delinquency* at 3-152 (2nd ed., 1977); Ellen Ryerson, *The Best Laid Plans: America's Juvenile Court Experiment* at 16-56 (1978); John R. Sutton, *Stubborn Children: Controlling Delinquency in the United States 1640-1981* (1988); Steven L. Schlossman, *Love and the American Delinquent: The Theory and Practice of 'Progressive' Juvenile Justice, 1825-1920* at 55-156 (1977); Sanford Fox, 'Juvenile Justice Reform: An

Historical Perspective' 22 Stan. L. Rev. 1187 at 1221-30 (1970); Ainsworth, *supra* note 5 at 1094-1101.

22. I have written elsewhere at greater length about the social and cultural factors that led to a reconfiguration of childhood and the evolution of adolescence during this period in American history. Ainsworth, *supra* note 5 at 1093-96. See also, John Demos, *Past, Present and Personal: The Family and the Life Course in American History* (1987); Joseph F. Kett, *Rites of Passage: Adolescence in America — 1870 to the Present* at 111-264 (1977); David Bakan, 'Adolescence in America: From Idea to Social Fact' 100 Daedalus 979 at 979-84 (1971); John Demos & Virginia Demos, 'Adolescence in Historical Perspective' 131 J. of Marriage & the Fam. 632 at 636-37 (1969).

23. Ainsworth, *supra* note 5 at 1094-96.

24. The belief that children differ in an essential sense from adults is of comparatively modern vintage. For further historical overviews of the history of childhood in Europe and America, see Philippe Ariès, *Centuries of Childhood: A Social History of Family Life* (1962); C. John Sommerville, *The Rise and Fall of Childhood* (1982) (childhood from ancient Greece to twentieth century); Neil Postman, *The Disappearance of Childhood* (1982) (childhood from the European middle ages to present-day America); Robert Bremner, ed., *Children and Youth in America: A Documentary History* (1970) (five volume collection of primary source materials on American childhood); David Rothman, 'Documents in Search of a Historian: Toward a History of Childhood and Youth in America' 2 J. of Interdisciplinary Hist. 367 (1971). See generally Miles F. Shore, 'The Child and Historiography' 6 J. of Interdisciplinary Hist. 495 (1976); LaMar T. Empey, 'Introduction: The Social Construction of Childhood and Juvenile Justice' in *The Future of Childhood and Juvenile Justice* 1 at 7-15 (LaMar T. Empey, ed., 1979).

25. In medieval Europe, 'the awareness of the particular nature of childhood ... which distinguishes the child from the adult ... was lacking'. Ariès, *supra* note 24 at 128.

26. Beginning in the sixteenth century, economic and technological changes in European society combined with new philosophical attitudes about human nature to create a perception of childhood as a separate stage of human development with specific characteristics. Arlene Skolnick, 'Children's Rights, Children's Development' in *The Future of Childhood and Juvenile Justice* 138 at 150 (LaMar T. Empey, ed., 1979); Postman, *supra* note 24 at 20-51.

27. Arlene Skolnick has traced the connection between early twentieth century beliefs about the psychological development of the child and the evolution of social and legal practices befitting those beliefs. Arlene Skolnick, 'The Limits of Childhood:

Conceptions of Child Development and Social Context' 39 Law & Contemp. Prob. 38 (1975).

28. Postman, *supra* note 24 at 67.

29. John and Virginia Demos have noted that '[a]dolescence, as we know it, was barely recognized before the end of the last century'. Demos & Demos, *supra* note 22 at 632. As described at the turn of the century, the adolescent was 'vulnerable ... pliant ... impressionable ... ', subject to a 'lack of emotional steadiness [and] violent impulses' (pp. 634-35). For an extensive social history tracing the development of adolescence in America as a culturally recognized stage of human development, see Kett, *supra* note 24 at 111-264 (1977); see also Skolnick, *supra* note 27 at 61-4; Bakan, *supra* note 22 at 979-84.

30. As Neil Postman observed, 'In a hundred laws children were classified as qualitatively different from adults'. Postman, *supra* note 24 at 67.

31. Twenty years after the founding of the first juvenile court system in Illinois, nearly every state had enacted legislation establishing similar juvenile courts. Platt, *supra* note 21 at 9-10.

32. One of the most articulate expositions of the theory underlying the juvenile justice system was written by Judge Julian Mack, a juvenile court judge in Chicago who became an influential advocate for separate juvenile courts. Julian W. Mack 'The Juvenile Court' 23 Harv. L. Rev. 104 (1909).

33. For female adolescents, one could add sexual activity to the list of behaviors that often resulted in lengthy incarceration in juvenile detention facilities. Steven Schlossman & Stephanie Wallach, 'The Crime of Precocious Sexuality: Female Juvenile Delinquency in the Progressive Era' 48 Harv. Educ. Rev. 65 (1978).

34. Ryerson, *supra* note 21 at 75.

35. I have written elsewhere in more detail about the reconfiguration of life stages, including childhood, in contemporary American culture. Ainsworth, *supra* note 5 at 1101-04.

36. See, e.g., Postman, *supra* note 24 at 120-34; Marie Winn, *Children without Childhood* at 3-7 (1983); Skolnick, *supra* note 26 at 164-65.

37. Postman, *supra* note 24 at 98-142.

38. Mack, *supra* note 32 at 119-20; Ryerson, *supra* note 21 at 38-39.

39. See, e.g., *In re Gault*, 387 U.S. 1 (1967), holding that due process in juvenile court required notice of the charges, the right to be represented by counsel, the right to confront adverse witnesses, the right to exercise the privilege against self-incrimination, and the right to appellate review; but see *McKeiver v. Pennsylvania*, 403 U.S. 528 (1971), plurality opinion, holding that juveniles accused of criminal law violations are not entitled to jury trial under either the Sixth Amendment or the due process clause of the Fourteenth Amendment.

40. For more detailed discussions of the recent shift in juvenile justice philosophy from rehabilitation to a more punitive 'just deserts' model, see Ainsworth, *supra* note 5 at 1104-12; Martin L. Forst & Martha-Elin Blomquist, 'Cracking Down on Juveniles: The Changing Ideology of Youth Corrections' 5 Notre Dame J. Leg. Ethics & Pub. Pol'y 323 (1991); Martin L. Forst & Martha-Elin Blomquist, 'Punishment, Accountability, and the New Juvenile Justice' 43 Juv. & Fam. Ct. J. 1 (1992); Barry C. Feld, 'The Transformation of the Juvenile Court' 75 Minn. L. Rev. 691 (1991); Martin R. Gardner, 'Punitive Juvenile Justice: Some Observations on a Recent Trend' 10 Int'l J. L. & Psychiatry 129 at 131-47 (1987); Barry C. Feld, 'The Juvenile Court Meets the Principle of the Offense: Punishment, Treatment, and the Difference It Makes' 68 B.U. L. Rev. 821 at 822-96 (1988).

41. Diana Fuss, *Essentially Speaking: Feminism, Nature, and Difference* at 2 (1990).

42. In contrast, social constructivism posits that the seemingly natural categories of essentialism are themselves historically and culturally contingent artifacts. A social constructivist perspective focuses on the interrelationship of complex cultural and ideological practices that together produce systems of classification. Thus, a constructivist denies that innate and invariant essences exist prior to their contingent social production. For a fuller treatment of social constructivism, see Ainsworth, *supra* note 5 at 1085-90.

43. In focusing on one attribute as primary in the constitution of identity, essentialism brackets other attributes as secondary. Many critics have, for example, pointed out that gender essentialism in feminist theory obscures differences among women such as race, class, sexual orientation, etc. See Elizabeth V. Spelman, *Inessential Woman: Problems of Exclusion in Feminist Thought* (1988); Angela P. Harris, 'Race and Essentialism in Feminist Legal Theory' 42 Stan. L. Rev. 581 (1990); Martha Minow, 'Feminist Reason: Getting It and Losing It' 38 J. Legal Educ. 47.

44. At every level of the process — from the initial police decision to cite or arrest, to pre-trial detention determinations, to the prosecutorial choice of charge, to the adjudication of delinquency, through to disposition and ultimate release from supervision — race plays a critical role in the functioning of the juvenile justice system, with African-Americans consistently over-represented in the system and subjected to more severe sanctioning than juveniles of other races. See, e.g., Richard Sutphen, P. David Kurtz, and Martha Giddings, 'The Influence of Juveniles' Race on Police Decision-Making' 44 Juv. & Fam. Ct. J. 69 (1993); Jeffrey Fagan *et al.*, 'Blind Justice? The Impact of Race on the Juvenile Justice Process' 33 Crime & Delinq. 224 (1987); Jeffrey Fagan *et al.*, 'Racial Determinants of the Judicial Transfer Decision: Prosecuting Violent Youth in Criminal Court' 33 Crime & Delinq. 259 (1987); Rogers McCarthy & Brent L. Smith, 'The Conceptualization of Discrimination in the Juvenile Justice Process: The Impact of Administrative Factors and Screening Decisions in Juvenile Court Dispositions,' 24 Criminology 41 (1986); Barry Krisberg *et al.*, 'The Incarceration of Minority Youth' 33 Crime & Delinq. 173 (1987); Dale Dannefer & Russell K. Schutt, 'Race and Juvenile Justice Processing in Court and Police Agencies' 87 Am. J. Soc. 1113 (1982); Terence P. Thornberry, 'Race, Socioeconomic Status and Sentencing in the Juvenile Justice System' 64 J. Crim. L. & Criminology 90 (1973). In this regard, unfortunately, the juvenile justice system mirrors the adult criminal justice system in the disproportionate presence of racial minorities among accused offenders. See generally, Coranne Richey Mann, *Unequal Justice: A Question of Color* (1993).

45. Historically, gender played a significant role in the decision to invoke jurisdiction over offenses unique to the juvenile court system such as stubbornness, sexual activity, and being a runaway. Female adolescents were far more likely than their male counterparts to be charged with these status offenses and incarcerated for long periods as a result. Meda Chesney-Lind, 'Guilty by Reason of Sex: Young Women and the Juvenile Justice System' in *The Criminal Justice System and Women* 77 (Barbara R. Price & Natalie J. Sokoloff, eds., 1982). This form of gender bias is less overt today, but can still be found in differential treatment of male and female offenders. Donna M. Bishop & Charles E. Frazier, 'Gender Bias in Juvenile Justice Processing: Implications of the *JJDP Act*' 82 J. Crim. L. & Criminology 1162 at 1183-85 (1992), finding that males are somewhat more likely to be incarcerated for criminal violations than similarly offending females, but females held in contempt of court for repeat status offenses are sharply more likely to be incarcerated than similarly offending males. See also Meda Chesney-Lind & Randall Shelden, *Girls, Delinquency, and Juvenile Justice* (1992); Daniel J. Curran, 'The Myth of the New Female Delinquent' 30 Crime & Delinq. 3486 (1984).

46. While it may appear so obvious as to go without saying, the socioeconomic status of the accused is a key variable at every level of discretion in charging, adjudication, and dispositions in juvenile court. Robert J. Sampson & John H. Laub, 'Structural Variations in Juvenile Court Processing: Inequality, the Underclass, and Social Control' 27 Law & Soc'y Rev. 285 (1993).

47. Fitzgerald, *supra* note 3.

48. *Ibid.* at 22.

49. *Ibid.* at 19.

50. *Ibid.* at 98.

51. The article in question does touch upon the juvenile justice system, but mainly focuses on the legal doctrines governing child custody and child welfare as her vehicle for discussing the legal status of children.

52. Professor Fitzgerald was not unaware that her analysis could be seen as essentialist. She further recognized that essentialism tends to mask differences among members of the class in question, so that an essentialist perspective on childhood masks differences among children based on race, class, gender, and so forth. *Ibid.* at 98, n. 548. Notwithstanding her disclaimer, however, her repeated insistence throughout the article on the absolute incommensurability between the adult and child's world views warrants considering her analysis as an example of essentialism.

53. The mismatch between the assumed attributes of the child and the perceived characteristics of some young offenders often leads to their expulsion from the juvenile justice system for being insufficiently 'child-like'. See *infra* notes 89-92 and accompanying text.

54. See generally George Lakoff, *Women, Fire, and Dangerous Things: What Categories Reveal About the Mind* (1987).

55. Basic-level categories have simpler names, greater cultural salience, and are learned earlier by children than higher or lower level categories. For example, 'tree' is a basic-level category, as compared with the higher level category 'plant' and the lower level category 'sugar maple.' *Ibid.* at 31-38.

56. *Ibid.* at 68-154 (1987); see especially Lakoff's analysis of the inferences entailed in the use of the category 'mother' as a basic-level idealized cognitive model, *ibid.* at 74-85.

57. *Ibid.* at 44-45.

58. Lakoff asserts that 'prototypes act as *cognitive reference points* of various sorts and form the basis for inferences.' *Ibid.* at 45 (emphasis in original, citations omitted).

59. *Ibid.* at 42.

60. This particular prototype effect, called asymmetry in generalization, is most clearly demonstrated in empirical research done by Lance J. Rips, 'Inductive Judgments about Natural Categories' 14 J. Verbal Learning & Verbal Behavior 665 (1975), discussed in Lakoff, *supra* note 54 at 42 and 45.

61. Observers of the juvenile justice system have been virtually unanimous in their condemnation of the system's tolerance of seriously inadequate defense lawyering. See, e.g., M. A. Bortner, *Inside a Juvenile court: The Tarnished Ideal of Individualized Justice* at 136-39 (1982); M. Marvin Finkelstein *et al.*, *Prosecution in the Juvenile Court: Guidelines for the Future* at 40-42 and 51-62 (1973) (describing Boston Juvenile Court); Barbara Flicker, *Providing Counsel for Accused Juveniles* at 2 (1983); Jane Knitzer & Merril Sobie, *Law Guardians in New York State: A Study of the Legal Representation of Children* at 8-9 (1984); Edwin M. Lemert, *Social Action and Legal Change: Revolution Within the Juvenile Court* at 178 (1970); Platt, *supra* note 21 at 163-75; Stevens H. Clarke & Gary G. Koch, 'Juvenile Court: Therapy or Crime Control and Do Lawyers Make a Difference?' 14 Law & Soc'y Rev. 263 at 297-300 (1980); David Duffee & Larry Siegel, 'The Organization Man: Legal Counsel in the Juvenile Court' 7 Crim. L. Bull. 544 at 548-49 (1971); Barry C. Feld, 'The Right to Counsel in Juvenile Court: An Empirical Study of When Lawyers Appear and the Difference They Make' 79 J. Crim. Law & Criminology 1185 at 1207-8 (1989); Elyce Z. Ferster, Thomas F. Courtless, & Edith N. Snethen, 'The Juvenile Justice System: In Search of the Role of Counsel' 39 Fordham L. Rev. 375 at 398-99 (1971); Fox, *supra* note 21 at 1236-37; Anthony Platt & Ruth Friedman, 'The Limits of Advocacy: Occupational Hazards in Juvenile Court' 116 U. Pa. L. Rev. 1156 at 1168-81 (1968).

62. See *infra* notes 66-81 and accompanying text.

63. In response to a survey undertaken in the mid-1980s in New York state, 85% of the juvenile defense lawyers described their role as a guardian *ad litem*. Knitzer & Sobie, *supra* note 61 at 8-9. See generally, Ferster *et al.*, *supra* note 61 at 398-401 discussing the tendency of defense counsel in juvenile court to adopt a non-adversarial guardian-like stance.

64. See Bortner, *supra* note 61 at 138-39; see also, David Bogen, 'Beating the Rap in Juvenile Court' 31 Juv. & Fam. Ct. J. (no.3) 19 (1980), criticizing those defense lawyers who value acquittals over ensuring that the juvenile court retains the authority to correct the social deviance of the juvenile offender.

65. Another rationalization for less-than-vigorous advocacy is that the typical length of confinement for juveniles is much shorter than the adult sentence imposed for the equivalent offense; lower stakes are thought to justify lesser standards in defense advocacy. This rationale for sub-standard lawyering should be rejected. Although exceptionally severe sanctions — the death penalty, life imprisonment without parole — may justify an extraordinary effort on the part of defense counsel, this should not legitimize providing inadequate defense simply because the penalties in a case are perceived as light. In any event, it is not necessarily true that juvenile sentences are invariably shorter than those in the adult criminal justice system. See, e.g., Hirschi & Gottfredson, *supra* note 2 at 270, noting studies that show that juveniles sometimes are incarcerated for longer periods than similarly-offending adults; see also Susan K. Knipps, 'What is a 'Fair' Response to Juvenile Crime?' 20 Fordham Urb. L. J. 455 at 460 (1993), citing recent New York study showing that only 4% of juveniles waived into the criminal courts received longer sentences than they might have received if jurisdiction had been retained in juvenile court.

66. Martha Minow, *Making All the Difference* at 299-300 (1990). Professor Mary Ann Glendon notes in her communitarian critique of contemporary American legal culture that American rights discourse presumes that the rights-bearer is 'a lone autonomous individual'. Mary Ann Glendon, *Rights Talk: The Impoverishment of American Discourse* at 45 (1991). Feminist legal theorists have similarly criticized legal doctrine for privileging the autonomous individual as the legal norm, to the disadvantage of those who place greater value on relationships than on independence. See, e.g., Mary I. Coombs, 'Shared Privacy and the Fourth Amendment, or the Rights of Relationships' 75 Calif. L. Rev. 1593 (1987), analyzing the influence of assumptions about autonomy and independence in search and seizure law and suggesting that these norms represent male values.

67. Robert H. Mnookin, 'The Enigma of Children's Interests' in *In the Interest of Children: Advocacy, Law Reform, and Public Policy* at 16 (Robert H. Mnookin, ed., 1985).

68. Only thirteen states guarantee jury trials in juvenile court. See the statutes and caselaw collected in Ainsworth, *supra* note 5 at 1121-22, n. 258-261, listing the statutes and cases in each jurisdiction regarding the right to jury trial in juvenile court. Even in those jurisdictions that do statutorily permit juveniles to elect trial by jury, jury trials are apparently extremely rare. The *parens patriae* ideology

shared by most lawyers and judges in juvenile court probably makes adversarial jury trials seem out of place, so that the formal statutory jury trial guarantee is seldom exercised by juvenile accuseds. *Ibid.* at 1122, n. 263.

69.   For a fuller explanation of the value of jury trials and of the many ways in which juveniles are at a disadvantage because they are denied jury trials, see Ainsworth, *supra* note 5 at 1121-26.

70.   In holding the Sixth Amendment jury trial guarantee applicable to the states, the Supreme Court noted its importance as a 'safeguard against the corrupt or overzealous prosecutor and against the compliant, biased, or eccentric judge'. *Duncan v. Louisiana* 391 U.S. 145 at 156 (1968).

71.   The most extensive comparative study is that of Harry Kalven and Hans Zeisel, in which they compared jury verdicts in over three thousand cases with 'shadow' verdicts that the judges would have given if the cases had been tried to the court. Overall, juries failed to convict more than twice as often as judges would have done. Harry Kalven Jr. & Hans Zeisel, *The American Jury* at 55-81 (1966).

72.   P. Greenwood *et al.*, *Youth Crime and Juvenile Justice in California* at 30-31 (1983).

73.   Ainsworth, *supra* note 5 at 1126.

74.   Professor Rosenberg, among all of the defenders of a separate juvenile court system, has most explicitly addressed what she sees as the relatively minimal consequences of the denial of the right to trial by jury. Rosenberg, *supra* note 2 at 109-10.

75.   Rosenberg, *supra* note 2 at 109-10.

76.   Rosenberg, *supra* note 2 at 109.

77.   See *ibid.*

78.   *Pasco v. Mace*, 655 P.2d 618 (1982).

79.   I am basing my assessment of the impact of jury trials in municipal court on my experience and that of my colleagues at the Seattle-King County Public Defender Association, where I was first a staff attorney and later the training coordinator.

80.   Stephen K. White, *Political Theory and Postmodernism* at 15-16 (1991); Joan W. Scott, 'Deconstructing Equality-versus-Difference: Or, the Uses of Poststructuralist Theory for Feminism' in *Conflicts in Feminism* at 134 and 137 (Marianne Hirsch & Evelyn Fox Keller, eds., 1990).

81.   'First principles ... are commonly defined by what they exclude'. Terry Eagleton, *Literary Theory* at 132 (1983). For example, a term thought of as primary such as 'man' defines what it means to be male only in contrast to the partner term of secondary status, 'woman.' As Professor Eagleton explains (*ibid.*): '[w]oman is the opposite, the 'other' of man: she is non-man, defective man, assigned a chiefly negative value in relation to the male first principle. But equally man is what he is only by virtue of ceaselessly shutting out this other or opposite, defining himself in antithesis to it, and his whole identity is therefore caught up and put at risk in the very gesture by which he seeks to assert this unique, autonomous experience.'

      This reversal of the polarity of binary oppositions is the central intellectual move of deconstruction. Of course, the new hierarchical relationship resulting from the deconstructed binary opposition can itself be deconstructed, and so forth, *ad infinitum*. Thus, the structuralist attempt to provide a foundation for meaning is shown through deconstruction to be chimerical, as meaning so generated is inherently indeterminate. White, *supra* note 82 at 15-16.

82.   *Cf.* Eagleton, *ibid.*, at 132-3, describing how the 'female' construct comes to define the supposedly primary 'male' construct as its inverse.

83.   See Rosenberg, *supra* note 2 at 163.

84.   I do not mean to suggest that the decline of rehabilitation as a goal of the criminal justice system is the sole result of the dichotomous adult/juvenile justice system. There are many reasons behind the increasingly punitive and retributive nature of American criminal justice. See Francis A. Allen, *The Decline of the Rehabilitative Ideal: Penal Policy and Social Purpose* (1981), discussing the disillusionment with the rehabilitative model in penology and the embrace of a more punitive criminal justice philosophy. See also Tonry, *supra* note 16 at 197, contending that one factor in the increasingly harsh sentencing policies of the United States is our 'remarkable ability to endure suffering by others'. What I do contend is that making the criminal justice system the complementary inverse of the juvenile justice system exacerbates these tendencies.

85.   *Cf.* Van W. Ellis, 'Guilty but Mentally Ill and the Death Penalty: Punishment Full of Sound and Fury, Signifying Nothing' 43 Duke L.J. 87 (1993), arguing against the trend in the criminal justice system towards hostility to lack of mental capacity as excusing criminal liability, including capital punishment.

86.   The Supreme Court has upheld the execution of mentally retarded offenders in *Penry v. Lynaugh*, 492 US 302, 340 (1989), holding that the imposition of the death penalty upon a mentally retarded defendant found competent to stand trial does not violate the Constitution. Since then, the state of Texas put to death a man with an IQ of 65. David Stout, 'Texan Who Killed Ex-wife and Her Niece Is Executed', New York Times Section A, p. 16, 18 January, 1995. About three percent of Texas' death row population currently awaiting execution are estimated to be mentally retarded. Malissa Wilson, 'Executing Retarded Convicts Fuels Moral Debate', Houston Post, p. A-25, 17 March, 1995.

87.   Barry C. Feld, 'The Juvenile Court Meets the Principle of the Offense: Legislative Changes in Juvenile Waiver Statutes' 78 J. Crim. L. & Criminology 471 (1987).

88.   For a survey and analysis of the variety of statutory mechanisms for automatic waiver of certain juvenile offenders into the criminal courts, see Feld, *supra* note 89; see also Ainsworth, *supra* note 5 at 1110-11, n. 173-177, collecting state statutes authorizing automatic transfer of juvenile jurisdiction into the criminal courts.

89.   Ainsworth, *supra* note 5 at 1111.

90.   Even sympathetic observers cannot see minority inner-city youths as 'children'. See, e.g., the tellingly-titled account by a middle-class white journalist of the story of two young African-American boys. Alex Kotlowitz, *There Are No Children Here: The Story of Two Boys Growing Up in the Other America* (1992). Less sympathetic observers are even less likely to see such youths as redeemable 'children' appropriate for treatment within the juvenile justice system. 'Most middle-class parents get second chances for their kids ... Society is increasingly intolerant, however, of the mistakes of children from lower-class families. The popular attitude is that they're lost causes.' Hartford Courant, 'Trying 14 Year Olds As Adults: An Exercise in Frustration', 2 January, 1995.

91.   This kind of all-or-nothing categorization is common in legal discourse, and is frequently the product of essentialism with respect to the nature of the category in question. '[L]egal reasoning ... not only typically deploys categorical approaches that reduce a complex situation, and a multifaceted person, to a place in or out of a category but also treats the categories as natural and inevitable.' Minow, *supra* note 66 at 22.

92.   Martha Minow has observed that the adult/child dichotomy in the law — constructing the adult as autonomous and powerful as opposed to the dependent, powerless child — acts to obscure the interdependence and lack of autonomy of many adults and to conceal the range of power and powerlessness in individual

adult lives. Minow, *supra* note 66 at 301-6. Feminist scholars have long observed that legal doctrine and theory promotes individualism and autonomy as legal norms, at the expense of the interconnected interdependence that many people experience as central to their identity. See, e.g., Coombs, *supra* note 66 at 1598; *cf.* Pierre Schlag, '*Fish v. Zapp:* The Case of the Relatively Autonomous Self' 76 Geo. L.J. 37 (1987), noting that even the socially and rhetorically constructed self constructs itself as autonomously choosing its degree of autonomy.

93. After examining the work of developmental psychologists, Arlene Skolnick concluded that '[t]he overemphasis on the differences between children and adults ... results from not only an underestimate of children's abilities, but an overestimate of that of adults.' Skolnick, *supra* note 27 at 56.

94. Minow, *supra* note 66 at 20-21.

95. Minow 'rejects the notion that our society should answer questions about children's legal status simply by asking how children differ from adults. That inquiry wrongly suggests that such differences are real and discoverable rather than contingent upon social interpretations and choices'. *Ibid.* at 303.

96. *Ibid.* at 283-306.

97. My vision of sentencing within a unified criminal justice system would appear to fly in the face of the current trend in criminal justice towards determinate sentencing, in which statutory sentencing guidelines provide narrow sentencing ranges for a particular offense without regard to the characteristics of the particular offender. For a recent symposium on determinate sentencing guidelines, see 78 Judicature no. 4, 1995.

   A critique of one-size-fits-all determinate sentencing policies is beyond the scope of this Article; however, such policies are not necessarily incompatible with the kind of sentencing that I advocate within a unified criminal court. Even within a strict determinate sentencing scheme, mitigating circumstances insufficient to provide a complete bar to criminal liability justify lower sentences than the standard range for an offense. Such factors as immaturity, relative lack of ability to appreciate the future consequences of one's actions, and the like could be considered as mitigating factors in sentencing.

98. Rosenberg, *supra* note 2 at 166.

99. *Ibid.* at 171-74.

100. Among the other visions that might provide the basis of an effective, humane, anti-retributive criminal justice system are feminist theory and civic republicanism. See Kathleen Daly, 'Criminal Justice Ideologies and Practices in Different Voices: Some Feminist Questions about Justice' 17 Int'l J. of the Sociology of Law 1 (1989) (feminist theory); John Braithwaite & Philip Pettit, 'Not Just Deserts: A Republican Theory of Criminal Justice' (1990) (civic republicanism). See also, Tonry, *supra* note 16 at 181-209, noting that the disparate racial impact of contemporary sentencing policies must be taken into account in reforming the criminal justice system to achieve more balanced and less cruel sentencing practices.

IV

The James Bulger Tragedy: Childish Innocence and the Construction of Guilt

MICHAEL FREEMAN*

THE MURDER OF TODDLER JAMES BULGER by two ten-year-old boys in Merseyside in February 1993 came — depending upon how one looks at it — at just the right or the wrong time. For the Right, it was an instantaneously recognisable symbol for a wider malaise. 1992 had stood out as a year in which there was a sense of panic about youth crime. There was rioting on out-of-town council estates. Car theft and ram-raiding received considerable public exposure. In Manchester, on Moss Side, a 14-year-old boy was shot dead, seemingly an innocent victim of so-called crack wars. In Manchester also, a 15-year-old girl was abducted, imprisoned and eventually tortured to death by her 'friends'. In South London, a 12-year-old boy was stabbed by another school child in his school playground. But concern turned to consternation and panic with the arrest of two ten-year-olds, revealed in photographs[1] after their trial and conviction, to look 'normal', even angelic, for the abduction and murder of a two year old who strayed from his mother's attention in a shopping mall. The Home Secretary's immediate response was to say that persistent and serious offenders under 15 would, in future, be locked up. He urged MPs to 'catch up with the mood of the people' and attacked 'laggard police authorities'. The Prime Minister called for a 'crusade against crime'. He blamed 'parents, the church and "opinion generally" for failing to disapprove of criminal behaviour'.[2] The Education Secretary proceeded one week later to announce a £10 million clampdown on truancy: 'Show me a persistent young truant; I will show you a potential young criminal.'[3]

As if not to be overtaken in sensing public mood, the Labour Party (for these purposes ideologically part of the Right) responded with similarly fatuous sound bites. The Shadow Health Secretary demanded the reintroduction of national service and Tony Blair, then Shadow Home Secretary, demanded a regime of 'tough love'. The phrase was Bill Clinton's and embraces a regime in which secure containment is tempered with responsiveness to an offender's needs.

The Bulger case could not have been more timely. A week after the murder, *The Daily Telegraph* published its annual 'state of the nation' Gallup poll.[4] It oozes despair and despondency. More than a third of the population could think of nothing about Britain to be proud of and nearly half said they would emigrate if they could. A panic of such epidemic proportions demands, as Cohen reminds us,[5] a 'folk devil' and the juvenile delinquent — now younger than ever — was on hand to fit the frame.

Only six months earlier, the House of Commons Home Affairs Select Committee had examined the problem of persistent young offenders. It heard that, although the number of 10- to 18-year-olds convicted or cautioned by the police had fallen by 25 per cent between 1981 and 1991, recorded juvenile crime had risen by 54 per cent. There was, so the Association of Chief Police Officers argued, 'a small hard core who have absolutely no fears whatsoever of the criminal justice system'. What empirical or other evidence they had for this is not vouchsafed. Hagell and Newburn, however, have concluded, to the contrary, that most persistent juvenile offenders seldom commit serious crimes and that those who do commit serious crimes are seldom persistent offenders.[6] The Home Secretary was nevertheless convinced, as he told the public in a television interview, that 200 juveniles between 10 and 15 were responsible for 60 per cent of all juvenile crime. If this were true, each would have to commit about 16,000 offences a year, or about 44 offences each day!

In a culture of panic, facts are of secondary importance. In a country 'in a state',[7] with deep fissures fracturing national life, with industry having disintegrated and one in three children growing up in poverty, in a society divided into 'us' and 'them', a gulf at least as great as in the days when class structure was clear, it is conventional to look for, find and blame victims.[8] Britain already imprisons more *per capita* of its population than any country in Western Europe. But adult penal policy, like almost every other policy pursued in Britain in the last decade and a half, has failed. Compared to the United States and many other countries, crime is actually a minor problem. So is illegal immigration. But, when discontented Conservatives were asked to explain a massacre of sitting Tories in recent local elections, they pinpointed both criminal activity and illegal immigration as areas of concern not addressed by 'their' government.

Moral panics feed on scandal. Whether fictionalised, such as that in Upton Sinclair's novel *The Jungle,* which led to food and drugs legislation in the United States — but not, of course, to improvements in the working conditions of the labour of 'Packingtown'; or through the whistle being blown eventually on endemic social problems such as child abuse, often after a particular graphic episode — a Maria Colwell, a Denis O'Neill, a Cleveland — action is often swiftly taken that otherwise might require lengthy deliberation over years. If the sad logo of Maria Colwell's face impressed itself upon the public imagination in 1973, and as assuredly influenced the package of child care measures in the *Children Act* 1975, then the faces of Robert Thompson and Jon Venables, the 11-year-olds convicted of James Bulger's murder, have become identified in the public's mind with the problem of youth crime.

I. THE BULGER CASE

THE BULGER CASE CAPTURED THE WORLD'S HEADLINES in February 1993, when the murder occurred, and again in November 1993, when the case came to trial. Murders by children are thankfully rare. Charles Patrick Ewing, who has collected case studies of juvenile murder in America, notes that most juveniles who kill are 15, 16 or 17 years old. Fewer than one per cent of those arrested for murder or non-negligent manslaughter have been under the age of 15.[9] Britain had its Mary Bell case [10] in 1968 and an interesting precedent in 1861 (in fact a striking contrast, as we shall see), but to find murderers as young as 10 is rare. That the prelude to the awful crime was captured on video added to the public's disbelief: the boys looked, and indeed were, ordinary, not demonic, and the site of the abduction, a modern shopping precinct, conveyed images of conventional normality. We don't televise our trials in England, but in this case we almost went one better — televising over and over again the two boy-murderers leading the innocent child to his death.

The trial, which took place in an adult court before a judge and jury some eight months after the murder, established very little. It lasted nearly three weeks, though nearly the whole trial consisted of prosecution evidence. The boys offered none and the defence case was condensed in the extreme. It cannot be said that the trial threw any insight into why the crime was perpetrated. It was not intended to do so. To describe the trial as a 'show trial', as a 'political trial' almost, is hardly an exaggeration. The result was a foregone conclusion: the presence of the boys in the court was a forensic irrelevance, though crucial in the construction of a demonology of deviance.

The boys were in detention, and separately detained, between their apprehension and trial. During this period they were examined by three leading psychiatrists, whose only function was to establish that the boys were capable of distinguishing right from serious wrong. There are two reasons for this. First, English law requires those who are aged between 10 and 14 to be *doli capax* — that is, capable of understanding the difference between serious wrong and mere naughtiness or mischief.[11] Secondly, it was important to establish that the boys were mentally responsible for the acts at the time when they committed them. But English law forbids any therapeutic involvement by psychiatrists before the trial. The explanation for this denying ordinance is — or so it is said — that intervention by psychiatrists which goes beyond matters of criminal investigation and approaches therapy would adulterate the evidence.

The police officers involved in the case were deeply interested in the boys' backgrounds but it was not their job to excavate these. As far as the law is concerned, their primary function is to prepare the evidence for the prosecution. They must establish that there is a case to answer. It is not their job, however personally and seriously interested they may be in the question, to unravel the causes of the crime, to discover why the boys behaved in the way they did.

Both these limitations cast light on what the criminal justice system understands to be its function and on the narrow time-frame within which the criminal law operates. But Kelman[12] and others have commented upon this and it need not be pursued further here.

Again, because — so it was said — the trial had to take place in open court and because many of its facts were distressing and would have devastated James Bulger's family and offended anyone else listening to the case, there was an agreement between prosecution and defence to the effect that once there was sufficient forensic evidence to prove the case against the two boys beyond reasonable doubt, the audience — it was said the jury — would be spared some of the more unpleasant details. The result of this is that events which may have taken place and would go some way towards explaining why the murder happened were discreetly veiled from the public eye. It was considered that, whilst what was hidden would greatly interest an inquisitive press and prurient public, these facts raised issues which went beyond what was strictly necessary to establish the boys' guilt. What results is a mismatch between forensic requirements and the need to 'know why'.

There can be little doubt that Thompson and Venables were deeply disturbed. James Bulger was not just murdered but brutally murdered, even tortured. Even when the two boys had savagely beaten the small child to pulp, they left his body on a railway line to be cut in two by a passing train. Additionally, and very significantly, it has emerged since the case (a little only came out during the course of the trial) that serious sexual assaults were perpetrated on James Bulger. In the trial it emerged that the boys had removed James's underpants and played with his foreskin. It now also appears to be the case that the batteries the boys stole from the shopping centre shortly before they abducted James were forced up the toddler's anus and used to mutilate his mouth.

The question must therefore be asked as to whether these boys, or at least one of them, had experienced sexual abuse. That there is a cycle of abuse, and that those who are abused frequently repeat this behaviour upon others, is established beyond any doubt. It is all the more unfortunate that therapeutic intervention had to be delayed until after the trial.

Of the boys themselves we know a little. And what we know points to deep disturbance and to unstructured, disorganised lives. They were, in a very real sense, damaged children. Venables was a head banger. There was an incident at school when he had to be physically constrained from a savage attack upon another child. His was a broken home, though, unlike Thompson, he did have contact with his father. Thompson came from a violent, disorganised home with other children of the family in local authority care. He was a truant and said to have a short temper. Neither boy was stupid: intelligence tests conducted before the trial by psychiatrists, allowed to establish that they were *doli capax*, showed Venables to be of average intelligence, and Thompson of 'good, at least average' intelligence.

It seemed to be assumed that they planned a killing on the fateful day in question. There had been a previous attempt at an abduction. But the pilfering of the batteries and the long, torturous route of the march before the attack suggest that if anything was planned, it was not murder *simpliciter*. If they had murder in mind, there were unquestionably easier ways of perpetrating the act. They passed a canal on the way and there were dangerous roads and heavy traffic. If murder was their intention, plenty of opportunities presented themselves on the way — and they could have easily covered their tracks. A small child could have fallen into a canal, or in front of traffic. It seems much more likely that, if anything, they or one of them planned a sexual attack. And, if this hypothesis is right — and it is certainly plausible — the decision to conduct the trial as involving a brutal murder, rather than a frenzied sexual attack, becomes particularly unfortunate.

It is doubtful whether an English Court would accept the defence of diminished responsibility (*Homicide Act* 1957, s. 2) which, if successful, would reduce the crime to manslaughter, because being traumatised by sexual abuse does not, it would be said, lead to an 'abnormality of mind' so as substantially to impair mental responsibility. However, it has to be accepted that the defence, like the concepts of responsibility generally, employ adult — specifically adult male — concepts of responsibility.[13] Challenging one of the law's 'truths' is difficult at the best of times, but it was not even tried in this case.

The trial itself made no concession to the age of the defendants. It was conducted in a traditional court room before a bewigged and robed judge and in the presence of a jury, though hardly one comprised of the boys' peers. The trial proceeded according to adult norms of behaviour, expression, procedure and style. The boys sat in a dock, accompanied, at least, by two male social workers. It is clear that they had little or no understanding of what was going on in the three-week trial to which they were subjected. Both seemed bored and bewildered during much of the trial. The judge, who had wide experience of criminal trials, had not any experience of appearing in juvenile courts. At times he adopted the view that the boys in this case were Victorian urchins, so that they had to be addressed as one might those in *Oliver Twist*. He even at one point purported to put on a mock scouse accent, as if conceding that the language of the trial was alien to the boys.

Neither of the boys gave evidence, though what they might have been able to tell a less formally-constructed forum might well have been revealing. They did not do so because they were unable to do so. They were psychologically traumatised. Their minds were confused, their memories blurred, they were fantasising in childish ways. Outside the trial, one spoke of James Bulger as a character in a chocolate factory and imagined that, as in some Disney-esque scenario, he might be brought back to life. The other also expressed the belief or hope — perhaps it is as well not to distinguish them — that James could be 'mended'.

This is not the world of Preston Crown Court where counsel address 'significant others' about responsibility and action. The disjuncture between the boys' world and that of the world constructed by law and lawyers is such that they might have been inhabiting different planets. 'Justice' demanded the presence of the boys — or so it was said. Their presence was important, just as the presence of the devil was important to the medieval mystery play. But it was politics also that demanded their presence. For Thompson and Venables were to become the visible representatives of the moral panic about crime, and juvenile crime in particular. It wasn't necessary to reveal their names — they were known throughout the trial as 'Child A' and 'Child B' — but the judge allowed this to be done after their conviction. A press eager to catch the mood of the time responded with the full blare of publicity. If the 'full' story was to be told, if the lessons were to be learned from the case were to be used to justify new and harsher ways of dealing with criminal activity by children, it was imperative that the public could put names and faces to new 'folk devils', rather than having to talk of Liverpudlian urchins or murderers from Merseyside. That the new devils looked like cherubs or at least ordinary school kids in neat school uniforms wasn't surprising. The devil always came in disguise, didn't he?

The press did, of course, hunt about for reasons to explain why the boys behaved as they did. In this they were 'assisted' by the judge who linked the boys' behaviour to the viewing of a particular 'video-nastie', *Child's Play 3*, and by statements by politicians and clergy which emphasised that both boys came from female-headed households, the implication being that the boys lacked role models or discipline or both, and that they perpetrated the murder when they should have been at school. Whether the boys had seen the video cannot be proved. Although the video does show an incident which uncannily resembles acts perpetrated upon James Bulger, hundreds of thousands of other 10 and 11 year olds will undoubtedly have seen it. That the male role models in Merseyside would almost certainly have been out of work and to have no prospects of work is hardly likely to encourage school attendance: the rate of youth unemployment on Merseyside is one of the highest in Britain, indeed in Western Europe. On the surface, the boys' upbringing was little different from that of other working class boys. If there was sexual abuse this would, of course, go a long way towards explaining what happened on the railway line in Walton. But it would not provide the underpinning for new penal policies. Nor would accepting the murder as a 'one-off', rare, ghastly and unpredictable.

For the Bulger case to become a vehicle for a reconstruction of juvenile penal policy, the boys had to be evil and had to be representatives of a new phenomenon — violent, ruthless, disorganised young thugs for whom tougher punishment was the only response. A government which was failing with its own constituency knew, or at least hoped, it could regain confidence by showing it was tougher on law and order and in particular on young, amoral or disrespectful criminals. The *Bulger* case thus became a symbol for more repressive control measures against the young.

II. TURNING THE CLOCK BACK

THERE IS SOME IRONY IN THIS. The *Criminal Justice Act* 1991 ended the imprisonment of children under 15. There had been a number of graphic and well-publicised child suicides, including that of Philip Knight in Swansea. The measure had been in operation only five months when, on 2 March, 1993, two weeks after the Bulger murder, Home Secretary Kenneth Clarke (a liberal in comparison with his successor Michael Howard) announced the introduction of the 'secure training order'. This was aimed at 'that comparatively small group of very persistent juvenile offenders whose repeated offending makes them a menace to the community'.[14] These young people were to be 12- to 15-year-olds who had committed three imprisonable offences, and who proved unable or unwilling to comply with the requirements of supervision in the community.

Michael Howard, within weeks of becoming Home Secretary, decided that even this reformulation was insufficient. In the summer of 1993, before the Bulger trial, newspapers began to report on the basis of a course of 'leaks' that Howard had ordered a rethinking of secure training centres when it had become clear that the scheme would be prohibitively expensive and would not address the explosion of youth crime. Thus, according to the *Daily Mail*, the mouthpiece of middle Conservative England, 'Ministers believe that hundreds more young thugs need to be locked up'. And by October he told the Tory party conference,

Prison works, it ensures that we are protected from murderers, muggers and rapists — it makes many who are tempted to commit crime think twice. This may mean that many more people will go to prison. I do not flinch from that. We shall no longer judge the success of our system of justice by a fall in our prison population.

The Tory press responded by finding just the stories upon which Howard could feed; Howard, in turn, did his best to nourish them and *vox populi*. There were stories about juvenile delinquents being taken on 'overseas jaunts' by social workers. When checked, the recipients of the 'holidays' were as often as not abused children rather than delinquent youth. But truth was not an important consideration. We were told that the probation service — apparently staffed by young Black women — had gone soft. Naturally, these jaunts were to be stopped and social work-trained probation officers were to be replaced with ex-soldiers and police officers.[15] A review in early 1995 was critical of the over-recruitment of ethnic minorities to the probation service, and proposed alternative routes for a new type of mature student. In March 1995, the Government published a Green Paper proposing the scrapping of the existing probation, community service and combination orders in favour of a 'community sentence', the details of which would be specified by the magistrates. The new two-pronged attack thus offered toughened teenage prison regimes and a more repressive rehabilitation system. Discipline had to be instilled into the young, barbaric underclass that Thompson and Venables were thought to symbolise.

It is to be noticed that in all this there is no mention of the causes of crime. Any suggestion that it might have social or economic causes is discreetly overlooked. Rather, crime is attributed to biological, psychological or intellectual deficiencies of individual offenders and/or to a lack of discipline. The former view derived its intellectual nourishment from the writings of James Q. Wilson[16] and Charles Murray.[17] Phrases like 'biologically predisposed man' and 'intellectually impaired man' were drawn from these authors, the latter from the notorious *Bell Curve*,[18] and used to support these reinvented penal policies. The latter view attributed blame to a loose network of counter-revolutionaries ranging from left-wing teachers to black probation officers and taking in for good measure on the way the Labour Party ('old Labour' as I suppose we must now call it).[19] Understanding a little less and condemning a little more became the bywords for this new policy.

Simultaneous with these developments — there is no need to believe in conspiracy theories to remark upon their coincidence — the Divisional Court purported to abolish the *doli incapax* presumption which has stood since at least the fourteenth century.[20] The House of Lords has since restored the presumption[21] but only because it believes that whether the presumption is retained or not should be a matter for Parliament rather than for judicial legislation. It is to be expected that Parliament will finally abolish the presumption at the earliest opportunity, perhaps as early as this year. To abolish the presumption will be to make 10 the age of criminal responsibility without the requirement to prove *doli capax*. Only Ireland, Switzerland, Cyprus and Liechtenstein (seven), Scotland and Northern Ireland (eight) and Malta (nine) believe in a younger age of criminal responsibility than England. All other European countries have a higher age of responsibility: for example it is 13 in France, 14 in Germany, 15 in Sweden and 16 in Spain.[22]

Speaking on a BBC radio programme which focused on the *Crump* case,[23] Susan Bailey, a forensic psychiatrist who gave evidence in the Bulger trial (she thought Thompson and Venables were *doli capax*) argued that most 10-year-old offenders have not reached moral maturity, and that there is a wide range between different children of the same age.

Between the age of 10 and 14, there is a tremendous range of developments within youngsters. They develop cognitively, emotionally and psychologically, and ... one of the many elements is that during that time most youngsters develop the capacity to move from concrete thinking to abstract thinking. The ability to have abstract thoughts is associated with your ability to think through what the consequences of the action are when you're committing a crime. So it is a critical and central area.[24]

Somewhat uniquely, the Crump boy himself was interviewed on the radio programme. The following extract from what he said gives, I believe, considerable insight into the problem and suggests the cut-off is not as clear-cut as some of the judges think (and, we may suppose, Parliament will as well). The question was whether the boy, when 12, knew that it was wrong to damage a moped.

Questioner: Do you have an idea in your mind of what is right and wrong?

C: Yeah.

Q: What is right and wrong?

C: Robbing cars is wrong.

Q: Why is it wrong?

C: It's taking somebody else's things.

Q: When you were 12, there was this incident, do you know what was right and wrong?

C: Yeah, and I never done nothing wrong. I was right, I was only looking. [The police] said I had a crowbar. I never had a crowbar. They was telling lies through their teeth.

Q: If you had been stealing or had been trying to take that motorbike would you have known that was wrong?

C: Yeah, of course.

Q: How would you have known that?

C: I'm not stupid.

Q: Where do you think you learned what was right and wrong?

C: In the infants, when I was younger.

Q: Do you think that most young people of 12 would know what was right and wrong?

C: I don't know. Some are thick. Some don't know the difference.

Q: Who taught you what's right and wrong?

C: My mum and dad, school, my nan, granddad.

Police told the BBC that he had been offending since he was nine. By 12, as part of a gang taking vehicles and stealing from shops, he had committed at least 20 offences of theft. Since 1992, the apprehension in question, he had continued to offend. Boy C was again asked why he had offended when he knew it was wrong.

C: Dunno, because everybody else was doing it. It's when you're there with all your mates and that, they're doing it, you do it.

Q: Do you regret it now?

C: Yeah, going to court and all that.

Listening to the broadcast or reading this transcript there is, to say the least, ambivalence in the boy's thinking and reasoning. He sees nothing wrong in lying or in offending if the peer group is also doing this. Nor does he regret attempting to steal a motorbike, only 'going to court and all that'. Different children will appreciate what is right and wrong at different ages: there are class, gender and intellectual and social maturity differences. In England both case law (the well-known *Gillick*[25] decision in 1985) and legislation (in particular, the *Children Act* 1989) in the area of civil law grade competence in terms of understanding with, unfortunately, too great an emphasis on 'book work' information rather than experiential knowledge.[26] Thus, rather than saying that a child can consent to medical treatment at a certain age (the question arises only with children under 16)[27] or seek a residence order (in effect choosing where he or she shall live),[28] we grant such rights to those with sufficient understanding of what is involved. It may readily be conceded that competence is difficult to assess and that it is far from value-free, all the more reason for not tying criminal responsibility to an inflexible standard. These arguments will not appeal to a government prepared to sacrifice children's interests to boost its flagging support. It knows its constituency and this does not consist of the (small) children's rights lobby.

Just how far these measures turn the clock back can be appreciated if we take a backward glance to the early 1980s, the early years of Thatcherism. Not that Thatcher and her supporters were soft upon crime.[29] The 1984 *Police and Criminal Evidence Act* increased police powers and the government tried the so-called 'sharp shock'[30] as a way of dealing with juvenile delinquents. 'Short, sharp shocks' didn't work. Perhaps they were not meant to. They pacified the Tory grassroots who were given the feeling that something was being done to curb rising crime. But in reality it was only a holding measure. It bought time and gave the new Thatcher government political credibility.

The 1982 *Criminal Justice Act* was sold as a vindication of Thatcher's promise to make Britain's streets safe. Actually, one of its aims was to limit the imprisonment of children and young people. In the light of the Bulger case it is worth remarking that part of the legacy the Conservatives inherited was an unfulfilled promise in the *Children and Young Persons Act* 1969 to raise the age of criminal responsibility to 14.[31] Labour having failed to do this, it was not to be expected that the Conservatives would. Had either government the courage to do this, Thompson and Venables could not have been prosecuted.

The Conservatives inherited this commitment. They also inherited the incoherence of the welfare-oriented *Children and Young Persons Act* and institutions such as borstals, detention centres and attendance centres which belonged to an earlier era and ideology.[32] It was this part of the system that was leading to more and more children and young persons being locked up. In the 12 years between 1965 and 1977, the number of young people between 15 and 17 sent to borstals by juvenile courts more than doubled. The detention centre population increased four-fold. But the number being supervised in the community by social workers or probation officers fell by more than a third.[33] An effect was a 'trickle up', with growing numbers of 17- to 21-year-olds filling adult prisons.

The 1982 Act was a failure. In 1983 the DHSS launched the Intermediate Treatment Initiative: £15 million was committed to providing 4,500 alternatives to custody over three years. This triggered the most extensive decarceration of the young this century: between 1981 and 1989 the number of juveniles incarcerated fell from 7,000 to 1,900 a year. This was accomplished by youth and welfare workers working with police and magistrates. By the late 1980s there was a nationwide structure of multi-agency juvenile justice panels. These were composed of representatives from welfare agencies, the youth service, police and education departments. They tried wherever possible to divert children and young people from court. Police cautioning was used extensively to divert first offenders from prosecution. A system known as 'cautioning plus' evolved to deal with more persistent offenders. Such persons were offered the inducement of further cautions on condition that they participated in additional educational, recreational or therapeutic activities. The success of this persuaded the government by the late 1980s to attempt a similar strategy with over-18s in the adult system.[34] The policy of punishment in the community crystallised in the *Criminal Justice Act* 1991.[35]

But Britain was already in economic recession. It can be no coincidence that recorded crime, which dropped by 5 per cent in 1988, the apogee of economic boom, rose sharply from the end of 1989, climbing by 17 per cent in 1990 and a further 16 per cent in 1991. The government blamed police, probation officers, social workers, even the public. At the 1991 Tory party conference the Home Secretary, Kenneth Baker, accused victims of crime of not taking sufficient care of their property. He was vigorously booed. The Home Secretary's speech is frequently a thermometer to take the temperature of 'middle' Britain. This time it demonstrated that the policies of the 1980s had run their course, and not just the penal policies. Whatever economic success the few had enjoyed had not 'trickled down' to the many. There was economic and, increasingly, social polarisation, growing crime and public disorder. In many senses the 'poll tax' riots symbolised the malaise. What began to be described by Charles Murray and others as 'underclass' had emerged. In *The Public Interest* in 1990, he wrote of a Britain that 'has a growing population of working aged healthy people who live in a different world from other Britons, who are raising their children to live in it, and whose values are now contaminating the life of entire neighbourhoods'.[36] A rising tide of teenage barbarism was described.

This offered an ideological underpinning for a government propelled back into an interventionist stance by a rising crime rate. If the 1980s policies had drawn on James Q. Wilson's world[37] in which rational people act to maximise their pleasure and minimise their pain, now the 'insights' of Charles Murray were making their mark. A free market in morality was being distorted by a welfare system which rewarded young women for having children outside marriage by giving them local authority housing and welfare benefits.[38] An underclass with separate moral values was being created. The language of Murray and Herrnstein's *Bell Curve*[39] with its talk of 'intellectually impaired man' synchronised with the feelings of a Conservative Party in Britain bent on reconstructing society, in creating a new social discipline.

Ironically, part of this was the rediscovery of rehabilitation. It was very different from the rehabilitative ideal we had become used to in the 1960s and 1970s with its use of 'psy' professionals to correct social and emotional difficulties. Now the goal was restoration of rationality, a reinjection of conformity, the teaching of discipline. Crime was attributed to intellectual deficiency and to lack of discipline. As so often rehabilitation went hand-in-hand with the urge to imprison and, as already described, the locking-up of the young, it became a key policy in the Howard era at the Home Office. Howard's decision to increase to 15 years the period for which Thompson and Venables are to be detained — the trial judge had recommended 8 years, the Lord Chief Justice 10 years — did not use the language of rehabilitation. He talked of public concern and the need to maintain public confidence in the criminal justice system.[40] But implicit in his directive is his belief that the murderers of James Bulger 'represent' a barbarism that needs to be tamed. They were to be made examples of, to restore a new social discipline.

III. A VICTORIAN MURDER

THAT THE BULGER TRIAL did not have to be seen this way, that there are other ways of approaching crimes, even horrific crimes, by children, is often remarked upon. Critics point justifiably to the recent Norwegian case which made headlines one day and disappeared the next as the children and their families were helped to come to terms with what was conceived of as a tragedy.[41] But it is not necessary to point to contemporary parallels in other countries. Gitta Sereny, the author of the leading book on the Mary Bell case[42] and commentator on the Bulger trial,[43] has recently excavated evidence of a similar case in England in 1861, the interest of which lies in the approach taken.[44]

Two Stockport eight-year-olds, Peter Barratt and James Bradley (the age of criminal responsibility then being seven) were convicted of the manslaughter of two-year-old George Burgess, a child they had, so far as is known, never laid eyes on before, just as in the Bulger case. Again, as in the Bulger case, the killing was particularly brutal. Nor do the parallels end there. The boys had both been disruptive at school shortly before the murder. It seems, at least initially, that Barratt and Bradley, like the children in Newcastle and Liverpool a century later, had no real concept of what they had done. The boys were charged with murder but convicted of manslaughter. The judge had told the jury that if they found that the boys did not understand the effect of the act they were committing, the presumption of malice would be rebutted and the crime reduced to manslaughter.

The similarities between the cases end with the verdict. James Bulger's killers were not given the opportunity of a manslaughter verdict and, whereas the judge in the Bulger trial seemed oblivious to the welfare of Thompson and Venables, in 1861 a judge could use this language:

[t]he prisoners will be sent to the Reformatory at Bradwall from whose excellent manager I received a letter stating that although the boys were younger than the generality of those under his care, under the peculiar circumstances of the case, he would have great pleasure in taking them and in looking after their future welfare.

In sentencing the boys, he said,

I am afraid you have been very wicked, naughty boys, and I have no doubt that you have caused the death of this little boy by the brutal way to which you used him. I am going to send you to a place where you will have an opportunity of becoming good boys, for there you will have a chance of being brought up in a way you should be, and I doubt not but that in time, when you come to understand the nature of the crime you have committed, you will repent of what you have done. The sentence is that each of you be imprisoned and kept in gaol for one month, and at the expiration of that period you be sent to a Reformatory for five years.

There was a leading article in *The Times*[45] on the case, and what a striking contrast it makes with the 'op-ed' columns of today! It argued that children of the age of Bradley and Barratt could not be held legally accountable in the same way as adults. 'What is the reason then', it notes,

why it should have been absurd and monstrous that these two children should have been treated like murderers? ... As far as it went [their conscience] was as sound and as genuine a conscience as that of a grown man: it told them what they were doing was wrong ... [But] conscience, like other natural facilities, admits of degrees: it is weak, and has not arrived at its proper growth in children, though it has a real existence and a voice within them; it does not speak with that force and seriousness which justifies us in treating the child as a legally responsible being.

IV. CONCLUSION

BUT THAT IS HOW THOMPSON AND VENABLES were treated 132 years later. There was no psychology or psychiatry in 1861. In 1993, with psychiatry well-established, it had to play a handmaiden's role to the masterful discipline of law.[46] It was the law which determined that Thompson and Venables could not be helped until after their trial. It was the law which decided that the role of the 'psy' sciences was to determine legal responsibility, but not to explain or excuse. From the perspective of the government, this was as well. Had the child psychiatrists' evidence failed to establish that the boys were unable to distinguish naughtiness from serious wrong, or found that they lacked the mental capacity to stand trial, where would they have been? With no trial, with identities and biographies suppressed, the killing of James Bulger could not have been used as an object lesson for pontificating about evil, nor could it have used to symbolise the mischief that new government strategies were designed to tackle.[47]

Notes

* Versions of this paper were given at Tulane Law School and the Universities of Illinois-Champaign and Tel-Aviv before its presentation to the Law and Society Conference in Toronto in June 1995. I am grateful to all those whose constructive criticism have helped me prepare this version for publication.

1. These appeared in every daily newspaper on 25 November, 1993.

2. *The Sunday Times*, 21 February ,1993.

3. *The Sunday Times*, 28 February, 1993.

4. *The Daily Telegraph* 22 February, 1993.

5. *Folk Devils and Moral Panics* (McGibbon and Kee, 1973).

6. *Persistent Young Offenders* (1994).

7. See Will Hutton, *The State We're In* (Jonathan Cape 1995). A revised edition has been published in 1996.

8. *Cf.* W. Ryan, *Blaming The Victim* (Vintage Books, 1976).

9. *Kids Who Kill* (Mondo, 1993; originally published by Lexington Books in 1990). See also Kathleen M. Heide, *Why Kids Kill Parents* (Sage, 1995).

10. See Gittta Sereny, *The Case of Mary Bell* (Pimlico, 1995, originally published by Eyre Methuen in 1972).

11. *C. v. Director of Public Prosecutions* [1995] 1 F.L.R. 933.

12. 'Interpretive Construction in the Substantive Criminal Law' (1981) 33 Stanford Law Review 591.

13. See for example, *R v. Tandy* [1989] 1 All E.R. 267. On women see Hilary Allen, *Justice Unbalanced: Gender, Psychiatry and Judicial Decisions* (Open University Press, 1987).

14. *The Independent*, 3 March, 1993.

15. Dewes and Wright, *A Review of Probation Officer Recruitment, Qualification and Training*, Home Office Probation Training Unit, 1994. Challenged as unlawful, judicial review was mounted but failed in February 1996.

16. *Thinking About Crime* (Basic Books, 1975).

17. 'The British Underclass', *The Public Interest*, No. 99, 4 (1990).

18. See Charles Murray and Richard Hermstein, *The Bell Curve* (Simon and Schuster, 1994).

19. But on the Labour Party's reactions to this see Angela McRobbie, 'Folk Devils Fight Back', 203 New Left Review 107 (1994).

20. *C. v. D.P.P.* [1994] 3 W.L.R. 888.

21. See *supra* note 11. The Lords thought the presumption anomalous and absurd, but believed its abolition ought to be left to Parliament.

22. And see J. Bourquin, 'The James Bulger Case Through The Eyes of the French Press' 1 Social Work in Europe 42 (1994).

23. Known as 'C' in the law report.

24. *The Independent*, 17 March, 1995, p. 3.

25. [1986] A.C. 112.

26. See Priscilla Alderson and Mary Goodwin, 'Contradictions Within Concepts of Children's Competence' 1 International Journal of Children's Rights 303 (1993).

27. Family Law Reform Act 1969 s. 8(1). But Courts have now decided that they can *refuse* consent (see *Re R.* [1992] Fam. 11 and *Re W.* [1993] Fam. 64).

28. On which see M. Freeman, 'Can Children Divorce their Parents?', in M.D.A. Freeman (ed.), *Divorce: Where Next?* (Dartmouth, 1996) 159.

29. See Martin Kettle, 'The Drift To Law and Order' in Stuart Hall and Martin Jacques (eds.), *The Politics of Thatcherism* (Lawrence and Wishart, 1983) 216.

30. See Michael Freeman, 'Short, Sharp Shocks' [1980] New Law Journal 130.

31. Allan Levy, *The Guardian*, 25 November, 1994, criticised this in the aftermath of the Bulger Case.

32. See M.D.A. Freeman, *The Rights and Wrongs of Children* (Frances Pinter, 1983).

33. See John Pitts, *The Politics of Juvenile Crime* (Sage, 1989).

34. See Anthony Bottoms *et al.*, *International Treatment and Juvenile Justice, Implications And Findings from A Survey of Intermediate Treatment Policy and Practice Evaluation Project*, Final Report (London H.M.S.O., 1990). See also John Pratt, 'Corporatism, The Third Model of Juvenile Justice' (1989) 29 British Journal of Criminology 236.

35. On the policy see Home Office, *Punishment In The Community* (London: H.M.S.O., 1989) and Home Office, *Crime, Justice and protecting The Public* (H.M.S.O., 1990).

36. *Supra*, note 18.

37. Described in *Thinking About Crime, supra* note 16.

38. On Peter Lilley's 'little list' of persons who would not be misssed (*cf.* Gilbert and Sullivan's *The Mikado*) in his speech to the Tory party conference in October 1992. See also N. Dennis and G. Erdos, *Families Without Fatherhood* (Institute of Economic Affairs, 1992). More rational but similarly directed is Melanie Phillips, 'Rediscovering The Values of The Family', *The Guardian*, 26 February 1993.

39. *Supra*, note 19.

40. This is being challenged at the European Court on Human Rights. See The Independent On Sunday, 22 May, 1994: see also the leading article in *The Independent*, 'A Challenge to The Bulger Trial', 23 May, 1994.

41. Five-year-old Silje Marie Redergard froze to death in a school playground after a 'game' with three boys (one aged 6, the other two aged 5). A striking parallel is that the T.V. programme 'Power Rangers' was widely blamed in Norway and broadcasts were suspended. But the differences in social attitudes are also noteworthy: James Bulger's parents have campaigned for Thompson and Venables never to be released: Silje Redergard's mother is quoted as 'forgiving the ones who killed my daughter. It is not possible to hate small children'.

42. *Supra* note 9.

43. *The Independent on Sunday*, 13 and 20 February, 1994 (reproduced as an appendix to Sereny, *The Case of Mary Bell, supra,* note 9).

44. 'A Child Murdered By Children', *The Independent on Sunday*, 23 April, 1995, pp. 8-12.

45. *Ibid.*

46. See, to like effect, Michael King, 'The James Bulger Murder Trial: Moral Dilemmas and Social Solutions' (1995) 3 International Journal of Children's Rights 167.

47. Nor as an atypical instance should it be. See, further, Stewart Asquith, 'When Children Kill Children', 3 Childhood 99 (1996), an article published too late for its valuable insight to be taken on board. Also valuable, but published after this article was written, is Colin Hay, 'Mobilization Through Interpretation: James Bulger, Juvenile Crime and the Construction of a Moral Panic' 4 Social and Legal Studies 197 (1995).

V

Therapies of Freedom: The Colonization of Aboriginal Childhood

ANNE McGILLIVRAY*

> *It would be wrong to say the soul is an illusion, or an ideological effect. On the contrary, it exists, it has a reality, it is produced permanently around, on, within the body by the functioning of a power that is exercised on those punished — and, in a more general way, on those one supervises, trains and corrects, over madmen, children at home and at school, the colonized ... The soul is the effect and instrument of a political anatomy; the soul is the prison of the body.*
>
> Foucault, *Discipline and Punish*[1]

BY THE LAST DECADES of the nineteenth century, childhood had become a primary locus of citizenship and the child a unit of moral exchange, severable and transformable. Canadian regimes for the reform of the dangerous child and the rescue of the perishing child (between whom little distinction was made) were imbued with an imperialism which envisioned as the highest aspiration of any child Anglo-Canadian citizenship in a Christian culture. This unitary vision of culture and acculturation dominated child welfare philosophy well into the twentieth century.

Nineteenth-century child welfare sought to erase the effects of wrong culture and nurture in the production of citizenship. This was a subjectivity derived less from Nikolas Rose's 'therapies of freedom', which 'align political, social, and institutional goals with individual pleasures and desires and with the happiness and fulfilment of the self',[2] than from earlier technologies of freedom in which Rose's matrix of the self must be plucked from deeper matrices of culture and relatedness in order to be remade. For Foucault, it was a coercive individualization in which the family became 'the privileged locus of emergence for the disciplinary question of the normal and abnormal'.[3] Where the family is 'abnormal', the child's normalization may be compulsory: the child is removed and subjected to a normalizing institutional regime. Where the abnormality to be eliminated is culture (as 'race'), normalization becomes cultural colonization, cultural genocide.[4] Where normalization is to be accomplished by 'forcibly transferring children of the group to another group', with the 'intent to destroy, in whole or part, a national, ethnical, racial or religious group', it is genocide, according to the 1948 *Geneva Convention on the Punishment of the Crime of Genocide*.

The colonization of Aboriginal childhood created a Foucauldian carceral archipelago whose institutions include the reserve, the residential school, the child protection system, young offender facilities and jail.[5] Results are seen in heightened rates of intimate violence, early death, poverty, substance abuse and, ultimately, alienation from kin and culture. Programs of assimilation were closely modelled after regimes developed to normalize or 'civilize' non-Aboriginal children. Removal of Aboriginal children for education and for protection were seen as remedies in subsequent generations for the inadequacies of the former. Education and child welfare are now, and historically have been, central sites of Aboriginal resistance to assimilation. Legacies of cultural destruction and intimate violence hold great symbolic power in the politics of self-government.

The Aboriginal peoples of Manitoba have been deeply marked by these programs of citizenship. The Manitoba experience embraces the first warnings by a government inquiry of cultural genocide in the massive apprehension of Aboriginal children, the first child protection agency managed and staffed by First Nations (Dakota-Ojibway Child and Family Services) and the first and only province-wide intertribal child welfare system in Canada. Manitoba is the first site of devolution of federal responsibility for Indian reserves from Indian Affairs Canada to First Nations government. Manitoba has gone further than any other Canadian jurisdiction in devising new regimes for the governance of Aboriginal childhood. The Manitoba experience discloses abuses of power and abdication of responsibility at every level of accountability at critical junctures of politics and culture. There has been no quick fix. Indigenous solutions, often promising and ingenious, have not overtaken official ones, nor are child protection decisions made in a context which equally accommodates the centrality of culture and the cultural destruction of child abuse.

At stake in the contested control of child welfare is childhood itself as product and repository of culture. State discourses of assimilation and counter-discourses of resistance and self-determination foreground culture in, or as, childhood and its governance.

Culture in a postcolonial context is about the construction of otherness and the inscription of difference in policy and law, a specular and often intimate relationship in which each is, to the other, alien. A 'high' or 'original' culture is lost or debased. A 'low' or 'debased' culture, having lost its utility for its Other, romantic, economic or otherwise, must be transformed. The experience of indigenous culture and of cultural colonization lies in what Certeau has called the practice of everyday life.[6] Here 'culture' is less about artefact or text than about '*a way of using* imposed systems' which

constitutes the resistance to the historical law of a state of affairs and its dogmatic limitations ... that is where the opacity of a 'popular' culture could be said to manifest itself — a dark rock that resists all assimilation.[7]

For those caught up in Foucault's disciplinary net, everyday life 'bring[s] to light the clandestine forms taken by the dispersed, tactical, and makeshift creativity of groups or individuals' operating on a small and daily scale to constitute the 'dark rock' of resistance. Tactics of resistance insinuate themselves 'into the other's place, fragmentarily, without taking it over in its entirety, without being able to keep it at a distance.' Such tactics are shaped by and, in turn, inform strategy. In carving out defined and possessed cultural locations, strategies of assimilation are revised, discarded and reinvented. Childhood is central in strategies of assimilation, tactics of resistance and post-1980 strategies of Aboriginal self-determination which draw on the symbolic capital of the colonization of Aboriginal childhood. Childhood is indeed the 'dark rock' against which Aboriginal childsaving vessels have, for almost two centuries, foundered.

This essay is an overview of the contested governance of Aboriginal childhood in the context of the Manitoba experience. The discussion brings together disparate discourses which address the governance of childhood. I begin with a broad outline of Indian relations with Canada, a history itself contested and incomplete, in order to establish the durability of assimilation policy. To suggest parallels between the governance of Aboriginal childhood and of other children identified as endangered or abnormal, Anglo-Canadian child welfare philosophy, residential schooling and 'catch-up' department politics of post-1960 reserve child welfare are surveyed. The Manitoba system of intertribal agencies, the disciplining of those agencies and the role of culture in contested child protection cases make up the remainder of the essay. The analysis is undertaken from an Anglo-Canadian historical perspective.[8]

The identification of academics and similarly privileged observers with the goals and norms of another culture contributes to the social hierarchizing of cultural values by co-opting and suppressing distance and difference. 'The Bororos of Brazil sink slowly into their collective death and Levi-Strauss takes his seat in the French Academy', as Certeau observed.[9] Trendy easy solutions where issues are as differently problematised in cultural terms as 'child welfare' do not advance either 'culture' or the goals of those whose culture is in question, even where observer solutions chime with cultural claims and observers adopt indigenous strategies of resistance. Certeau's fears are based on a covert agenda of 'elimination of a popular menace' which masquerades as the search for 'authentic' culture. This characterizes earlier stages of European contact with Aboriginal cultures ('The ethnologist and the archeologist arrive at the moment a culture has lost its means of self-defence') but academic identification with cultural claims also presumes 'we' know what 'they' are talking about, need and want. This imperils self-realization. What, if any, responsibility does the dominant culture have in cleaning up its mess? Is it enough for 'Whiteman' to just get out of the way? Does it make a difference if the mess is destroying the most powerless as well as the most contested constituency of The Other? Which is the greater destruction, infant body or cultural soul? and does that body or 'soul' rest in the hands of political bodies, however constituted? I cannot exempt myself from this critique or resolve its contradictions, nor can any external observer.

I. CIVILIZING THE INDIAN[10]

WHERE DIFFERENCE IS USEFUL, cultural interference is minimal and reciprocal.[11] Where difference is a problem (as 'the Indian problem'), the choices for nineteenth-century colonial governments were annihilation, the stop-gap measure of relocation, or assimilation. This chapter is an overview of the history of Anglo-Canadian assimilation strategies and tactics of resistance which frame and account for the colonization of Aboriginal childhood.

Nineteenth-century imperialism infused the emergent sciences of cultural anthropology, criminology, phrenology and social Darwinism with particular views of determinacy and deviance. These in turn justified imperialist projects of structural and cultural colonization and provided a mythology of inevitable cultural desuetude.[12]

The invaders invoked certain myths to legitimize and justify the colonization, displacement, and exploitation of aboriginal peoples in the name of evolutionary progress and national development. Terms such as the 'vanishing American' were coined to describe the demographic plight of the American Aboriginal. The situation was viewed with both alarm and ethnocentric complacency, as if the extinction of aboriginal peoples were the inevitable price of 'progress' ...

The Indian did not disappear through attrition, nor did an 'obsolete' culture yield to a 'progressive' Anglo-Canadian one as the mythology predicted. The 'weird and waning race' celebrated in the poetry of Indian Affairs Superintendent Duncan Campbell Scott[13] is now a powerful force in Canadian politics and in the politics of child welfare.

The Aboriginal population of the Americas had decreased by 1930 from a pre-contact total of about 19 million to under one million. The largest population decrease took place after 1800. By 1960, the Canadian Aboriginal population was restored to pre-contact levels[14] and continues to increase at 2.5 times the national average; 58 per cent of the population is under the age of 25.[15] Registered or 'status' Indians total 554,000 or 2 per cent of the Canadian population and 8 per cent of the population of Manitoba, the highest proportion of any Canadian province. There are some 601 bands occupying 2,261 reserves.[16]

Pre-1800 relations between European and Aboriginal peoples were based on a variety of forms of partnership. Aboriginal peoples in the new world were for the most part 'active agents of commercial, diplomatic, and military relations'.[17] The waning fur trade, resolution of European hostilities and European settlement shifted relations from partnership to social (and moral) burden. Extermination of Aboriginal peoples was ruled out by Anglo-Canadian humanitarianism and lack of entrenched hostility toward Aboriginal peoples.[18] The United States, by contrast, fought some 67 Indian Wars, many followed by genocide.[19] Anglo-Canadian political culture, in contrast with the United States, supported a strong government role in economic and social policy, making the shift from commercial and military jurisdiction to civil jurisdiction a comparatively easy one. 'The Indian' had been exploited in times of war; he must now be reclaimed from barbarism and taught the habits of civilized life. The English Secretary of State for War and the Colonies wrote in 1830,[20]

It appears to me that the course which has hitherto been taken in dealing with these people, has had reference to the advantages which might be derived from their friendship in times of war, rather than to any settled purpose of gradually reclaiming them from a state of barbarism, and of introducing amongst them the industrious and peaceful habits of civilized life.

Civilization centred on two systems, the establishment of reserves to clear the path of settlement and 'gradual civilization'. Conditions of enfranchisement — full citizenship upon revocation of Indian status — were set out in the 1857 *Act for the Gradual Civilization of the Indian Tribes in Canada,* which stated that 'it is desirable to encourage the progress of Civilization among the Indian Tribes ... and the gradual removal of all legal distinctions between them and her Majesty's other Canadian Subjects'. Conditions of citizenship or enfranchisement included military service, college graduation, sale of Treaty rights and a woman's marriage to a non-Indian. A tribal leader objected to the Act as an attempt 'to break them to pieces' but the Indian Department replied that 'the Civilization Act is no grievance to you'.[21] Offers of private landholding made by the Indian Commissioner, (only a handful of Aboriginal people accepted) reflected the 'policy of destroying the tribal or communist system and every effort made to implant a spirit of individual responsibility instead'.[22]

The terms of confederation in 1867 granted exclusive jurisdiction over 'Indians and lands reserved for Indians' to the federal government under s. 91(24) of *The British North America Act.* The 1869 *Act for the Gradual Enfranchisement of the Indian*[23] amalgamated and extended pre-confederation statutes. Individual title to reserve 'location tickets' was offered, on conditions of a three-year probation and band consent, with retention of band annuities and interests. Even on these more generous terms, few accepted. The 1876 *Indian Act* consolidated a variety of federal statutes in order to better govern the 'upwards of 60,000 Indians' brought into confederation, according to the 1867 Report of the Department of the Interior. In his *Annual Report* for 1876, Indian Affairs Deputy Superintendent General Vankoughnet

trusted that many Indians will avail themselves of [the Act's] liberal provisions for enfranchisement — framed as they were, with the object of aiding the Indian to raise himself from the conditions of tutelage and dependence; and of encouraging him to assume the privileges and responsibilities of full citizenship.

As only 57 of 90,000 Indians had been enfranchised, assimilation policies were again reconsidered. During the 1879 Indian Act debates, a Member of the House of Commons commented on the resistance to assimilation.[24]

The object of the [Indian] Act was to break up the Aboriginal system, but the system was endeared to the Indians by many associations, and it was the last remaining protection which they had against the capacity of the white man. They were attached to it because it was inherited from their ancestors, because it had become part of their very nature and entered, in all its ramifications, into their everyday life. They would never cease to adhere to the Aboriginal system until they ceased to be Indians.

Despite this trenchant insight, assimilation through enfranchisement remained the focus of government policy.

The 1880 Indian Act fully bureaucratized Indian mangement, enabling Indian Affairs to create Indian bands and entrenching a municipal system of band government by elected chief and council. This system had been introduced in the 1869 Act and expanded in the 1876 Act. It was intended to teach 'civic responsibility' by instituting elections, taxation and by-lawmaking powers. The system was based more on exotic fantasy about 'Chiefs' and 'Braves' — and on bureaucratic expedience[25] — than on the traditional governments and indigenous discourses it replaced. It created petty fiefdoms in place of tribes and nations and promoted individualism over 'tribal or communist' systems. It was laid over a complex and highly functional kinship structure, inviting excesses of nepotism. It embodied a Victorian patriarchy which disregarded matriarchal governments and erased women and children from the new band politics.

Crown treaties with First Nations in what are now the provinces of Manitoba, Saskatchewan and Alberta followed the pattern set in the rest of Canada, with important differences. The southern nations of the Cree, Chipewyan, Saulteaux, Nakota (Assiniboine), Dakota (Sioux), Siksika (Blackfoot), Kainai (Blood), Piegan and Sarcee were, arguably, relative latecomers to the Prairies, the Assiniboine and Cree arriving by the late seventeenth century and the Ojibwa (named Saulteaux for their trade at the Sault Rapids) by the eighteenth century. These groups did not constitute a unified culture, linguistically or otherwise, nor were entrenched hostilities and alliances *inter se* obliterated by Crown Treaty, as nineteenth-century Indian policy necessarily supposed. Smallpox epidemics, United States Indian policy — forcible relocation, war, the whisky trade, army buffalo slaughter — blocked the route south for Plains Aboriginal peoples. Massive buffalo slaughter by hunters after hides and tongues eliminated the buffalo on the Canadian Plains, opening the way to large-scale agriculture. By the 1860s, the economy of the buffalo was over.

The tribes were under pressure to settle land claims, having lost their livelihoods and fearing for their children's lives, a fear expressed at each Treaty signing. The new Dominion of Canada required speedy resolution of land claims in order to attach the Northwest for European settlement and block United States encroachment and military action against the Indians Plains First Nations entered into the 'Numbered Treaties', beginning at Red River (Winnipeg), Manitoba, in 1871 — the year after the Metis Rebellion and Manitoba's entry into confederation — and ending in 1877 at Bow River, Alberta, where the last of the wild buffalo had been seen a year earlier.

The North-West Rebellion of 1885, a continuation of the Red River Rebellion and Louis Riel's mythic vision of the Metis, resulted in Riel's hanging and the deliberate crushing of the last vestiges of Aboriginal leadership by Indian Affairs. The Indians under the Numbered Treaties were now to become farmers. This assimilationist 'policy of the plough' was geared to peasant farming in a machine age. While western grain farmers bought and shared the new gigantic steam engines for the agricultural conquest of the Plains, reserve farmers worked with horse and hand tools. Reserve lands were non-mortgageable, meaning that the new technology was unaffordable. Those who succeeded as farmers were denied marketplace competition by a variety of local tactics. Where land turned out to be useful, bands were removed and resettled in more remote and desolate locations, and arable reserve lands were sometimes sold to non-Indians by the federal government. The policy of the plough was not a success.

Reserves were not viewed by Canada as Treaty entitlements or cultural preserves, but as protective holding stations until full assimilation could be achieved. This is borne out by persistent failure to meet the spirit, and sometimes letter, of Treaty terms (when ploughs wore out they were replaced not with new ploughs or newer technology but with welfare); in involuntary enfranchisement policies; and in allocations of reserve lands which were less than agreed, economically marginal and geosocially isolate. Assimilating the Indian was the 'great aim' of Canadian civilization, according to Canada's first Prime Minister, Sir John A. MacDonald, in 1887.[26]

The great aim of our civilization has been to do away with the tribal system and assimilate the Indian people in all respects with the inhabitants of the Dominion, as speedily as they are fit for the change.

But the speed was slow and change did not materialize. Commanding assimilation is not the same thing as achieving it.[27] Indian Affairs officer Duncan Campbell Scott wrote 33 years later, in 1917,

I want to get rid of the Indian problem ... it is enervating to the individual or to a band to continue in that state of tutelage, when he or they are able to take their position as British citizens or Canadian citizens, to support themselves, and stand alone. That has been the whole purpose of Indian education and advancement since the earliest times ... Our object is to continue until there is not a single Indian in Canada that has not been absorbed into the body politic, and there is no Indian question, and no Indian department.[28]

By 1920, only 250 people had chosen enfranchisement, although many lost status through involuntary enfranchisement.

The 1969 federal White Paper *Statement of the Government of Canada on Indian Policy* called for full assimilation through abolition of Treaty rights, Indian status, the *Indian Act* and the reserve system. Prime Minister Pierre Trudeau summarized the views of his Liberal government in 1968. Compensation for Treaty lands must be made but the 'apartness' of Indians must end.[29]

We have set the Indians apart as a race. We've set them apart in our laws. We've set them apart in the way governments deal with them. They're not citizens of the provinces as the rest of us are. They are wards of the federal government ... we won't recognize aboriginal rights. We will recognize treaty rights ... It's inconceivable, I think, that in a given society one section of society has a treaty with the other section of society. We must be equal under the law ...

To solicit Aboriginal support for the proposals, Indian Affairs established and directly funded — and continues to fund — the National Indian Brotherhood, since 1980 the Assembly of First Nations, and constituent provincial all-chiefs associations. Assimilation was vigorously opposed by these associations. The last official vestiges of overt assimilation were abandoned in 1973 in face of resistance by organizations created and paid for by Indian Affairs. Increasing political activism focused on recognition of Treaty obligations and cultural rights. By the late 1970s, the foremost 'cultural right' had become control of childhood through control of education and child welfare.

By order-in-council signed 22 November, 1994, Manitoba became a testing-ground for self-government. The framework agreement commits Canada to dismantling Indian Affairs powers, recognizes the inherent right of First Nations to exercise full government powers, legislative, judicial, executive and administrative, and in effect creates a new level of government.[30] Local control is the ultimate aim, with bands setting their own pace for block funding and self-government within the framework of the agreement. Before this can take place, financial management will 'devolve' not to the bands created by Indian Affairs or to the original Nations which signed the treaties but to a political organization created by Indian Affairs, the Executive of the Assembly of Manitoba Chiefs, which will progressively 'devolve' control to the bands. This may be the first step to self-government. It may represent a new sort of assimilationism, as traditional relations between status Indian and Crown are progressively severed.[31] Canada, or at least Manitoba, stands at a critical nexus in which self-government may become the reality consistently claimed through centuries of European contact.

After a century and a half of active assimilation policies, Aboriginal peoples in Canada remain a fourth world within, yet unabsorbed by, a first-world nation, culturally distinct and politically active. They did not, however, remain unmarked by the experience. Whatever the forces shaping perceived characteristics of the Indian, Aboriginal adults had proved intransigent to manipulation on the scale needed for effective assimilation.[32] The focus of transformation shifted in the latter part of the nineteenth century to Indian childhood and to Anglo-Canadian technologies of normalization.

II. CIVILIZING CHILDHOOD

EIGHTEENTH-CENTURY UTOPIAN CONSTRUCTS of innocence uncontaminated by civilization made the 'noble savage' a cognate of childhood. As Sir Hector Langevin observed during the 1876 Indian Act debates, 'Indians were not in the same position as white men ... they were like children to a very great extent. They, therefore, required a great deal more protection'.[33] Nineteenth-century assimilation policies infantilized the Indian, remaking the adult in the image of childhood. Indians were in law state wards under the *Indian Act*, confined to the reserve, subject to protectionist policies (Indian agents, pass systems, liquor prohibitions),[34] forbidden religious and cultural practices,[35] subjects of projects of improvement, objects of pity, finally welfare-dependent.

The equation of Aboriginal peoples with childhood and dependency in English foreign policy was reflected in two reports: the 1834 *Report from His Majesty's Commission for Inquiring into the Administration and Practical Operation of the Poor Laws* and the 1837 House of Commons *Report of the Select Committee on Aborigines*. The Select Committee was concerned with 'Native Inhabitants of Countries where British Settlements are made ... to promote the spread of civilization among them', while the Commission on the Poor Laws was concerned with problems of the outcast closer to home. Both reports provided for special overseers or protectors, proposed training programs aimed at low-level employment and emphasized assimilation of their respective target groups into the larger society. Both reports stressed childhood and the need to educate, civilize, and bring into Christianity the young pauper or Aborigine. As the Select Committee on Aborigines noted, 'True civilization and Christianity are inseparable: the former has never been found, but as a fruit of the latter.'

If the adult 'Aborigine' was infantilized in the process of assimilation, the child was literally to be pressed into its service. This arose from a series of changes in Anglo-Canadian ideas about the governance of childhood. This chapter introduces these ideas, taking as illustration two childsaving projects which shared the civilizing vision which came to centre on Aboriginal childhood: the English child migration movement and the Winnipeg Home of the Friendless.

Childhood is both focus and creation of civilization, a life stage dedicated to the inculcation of a sociospecific citizenship. By the close of the eighteenth century, childhood had fully emerged as a legally and socially distinct life estate and numerous European constructs of childhood were extant.[36] By the last third of the nineteenth century, childhood was identified as both social problem and locus of charitable and state projects of citizenship. The health, welfare and rearing of children, as Rose observed, was 'linked in thought and practice to the destiny of the nation and the responsibilities of the state',[37] an association which was to make childhood 'the most intensively governed sector of human existence'. In the late nineteenth-century shift from government *of* the family to governance *through* the family,[38] the child became a symptom of relational problems within the family and between family and state, a major point of entry into the family for the new complex of family-oriented tutelary disciplines and agencies empowered to remove children from 'abnormal' environments.   Intervention and removal primarily affected families of marginal social status, while expert tutelage, being 'voluntary, was to have a broader impact. Childhood was, in effect, colonized by the state.

The governance of childhood was aimed at the induction of a docile citizenship, the creation of a disciplined soul. What motivated the 'great project', Rose argues, was not the 'repressive desire for surveillance and control' initially posited by Foucault. It was, rather,

a profoundly humanistic and egalitarian project, one that searched for the causes of failure of citizenship and sought to provide the knowledge that was to ensure the extension of the benefits of society to all its members.[39]

Where the 'members' had no perception of themselves as such, and no desire to join, this humanistic project of reform might well be perceived as 'repressive surveillance'.

The shift in relations between 'childhood' and state was reflected in the massive expansion of child welfare powers and programs in late nineteenth-century Canada.[40] The province of Manitoba, carved out of the North-West Territories in 1870, based its child welfare legislation on that of Ontario. The Ontario *Humane Societies Act* had been amended to give animal protection groups the power to remove children from the lawful custody of parents and guardians for neglect or mistreatment (*qua* the New York *Mary Ellen* case) but the need for separate societies and legislation became apparent. Canadian child law reformer J.J. Kelso wrote in his diary 10 January, 1890, 'The difficulty is cropping up of keeping the animals and children from clashing, the two having their separate and distinct friends'.[41] Ontario legislation was appropriately amended and Manitoba followed suit, instituting a system of quasi-charitable Children's Aid Societies in 1891 and enacting its *Child Protection Act* in 1898. (The Children's Aid Society model is extant in Manitoba and Ontario but was never adopted by provinces further west.)

The spate of reform continued in Manitoba, as elsewhere, into the next century. In place of a single statute based on the Tudor Poor Laws (the Manitoba *Apprentices and Minors Act*, 1877), there were by 1913 a multitude of statutory provisions in Manitoba empowering agencies to apprehend children for parental delict (neglect and abuse, immoral conduct) and delict of the child (vagrancy, truancy, expulsion from school, petty crime, exposure to immorality). The apprehended child would be placed in a normalizing environment, at first the industrial school; later, under the Kelso family model, in a foster family. By the 1920s, child welfare philosophy was moving away from child apprehension and institutional regimes, instead favouring family therapy and family-based settings.[42] Professional social workers and university-based experts were replacing the charitable amateur, to become the new 'owners' of child welfare. To honour the new therapeutic commitment, 'child protection' was renamed 'child and family services'.

The new childsaving, despite the renaming, shared much with the old.

> Despite the advancement of new ideas and procedures, the ultimate goal ... remained unchanged from that of earlier generations of middle-class child-savers: to avoid present and future expenditures on public welfare and to guarantee social peace and stability by transforming dependent children into industrious, law-abiding workers.[43]

The new expertise legitimated the middle-class bias of child welfare established by nineteenth-century moral crusaders and poor and non-anglophone families continued to be singled out. The new agencies and experts defined the normative family according to certain assumptions,

> first, that the natural, inevitable, and highest form of the family is a particular type of household arrangement — a nuclear unity comprising two adults in a monogamous, heterosexual, legal marriage, and their dependent children; second, that the family is premised on the biological or sexual division of labour that gives each member a different, but complementary, role with attendant obligations; third, the family is a private haven that operates on the basis of consensus as opposed to the public sphere of the marketplace where competition and conflict prevail.[44]

The construct has central implications for Aboriginal child welfare: it omits the childcare networks of kith and kin which function in pre-industrial societies to intervene in times of difficulty and provide alternate caregiving[45] and it ignores the complex extended-family structure of original societies. It is a monolithic construct[46] tailored to justify state intervention in 'abnormal' families.

Canadian child welfare philosophy prior to the Second World War was imbricated in a social Darwinism which read into 'survival of the fittest' a Canadian imperialism aspiring to equal partnership with England in the Empire.[47] The Canadian social purity movement embraced this vision of citizenship in its therapeutic focus on cleanliness and purity, medical and moral hygiene. The movement evangelicized a nativism which excised Aboriginal peoples from the Canadian landscape and viewed childhood as a blank slate upon which could be inscribed a chosen character. While the child might be irredeemably tainted by parental shortcomings, ethnicity or race, the enterprise, due to much confusion about eugenics and determinism, was nonetheless worth the try. Child welfare in the age of moral hygiene was characterized by an 'unabashed' interventionism in which sociology and religion formed a seamless web: 'the perfect sociology, perfectly applied, will realize the Kingdom of God on Earth'.[48]

The English child migration movement exemplified the imperialist project of citizenship and provides parallels to the 'normalization' of Aboriginal children. Beginning in 1618 with a group of 'orphaned and destitute' children sent from England to Virginia and lasting 350 years, 150,000 British children aged four to fourteen were exported to the colonies for apprenticeship as farm and household labourers.[49] Two out of three were sent to Canada, the 'healthiest' colony, between 1870 and 1925 in the evangelical entrepreneurship of such Victorian childsavers as 'Dr.' Thomas Barnardo and the infamous Maria Rye. Under banners of Empire and child-saving, health and opportunity, children were exported to save public welfare costs and costs of future delinquency, and to fill colonial needs for cheap labour and English stock. Fear of uncivilized children was also a motive. A contemporary poem urged, perhaps tongue-in-cheek,[50]

Take them away! Take them away!
Out of the gutter, the ooze, and the slime,
Where the little vermin paddle and crawl
Till they grow and ripen in crime.

The conclusion reflects nineteenth-century beliefs in the restorative powers of the New World: 'The new shall repair the wrongs of the old.'

At least two-thirds of child migrants were not orphans, as the public and the publicity supposed, but children placed in institutional care, primarily by parents and often on a temporary basis, and exported without consent. Many lost all contact with family. Despite sharing a language and 'mother' culture with the colonies which received them, the children experienced cultural disorientation, discrimination as the 'offal of the most depraved characters in the city of the old country', much physical and sexual abuse, emotional loss and inadequate and sometimes deadly living conditions. Moral panics circled about the child migrants. 'Much crime, drunkenness and prostitution was seen as a result', wrote a late nineteenth-century Winnipeg correspondent, although the *Winnipeg Free Press* observed that most of the 'crimes' in question were committed by local children. Labour unions complained that the child migrants were driving the working man out of the workplace.[51] The children were morally and genetically unfit to associate with Canadian children, wrote the prestigious Dr. Kenneth Clarke after sharing a train with a new shipment. 'In Canada we are deliberately adding to our population hundreds of children bearing all the stigmata of physical and mental degeneracy' and the government should be held criminally liable. The 1893 'Highways and Hedges' magazine of the English National Children's Homes Society was in accord.

For some of them are of poor human material; their constitution — physical and mental — is of inferior texture; they are naturally deficient in force of character and moral stamina; their antecedents were once vicious or at least unpromising; the sad entail of hereditary weakness or wickedness makes these unfortunate juveniles peculiarly the objects of our compassionate and continuous care ... Canada is no place to shoot rubbish. It is a magnificent British colony waiting for development ...

The majority of children were sent to Ontario and Manitoba and were a common feature of rural life.[52] These provinces not being places 'to shoot rubbish', restrictive legislation was enacted in 1897 which prohibited, under penalty of a fine of $100 or 3 months' imprisonment, immigration of any child

who has been reared or who has resided amongst habitual criminals, or any child whose parents have been habitual criminals, lunatics or idiots, or weak-minded or defective constitutionally or confirmed paupers, or diseased ...

Canada stopped accepting the children in 1925 due to new and more expensive ideas about child welfare management (vetted placements and follow-up visits, for example) at the onset of the Depression.[53] These new ideas about child welfare were not without their opponents on the homefront.

The Winnipeg Home of the Friendless, an evangelical 'Christian refuge of last resort' for 'orphaned or destitute' children and unwed mothers, was founded and run by Kansas evangelist Laura Crouch from 1900 to 1929. The Home was exempted from child welfare legislation by certificate of incorporation in 1913, a timely move as provincial powers of investigation and apprehension were reaching a temporary zenith. Empowered to refuse direct access of any 'person or agency' (including parents) to child inmates, and toapprentice or adopt out any child without consent of child or parent, the Home was privately funded by a wealthy grocer (Crouch testified she began operation with $5.00 and prayer provided the rest), held impressive rural and urban properties and operated two farms run on child labour.[54] Sixty-three former inmates testified before a provincial inquiry to beatings with straps, laths and switches — some 'for cause', others ritual; to fear and intimidation, inadequate diet, isolation in cellars for up to four weeks at a time, 15 to 20 hour workdays, badly crowded dormitories, forced religious observance (Crouch evangelized a doomsday 'holy roller' cult), lack of medical help and inadequate education. All complaints were dismissed.

Those who managed the Home were 'extremely earnest Christian people' while 'retrospective recollections of happenings in youth are apt to be distorted, unduly favorable or the reverse', wrote Deputy Minister of Education Dr. Robert Fletcher in his 1927 report. The corporal punishment described by witnesses was deserved, exaggerated or fabricated. Fletcher mused on the religious benefits of such punishment.

Notwithstanding that physical punishment is no remedy at all for the disease of mind and body complained of, we are further impressed with the religious possibilities in the matter. The strictest mentor is he or she who lives by the letter rather than by the spirit ... The true object of all punishment is to reform the mind of the victim.

Fletcher viewed the conflicting views expressed before his inquiry — 'Social investigators claim to have been refused admission to the premises, the Home officials say they have been spied upon' — as conflicts of ideology caused by a 'fundamental difference in policy' between the new social work and the religious mandate of the Home.

Social workers today have as objective the placing of every homeless child with a family in a home with adoptive or foster parents ... The Home of the Friendless is conducted on diametrically opposed lines. It is not only an institutional home for children but also it endeavours to absorb those children for life as workers ... and in the religious work [of the Home] ...

Fletcher was sufficiently impressed by Crouch and her staff that he recommended that the Home continue operation and be given a tax bailout by the province. This was not done. The Home was closed in 1929 for failure to pay taxes. Its huge property holdings — 'The farm equipment alone is large even in western conception' — became the object of a series of disputed property grabs by city and province. The children were seized by provincial authorities. Crouch took the remainder of her flock to British Columbia, where her Burnaby operation was shut down ten years later amid similar controversy.

The history of the Home of the Friendless illustrates the endurance and sanctioning of the nineteenth-century institutional model well into the Progressive Era of professional childsaving and foster care. It further illustrates inadequacies of the new child welfare legislation and philosophy. Children's Aid Society workers had attempted over a ten-year period, without success, to gain access to Home records and child inmates. Questions were raised in the Manitoba legislature. Affidavits of former inmates were taken by Percy Paget, Chair of the Board of Welfare Supervision and it was these, together with the direct testimony of former inmates, which formed the basis of evidence before the inquiry. Claims of inadequate educational curriculum rather than of child maltreatment may have finally attracted government action, as child welfare and education were a single department at the time. The Fletcher report did recommend that 'no new child-caring institution be permitted to commence operation in Manitoba until it shows itself willing to subscribe to ... lawful Government requirements'.

The Home's practices of isolation, corporal punishment, child labour, minimal education, regimentation, evangelicism and cultural devaluation — many of its inmates were the children of immigrants — illustrate strategies for the governance of childhood which disabled distinctions between corporal punishment and abuse, child labour and exploitation, minimal education and inadequate education. These distinctions were unclear even to government policy-makers, as the competing views of Fletcher and Paget demonstrate.

Child migration and the residential schooling exemplified in the Home of the Friendless were designed to normalize childhood by instilling values of Anglo-Canadian Christian citizenship in the children of the poor. The fact that they were challenged by the 'new' childsaving of the first decades of the twentieth century illustrates competing modes of child management — foster care and family support versus the orphanage, industrial school or reformatory; family model versus institutional model — rather than a fundamental disagreement with earlier technologies of transformation and normalization. The perishing child and the dangerous child were to be reformed by corporal punishment, regimentation and surveillance, isolation from kin and culture, cultural devaluation, religious indoctrination, education tailored to social status and child labour, whatever the model. These technologies were appropriated for assimilating the Aboriginal child. Indian residential schools were closely modelled on mainstream nineteenth-century institutional regimes for normalizing childhood. Like the Home of the Friendless, Indian residential schools escaped the attentions of the new childsaving by virtue of an insulating legal regime.

III. EDUCATION AND NORMALIZATION: THE RESIDENTIAL SCHOOL

ABORIGINAL PARENTING PRACTICES shocked early observers. The Jesuit missionary Le Jeune spent the winter of 1633-34 with the Montaignais, a Quebec Algonkian people linguistically and culturally related to the Plains Cree. His observations of Aboriginal childhood point to an unusual freedom to experiment, inclusion in the adult activities of the community and, worst of all, no corporal punishment but only a single reprimand as a last resort. Le Jeune concluded that removal from family and tribe was essential to the institution of a proper educational regime. In his imagined regime, the children would have a period of complete freedom to accustom them to the pleasures of European food and clothing such that 'they will have a horror of Savages and their filth'. A disciplinary regime, with appropriate corporal punishments, would then be introduced.[55] Le Jeune's was perhaps the earliest example of a normalization scheme for Aboriginal childhood based on residential schooling and corporal punishment. This chapter is a brief survey of Indian residential schooling in Canada.

The foundations of a mission school which would board Aboriginal children at Red River were laid by Hudson's Bay Company chaplain John West on his arrival at the trading post of York Factory in August 1820.[56] West was immediately impressed with the need for his services. The 'corrupt influence and barter of spirituous liquors at a Trading Post' made it 'peculiarly incumbent upon me to seek to ameliorate their sad condition, as degraded, emaciated, and wandering in ignorance'. Further, 'some spoke of impossibilities in the way of teaching them Christianity or the first rudiments of settled and civilized life'. West had a ready answer for this problem on his first contact with the new world and its indigenous inhabitants. The answer was childhood.

If little hope could be cherished of arresting the adult Indian in his wanderings and unsettled habits of life, it appeared to me, that a wide and most extensive field, presented itself for cultivation in the instruction of the native children. With the aid of an interpreter, I spoke to an Indian called Withaweecapo, about taking two of his boys to the Red River Colony with me to educate and maintain. He yielded to my request; and I shall never forget the affectionate manner in which he brought the eldest in his arms, and placed him in the canoe on the morning of my departure ... I considered that I bore a pledge from the Indian that many more children might be found, if an Establishment was formed in British Christian sympathy, and British liberality for their education and support (15 August, 1820).

West sought Hudson's Bay Company support for his 'Establishment'. His argument was not based on Christian sympathy for the noble savage but, more cleverly, on the threat to social order posed by deserted 'Half Caste children' who must 'equally claim the attention of the Christian Philanthropist with those who are of pure Aboriginal blood'.

I have suggested to the Committee of the H.B. Company the importance of collecting and educating the numerous Half Breed children, whose parents have died or deserted them, and who are found running about the different Factories in ignorance and idleness. Neglected as they hitherto have been, they grow up in great depravity, and should they be led to "find their grounds" with the Indians, it cannot be a matter of surprise, if at any time collectively, or in parties they should threaten the peace of the country and the safety of the Trading Posts (12 August, 1822).

This was an astute appeal to the widespread fears of unmediated childhood which propelled nineteenth-century evangelical childsaving.

Parents posed a problem. Like Le Jeune before him, West saw the need to separate child from mother culture and from the mother.

[T]he last two Indian Saulteaux boys have given us a little trouble in disciplining them to the school, from the mother living constantly about the settlement, and occasionally visiting them, when they have run off with their sisters to the wigwam (20 April, 1823).

This convinced him that 'it is far better to obtain the children from a distance, as those who are in the school and at a distance from their parents soon become reconciled to the restraint, and happy upon the Establishment'.[57] West returned to England disappointed by the failure of the Hudson's Bay Company to support his efforts. His Mission, however, was not lost.

The 1842 Bagot Commission recognized the difficulty of assimilating Aboriginal children who remained in contact with families. The Commission recommended as antidote the establishment of farm-based boarding schools far away from parental influence and interference. Residential schooling was approved by the Upper Canada Chiefs gathered at Orillia in 1846 who agreed to pay one-fourth of their annuities for 25 years in support of the school, although they objected to its assimilationist agenda. The system was extended in Upper Canada in the 1850s and 1860s. The Indian Department sent lawyer-journalist Nicholas Davin to investigate the United States model of 'aggressive civilization' which removed Plains Aboriginal youth 'from the tribal way of life' for industrial school training. Davin's 1879 *Report on Industrial Schools for Indians and Half-breeds* reflected the Bagot Commission conclusion that the schools worked best when farm-based and church-run.

The Canadian system was designed for Indian Affairs by Egerton Ryerson, Chief Superintendent of Education for Upper Canada. Ryerson led the campaign in the latter half of the nineteenth century for the establishment of a system of free universal compulsory education which would, he believed, create social cohesion by inculcating a common morality. Ryerson objected in principle to industrial schooling, as it segregated the children of the poor, but conceded it would do for the 'worst' children. These presumably included Aboriginal children. His 'Indian industrial schools' 'were to give [the Indian] a plain English education adapted to the working farmer and mechanic' and would include a strong Christian component because 'nothing can be done to improve and elevate [the Indian's] character without the aid of religious feeling'. The schools were to be joint undertakings of the federal Indian Department and major Christian denominations, supported by contributory child labour.

Although the precedent system of small mission schools like West's proposed 'Establishment' continued, Indian Affairs policy shifted in favour of industrial and boarding schools (a distinction dropped in 1923 for the term 'residential school'). Beginning in the 1880s in fulfilment of the Numbered Treaty obligations to educate Indian children, the residential school system expanded throughout the Northwest, the former territory of the Hudson's Bay Company and West's original mission. West's 'Half-breed children' had no place in official Indian policy. In total, 80 schools were constructed, most in the Prairie region. Between 1901 and 1961, the percentage of registered Indian children enrolled in residential schools fluctuated between 12 per cent and 37 per cent. In 1936, 42 per cent of Manitoba Indian children were registered in a residential school. This compares with 3 per cent in Quebec, 36 per cent in Ontario, 77 per cent in Saskatchewan, and 98 per cent in Alberta.[58]

The schools were to be located as far as possible from the Indian bands. As a member of Parliament explained in 1883,[59]

[i]f these schools are to succeed, we must not have them too near the bands; in order to educate the children properly we must separate them from their families. Some people may say this is hard, but if we want to civilize them we must do that.

Children between the ages of three or four and 14 were taken from their parents and 'villages', by now 'reserves', to schools hundreds of kilometres away. Their hair was cut or shaved off, they were separated by age and gender, denied sibling contact and given new names. The curriculum consisted of morning classes, rarely above a grade 3-5 level, with field or house work for the rest of the day. Only English speech was permitted, reflecting conscious assimilation and unconscious racial superiority. The poet Matthew Arnold, then British Inspector of Schools, had written in 1852 of the link between language and empire.[60]

It must always be the desire of a government to render its dominions, as far as possible, homogenous. Sooner or later the difference of language ... will probably be effaced ... an event which is socially and politically desirable.

A similar philosophy underlay residential school policy. Speaking an Aboriginal language was prohibited or severely restricted and punishment for infraction could be severe.[61] The efficacy of a residential school education depended equally on removal from family and culture, and on 'precept and example'. According to the 1889 Indian Affairs Annual Report,[62]

The boarding school disassociates the Indian child from the deleterious home influences to which he would otherwise be subjected. It reclaims him from the uncivilized state in which he has been brought up. It brings him into contact from day to day with all that tends to effect a change in his views and habits of life. By precept and example he is taught to endeavour to excel in what will be most useful to him.

Removal of children from 'the demoralizing and degrading influence of the tepees', as the Calgary Herald rather crudely put it in 1892, was necessary to the program. But a Presbyterian missionary wrote home in 1903 that the schools were no more than an attempt 'to educate & colonize a people against their will'.[63]

Nineteenth-century imperialism was carried into twentieth-century Indian Affairs policy under the stewardship of Duncan Campbell Scott, whose service lasted from 1878 to 1932. By 1909, assimilation was becoming less 'aggressive' due to cost, tactical resistance and the successful marginalization of Plains Indians. The path of Prairie settlement having been cleared, the path of assimilation was less important and citizenship through protective segregation — a slower assimilation — now became the justification for continuing the Indian Affairs policy of apartheid. Scott, mid-career as Indian Affairs Superintendent of Education, wrote of the change in 1909.[64]

The government and the churches have abandoned, to a large extent, previous policies which attempted to 'Canadianize' the Indians. Through a process of vocational, and to a smaller extent academic training, they are now attempting to make good Indians, rather than poor mixtures of Indians and whites. While the idea is still Christian citizenship, the government now hopes to move towards this end by continuing to segregate the Indian population, in large measure from the white races.

Despite a gradual relaxation of policy — newer schools were located closer to the bands; language restrictions were eased — resistance to schooling increased. In summer breaks, familial and cultural norms were confusingly reasserted. Some children had lost their Aboriginal language and skills but by summer's end had lost their English. Children resisted by speaking their own languages, playing truant or avoiding the Indian agent who collected children at summer's end. A few engaged in acts of violence or arson. Parents resisted, visiting against the rules (one Saskatchewan school built a sleeping porch for parents, to the consternation of the Bishop), withdrawing children because of corporal punishment practices, removing instructors for physical or sexual abuse, boycotting schools with overt assimilationist policies, fighting for the establishment of schools which would give their children a European education without Christian indoctrination, refusing to enrol their children without assurance of non-conversion. Although an 'English' education was sought and valued by Aboriginal peoples who recognized the inevitability of change, assimilation was consistently rejected.

Some children may have been assimilated, depending on how success is here defined. Certainly the schools produced children who had learned enough for effective resistance and who became twentieth-century social and political leaders — 'the most promising pupils are found to have retrograded and to have become leaders in the pagan life of the reserves', Scott wrote in 1913. Up to one half of all children enrolled prior to 1914 never went home. Indian Affairs medical officer P.H. Bryce reported in 1912 that 'It is quite within the mark to say that fifty per cent of the children who passed through these schools did not live to benefit from the education which they received therein'.[65] There are rumours of unmarked graves behind residential schools, said to hold the infanticided offspring of nuns.[66] If such graves exist, it is probable that they hold the unclaimed bodies of child victims of tuberculosis. The disease was spread in the stifling conditions of crowded and airless dormitory life during the long harsh Prairie winters and by the English love of brass bands, the instruments being vectors of the disease. 'TB' sanitariums still dot the Prairie landscape. These child deaths were an unforeseen example of resolving 'the Indian problem' by extermination, not by war, genocide, starvation, ignorance or neglect, but by 'doing good'.

Other children graduated to a life which did not accommodate their skills and whose skills they had lost. The non-nurturing attentions of instructors, early and prolonged separation from parents and siblings and the experience of institutional life did not teach residential school pupils either Aboriginal or Euro/ Anglo-Canadian parenting norms. Corporal punishment, a longstanding feature of European education,[67] was an important part of the regime and came to symbolize the cultural and social destruction of the residential school experience. Some schools had a 'discipline officer' whose rod required a certain number of weekly strokes.[68] William Clarence Thomas, Superintendent, Peguis School Board, told the Kimelman Inquiry in 1985 that[69]

[o]ne school principal in Brandon used to call us God's children three times on Sundays at the three services and the rest of the week call us dirty little Indians. No one ever told us they loved us. We were mere numbers. Strapping, beatings, hair cut to baldness, being tethered to the flag pole, half day school with unqualified tutors, and slave labour the other half ...

Janet Ross told the 1991 Manitoba Aboriginal Justice Inquiry that

[t]he boarding school is where the alienation began. Children were placed there, plucked out of their homes. The bond between parents and children was fragmented severely - some lost forever... The boarding schools taught us violence. Violence was emphasized

through physical, corporal punishment, strapping, beatings, bruising and control. We learned to understand that this was power and control.

Many children were sexually abused by teachers and clerics or by older children who had been similarly abused; most were controlled through abasement, cultural devaluation, humiliation and corporal punishment. The Aboriginal Justice Inquiry summarized the experience as one 'marked by emotional, physical and sexual abuse, social and spiritual deprivation, and substandard education ... Aboriginal communities have not yet recovered from the damage.'[70] Sexual use of children, corporal punishment and damaged parent-child bonds, recognized precursors of abuse, infiltrated reserve childhood. Economic disintegration leading to apathy and substance abuse provided the conditions of neglect and an environment in which child abuse as defined by child welfare policy and legislation could flourish.

The residential schools were maintained far beyond their time, when child welfare policy had moved toward family-centred solutions and interventions were at least overtly based less on class and 'race' than apprehension of harm. The project 'failed dismally' due in large part to Indian resistance[71] and the last schools (excepting a few which were turned over to First Nations management) were closed in the 1960s. The dream of empire which fuelled the assimilation of Indian childhood, as it fuelled assimilation of the children of poor and the marginalised through child migration and nineteenth-century child welfare, backfired. The imperialist mission of reconstructing Indian childhood on an Anglo-Canadian model made residential schooling an important symbol of assimilation and cultural destruction. A second system has emerged as an equally powerful symbol: of cultural genocide: the twentieth-century child protection system.

IV. DOMINATION AND RESISTANCE: CHILD WELFARE

STRATEGIES OF ASSIMILATION which focussed on the colonization of Aboriginal childhood inspired a variety of tactics of resistance and the agenda of self-determination. Band organizations in Saskatchewan and Manitoba chose two arenas of self-government to be forged out of the unique constitutional relationship of Indians with Canada and the provinces. These are control of education funding, including reserve day schools, high school and post-secondary school funding, and child welfare.[72] Child welfare control was the more far-reaching and the more emotive. The argument for band control of child welfare is multi-tiered. On the first level are arguments based on genocide and cultural survival. Children are a people's hope for the future. Children removed from their cultural matrix lose their own culture and represent an incalculable loss to their original cultural groups. This is cultural genocide. On the second level are arguments based on the child's interests. A healthy self-concept requires rearing by like parents for transmission of cultural identity. The 'bicultural' child belongs to neither culture and will fail to develop the ethnic pride which protects against racism. On the third level is the end to which Aboriginal control of child welfare is a means: self-government.[73]

The problematic politics of shared federal-provincial responsibility for Indian child welfare, the unsatisfactory and sometimes deadly provincial intervention record and the adopting-out of thousands of Indian children to non-Aboriginal families created a climate in which every form of intervention by any agency, however constituted, is 'child abuse'. The moral and political valence of child abuse in its post-1960s reconstructions, and the confusion and guilt surrounding Indian child welfare management, have made child welfare control the leading argument for self-government.[74]

The 1867 *British North America Act* granted exclusive federal jurisdiction over 'Indians and lands reserved for Indians' and exclusive provincial jurisdiction over child welfare. Provincial child welfare agencies had no jurisdiction on reserve. Reserve children at risk were cared for by relatives, sent to residential school or placed in an alternate reserve home by the federal Indian Agent.[75] Post-Second World War agency expansion and the increasing visibility of Aboriginal peoples as a result of population increase, northern development, urban migration and political resistance brought Indian child protection to mainstream attention. In 1947, the Canadian Welfare Council and the Canadian Association of Social Workers presented a brief to the Parliamentary Subcommittee on the *Indian Act*. The brief described inadequate living conditions and lack of comparable social services to reserve children, and condemned residential schooling. The practice of Indian adoption, the Council noted, 'is loosely conceived and executed and is totally devoid of the careful legal and social protection afforded to white children'.[76] The brief officially ended the silence imposed by federal Indian policy. The federal government responded by amending *The Indian Act*.

S. 88. Subject to the terms of any treaty and any other act of the Parliament of Canada, all laws of general application from time to time in force in any province are applicable to and in respect of Indians in the province, except to the extent that such laws are inconsistent with this Act ...

This gave the provinces the required constitutional authority to provide protection and adoption services to children on federal Indian reserves.

The provinces were reluctant to extend cost-intensive child protection programs onto reserves — understandable in face of the remoteness, culturally and physically, of many — and so continued to claim federal responsibility for reserve child welfare.[77] The 1966 Indian Affairs *Hawthorn Report* described conditions for Indian children as 'unsatisfactory to appalling'.[78] Later that year Indian Affairs signed cost-sharing agreements with the provinces for reserve child welfare. Aboriginal peoples were not consulted and no allowance was made for agency protection of culture and language or for employing Aboriginal child protection workers. As assimilation remained a federal goal until the demise of the 1969 Trudeau White Paper, the omissions are unsurprising. In Manitoba, as in other Prairie provinces, a patchwork of service delivery was put in place. The Children's Aid Societies of Central, Eastern and Western Manitoba contracted with the federal government for service provision to 14 southern bands. This left northern reserves, and the majority of registered Manitoba Indians, eligible only for life-and-death intervention.

Protective apprehension of Indian children was essentially a smash-and-grab operation, strongly resisted.[79] Failure to intervene early and provide family support, and a system bias in favour of apprehension and permanent placement, meant that few children were returned to their families. Families might be told nothing of what happened to their children; children might be returned a year later without explanation or not returned at all. Clear cases of abuse were overlooked with tragic results for the children concerned; children were apprehended in 'cases' resulting from cultural confusion: 'There were horror stories both ways'.[80] By 1976, 6.5 per cent of reserve children were in care. By the late 1970s to early 1980s, one in seven status Indian children were not in parental custody and one in 21 spent a significant period of childhood away from home.[81] The number in care dropped to just over three in 100 or 3.2 per cent by 1987, in the overall decline of children in care, but the rate was still four times that of non-reserve children, of whom 0.8 per cent were in care.

Adoption was the ideal fix. Adoption by legislation was a relatively recent addition to case disposition alternatives available to agencies. Provincial adoption law and policy forged shortly after the turn of the century was geared to concealment of adoption. The legislation recreated childbirth and rewrote genealogy by extinguishing prior records and entitlements of the child 'as though the child were a child born to the adopting parent in lawful wedlock'. Policies favoured adopters who most closely approximated the normative family: nuclear, financially comfortable, of child-bearing age, heterosexual and, usually, white and middle-class.[82] There was little interest in transracial adoption unless 'race' was disguised by light skin and eyes.

By the late 1960s, the situation had changed. The adoption market could no longer supply 'like' children to prospective adopters due to decreased birthrate and an increase in white single mothers, who had supplied the market, keeping their babies. The United States civil rights movement stimulated interest in transracial adoption and 'exotic' children.[83] For Aboriginal children seized under new provincial mandates, transracial adoption was the perfect, and politically trendy, solution.

Early warning of cultural destruction by adoption policy was sounded by the *Report of the British Columbia Royal Commission on Family and Children's Law* 1975.[84]

The *Adoption Act* is sometimes viewed as one more weapon employed by white society to destroy the Indian culture. It is seen as a means of taking away the right of Indian bands to take care of their own children and as a means of placing Indian children in white homes where they would lose contact with their own race.

Agencies were confronted with fourth-world living conditions and the legacies of institutional abuse and economic deterioration which visibly injured and killed children. Agency access to reserve children was compromised or denied by geography, culture and a legacy of profound anger. Budgets were limited. The therapeutic family model to which agencies aspired was inoperable under such conditions. Smash-and-grab apprehension seemed necessary and inevitable. Despite warnings of cultural destruction, agencies in Western Canadian provinces mounted aggressive advertising campaigns focused on the transracial adoption of Aboriginal children through the 1970s and early 1980s. Between 1971 and 1981, over 3400 Aboriginal children — 70 to 80 per cent of whom were Manitoba status Indian children — were adopted by non-status parents.[85] In 1981, 38 per cent of status Indian children and 17 per cent of Metis children placed for adoption in Manitoba were sent to the United States[86] where Canadian Aboriginal Indian children found a better market (African-American children similarly found a better market in Canada, on a much smaller scale). Manitoba agencies, flushed with success, continued to make extra-provincial placements long after the practice was terminated in other provinces.

Extra-provincial adoption negated agency follow-up. The child's contact with birth culture was prevented by adoption confidentiality and geocultural distance. Those adopted children who made their way back to their Manitoba home reserves found transition difficult.[87] Aboriginal children under provincial child welfare systems remained transferable and transformable commodities. When the legacies of nineteenth-century child-saving met late twentieth-century social work, the result was the massive neo-colonization of Aboriginal childhood. Disclosure of the magnitude of this intervention, whatever may have been the needs or endangerment of the children involved, led to moral panic and political opportunism across the entire 'stakeholder' spectrum — politicians, federal and provincial government bureaucrats, program directors, Aboriginal leaders, all-chiefs associations, academics, the 'psy' professions, Aboriginal communities. The result was the foundation of a compromise system for Manitoba which would be dually driven by Aboriginal cultural values and Euro-Canadian child protection expertise.

V. INTERTRIBAL AGENCIES: THE MANITOBA EXPERIENCE

ALL ON-RESERVE MANITOBA CHILDREN are served by intertribal child protection agencies under Indian management and control, a situation unique in Canada.[88] This chapter looks at the origin and functioning of these agencies.

Claims of genocide and the expense of reserve service delivery made federal and provincial governments as anxious to divest themselves of responsibility for reserve child welfare as the bands were for its control. The Manitoba Court of Queen's Bench in *Director of Child Welfare for Manitoba* v. *B.* (1979) 6 WWR 229 made clear the extent of provincial government responsibility for child protection services on reserves.

Irrespective of any views that the provincial government may have as to the historical, political, financial or moral responsibility of the federal government to provide health and social service care, it is now absolutely clear that it is the legal responsibility and duty of the province to supply child welfare services ... to the treaty Indian on the same basis and criteria as such services are supplied to the other residents of Manitoba.

No longer could the province rely on federal agreements, the court stated, to limit protective intervention for reserve children to ' "life-and-death" situations'. The writing was on the wall and the legislative loophole was there, in an anachronistic provision of the Manitoba *Child and Family Services Act* which allowed the Minister to establish new child welfare agencies without legislative debate.[89]

A 1980 report jointly authored by the federal and provincial governments and the Manitoba Indian Brotherhood agreed on the need to protect 'Indian cultural identity' and to involve Indian people in service provision. In 1982, a tripartite agreement between federal, provincial and Indian governments, *Political Accord on Manitoba Indian Child Welfare Negotiations*, established the first system of Aboriginal agencies mandated to apprehend children. It was signed by the federal Minister of Indian Affairs, the Minister of Community Services Manitoba, the Brotherhood of Indian Nations, First Nations Confederacy and the Southeast Resource Development Council.[90] Dakota-Ojibway Child and Family Services, established by special tripartite agreement in 1981, received its mandate to apprehend under this agreement. Further agreements were signed with six tribal councils, giving each an agency to serve the reserves in its area.[91] The *Child and Family Services Act* was revised in 1986 to incorporate the tripartite agreements[92] and a section stating that preservation of cultural and linguistic heritage is a criterion of the child's best interests was added to protect the cultural interests of off-reserve and non-status Aboriginal children. Under the agreements, Indian Affairs funds child welfare services at the provincial rate while the Manitoba Director of Child and Family Services retains control over 'standards of services and practices and procedures' including powers of review and dissolution.

All parties agreed on the massive failure of mainstream agencies to protect either child or culture, and on the desirability of 'devolving' child welfare control to intertribal councils. 'The road to hell was paved with good intentions, and the child welfare system was the paving contractor,' Judge Kimelman had written in his 1985 report on Aboriginal child welfare in Manitoba. The new intertribal agencies were to remedy the 'genocidal' practices of child apprehension and out-group fostering, adoption and extraprovincial placement of Aboriginal children.[93]   The agencies would incorporate into social work practice, structure and ideology such Aboriginal norms as consensus decision-making and shared multi-generational childcare. The structure would maintain cultural heritage and introduce Aboriginal control.

In effect, a community-based 'Aboriginal' model was tacked on to the provincial statutory structure and flow of authority (Minister, agency board, supervisor, staff). Each reserve has a worker stationed on-reserve and a Child Care Committee to advise the worker and help implement service plans. Chiefs by right have a seat on the intertribal agency council. The structure invited nepotism. Whether Chief, Chief and Council, agency supervisor or Child Care Committee is ultimately responsible for approving the decisions of child-care workers was contested from the beginning. Some Chiefs believed they were to make final childcare decisions as a legitimate exercise of their existing powers.   Many viewed their new child protection mandate as an exercise of the right to self-government.[94] Warnings of   professional shortcomings and ideological conflicts in the new agencies, and of children endangered or killed under the new policies, appeared in studies of the new system conducted during the 1980s by business and academic consultants. These oberservations were downplayed or ignored in the conclusions of the studies, in the enthusiastic embrace by consultants of an 'Indian' child protection system.

There were problems. Intertribal agencies were responsible virtually upon establishment for full service delivery without lead time to develop internal structures, procedures or staff. Few Aboriginal people had social work credentials and, it was argued, a social work degree did not include courses in Aboriginal child rearing or reserve life. Untrained workers were hired and start-up training programs hastily set up. The high turnover rate endemic to front-line child protection vitiated the educative value of fieldwork, while many of the new workers failed to internalize a professional discourse and discipline in a field which requires formal self-directed upgrading. The tension between 'Aboriginal' norms and child protection philosophy and legislation was apparent from the start.

The situation had not markedly changed ten years later. The 1988 suicide of a 13-year-old Ojibway child became the subject of the longest inquest in Manitoba history, held three years after his death. The report canvassed agency governance and agency failure. The agency responsible for the care of the child suicide Lester Desjarlais, a victim of profound and multiple abuse in the short course of his life who unsuccessfully sought reunification with his alcoholic mother, was Dakota-Ojibway Child and Family Services, the first Aboriginal child welfare agency in Manitoba. In his 1992 report,[95] Giesbrecht P.C.J. found DOCFS worker training inadequate, worker accountability lacking, record-keeping procedures all but useless, improper and ineffective intervention and record-tampering. Further, the provincial Minister failed to take action on any one of a long series of reported agency disasters and delicts out of fear of being labelled 'racist'.

Criticism of ministerial inaction was not new in Manitoba.

The Act gives the Director the authority to develop and maintain standards for child welfare services and to ensure the agencies are acting in accordance with those standards. In fact, the Director has not exercised that authority. ... It is not clear why the Director of Child Welfare has failed to exercise the legislated authority. It is clear, however, that such supervision of child care agencies is long overdue and must be put into effect.[96]

This was not the 1992 Giesbrecht Report but the 1985 Kimelman Report which found systemic bias in the child welfare system amounting to 'cultural genocide'. Ministerial indifference, poor training, lack of worker accountability, improper and ineffective intervention, inadequate record-keeping and record-tampering and a bias toward extra-cultural placement were destroying Aboriginal childhood.[97] The criticisms of the Giesbrecht Report of the new 'Aboriginal' agencies were an uncanny parallel. In too many respects, the new agencies shared much with the old. The Report, however, pointed to a new problem with the new agencies: Chiefs and band council members were interfering with agency decisions, using *Indian Act* jurisdiction over reserve residency to threaten expulsion[98] of workers who intervened in cases involving Chiefs, council members or their relatives. For local child care workers, expulsion meant loss of home and community. The disjunction between ideology and its exercise was expressed by a teacher blocked for years by Chief and council in her efforts to obtain protection for sexually abused children at the school, who told the *Winnipeg Free Press*: 'Let them cry cultural genocide. They do that on a daily basis anyway.'[99]

Nor was the Giesbrecht Report the first public intimation of nepotistic abuses of power. An earlier inquest into another child suicide concluded that Anishinaabe Child and Family Services ignored abuse reports because the child was the Chief's son. The Chief made an unsuccessful application to quash the report; see *Swan* v. *Manitoba* [1992] M.J. No. 90 (Man. Q.B.). In *Dakota-Ojibway CFS* v. *Anishinaabe CFS* [1989] M.J. No. 679, the Court of Queen's Bench found 'rank political interference' when a Chief used workers who were his close relatives to circumvent a no-contact order in order to continue the sexual abuse of his daughter. The case arose from a jurisdictional dispute between two intertribal agencies, Dakota-Ojibway and Anishinaabe. 'Workers were taking their instructions from the Band itself', the judge concluded.

The Giesbrecht Report focussed on the suicided child's cousin, a seven-year-old girl sexually abused, as was Lester Desjarlais, by the pedophile 'bogeyman of Sandy Bay' who had terrorized children for many years. The 'bogeyman' was a close relative of a band council member. In February 1988, the girl came to school with writing on her stomach in felt marker saying she and the 'bogeyman' were lovers. She was placed in a reserve foster home by Dakota-Ojibway workers but was forcibly removed that night by family members. Despite repeated reports of sexual abuse, no further action was taken.[100] Former Dakota-Ojibway supervisor Marion Glover, a key witness at the inquest, was fired for attempts to intervene. (The 'bogeyman' was later arrested and tried on other child sexual assault charges.)[101] Aboriginal leaders were collectively criticized as being 'in denial' both of their own childhood experiences of sexual abuse and of the fact, extent and damage of sexual abuse in their communities. Child protection advocate Dr. Charlie Ferguson, chief medical officer of the Winnipeg Children's Hospital Child Protection Centre, testified at the inquiry that the reserve was 'infested with incest'.[102]

The Giesbrecht Report did not resolve the problem of political interference inherent in the intertribal agency structure and in the history and politics of Aboriginal governance. The province responded by calling yet another review.[103] The November 1993 Report of the First Nations Child and Family Task Force, titled *Children First — Our Responsibility*, glossed over the central issues of child abuse and the politics of ignorance and interference, and set an agenda for full local reserve control by individual band councils. No action has been taken on the report. Political interference remains a problem.

In 1993, Jackhead Reserve withdrew from its intertribal protection agency, with the support of the Assembly of Manitoba Chiefs. The Assembly unanimously resolved that the province has no authority on Jackhead and Grand Chief Phil Fontaine stated that the goal of the Assembly of Manitoba Chiefs is Indian control of child welfare.[104] In 1994, a group of Chiefs filed injunctions to stop all Anishinaabe agency service provision and banished workers from their reserves. Only Indian Affairs and the Royal Canadian Mounted Police are immune from banishment (although individual officers can be, and have been, banished). In May 1994, Anishinaabe, and the 212 children under its care, was put under the control of an acting executive director appointed by Indian Affairs. Staff were instructed by memorandum dated 24 May, 1994

to follow the direction of your supervisor & myself and not that of some Chiefs that are entertaining the idea of using their Political influence to interfere in the business of Anishinaabe ... Politics of Band Elections should not in any way, have a bearing as to the operations or functioning of the Agency.

Chief Yellow Quill of Long Plains First Nations was charged under the *Child and Family Services Act* for abducting a newborn infant from hospital in the course of an agency custody dispute, in August 1995.[105]

The major change between the eras examined in the Kimelman and Giesbrecht Reports is the focus on preservation of culture and culturally appropriate child placement. Optimistic predictions that the creation of Aboriginal agencies and the legislative enshrinement of cultural standards would reduce the number of Aboriginal children taken into care were not borne out.[106] A 1991 evaluation of Manitoba child services estimated that Aboriginal children account for 60 per cent of children in Manitoba care.[107] Between 1986 and 1989, the number of children in care of intertribal Awasis Child and Family Services Agency increased by 30 per cent.[108] Aboriginal children taken into protective custody are unlikely to get out, a problem identified in the Kimelman Report. The system remains biased toward apprehension. The Director Ma Mawi Wichi Itata, a leading Aboriginal agency, observed,[109]

It's easier to help by plugging in the resources that the agency readily provides. It's easier for the professional social worker to document and justify the no-risk choice. That's what we do best: document, justify, substantiate. Native agencies operate under the same impetus to place ...

Cases involving adolescent children are rarely taken on, homes for damaged or disturbed children are inadequate and there is little funding for abuser treatment which would expedite return. Abused children suffering emotional or behavioural problems are moved from place to place as successive foster homes prove inadequate to deal with them, further endangering their sexual, emotional and physical safety.[110] According to Margo Buck, senior psychologist with the Winnipeg Children's Hospital Child Protection Centre, 'Children in foster care move 10 to 14 times. We just saw a child who had been moved 32 times in the 18 months since the permanent order was granted at the age of two.' Worker training in some agencies is still substandard, while others have made huge strides in the last few years.[111]

There is little guarantee of protection within the system. One quarter to one half of Manitoba child abuse cases arise in foster homes.[112] Early practices of intertribal agencies heightened the risk. Foster placements on home reserves exposed children to their abusers because foster placements were chosen for cultural connection rather than the child's protection. Agencies were successfully sued for placements which led to the child's injury or death. Jurisdictional disputes between urban and intertribal agencies are still common, as reserve connections for many urban families remain strong. An application by Anishinaabe for intervenor status in a Winnipeg agency case, for example, was refused by the court; see *Northwest CFS* v. *S.J.I.* (1991), 70 D.L.R.(4th) 418 (Man. Q.B.). In a case of contested guardianship case between two child protection agencies, six siblings had been removed by Anishinaabe from the custody of their physically and sexually abusive parents and placed in an Aboriginal foster home. The children were raped and beaten by other foster children and one was killed by a son of the foster parents. Custody of the remaining children was given to a mainstream Winnipeg agency in a dramatic courtroom transfer. The judge ruled in *Anishinaabe CFS* v. *D.M.O.* [1992] No. 492 (Man. Q.B.) that the children 'have not received the level and quality of service they desperately need, nor have I any confidence that they will'.

Judicial discipline of child protection agencies in the Kimelman and Giesbrecht inquiries and in the Manitoba courts gives an overly simplified view of the debate. 'Culture' is at the centre of the question, yet culture is rarely addressed in any meaningful way. It is a term used primarily for its political valence. Most of the reports and articles dealing with the Manitoba intertribal agencies place normative claims of communal child-caring side by side with the facts of severe child neglect and abuse. This is intended somehow to make the argument that responsibility for child protection should be returned to Indian communities. The disjunction is not resolved. McKenzie and Hudson, for example, conclude that policy and practice must 'emphasize principles of cultural autonomy and local control' and wonder 'whether community concern and support for children as their most important resource occurs as a result of this change.'[113] Yet this is the central issue. It is the reason why Aboriginal child welfare remains a highly contested domain. Does local control create concern for children or does demonstrated concern for children merit local control?

A related question in these debates which has not been addressed publicly is whether self-government under the 1994 Manitoba framework agreement means that bands will be able to opt out of provincial child protection systems and intertribal agencies. Could a band choose to have nothing at all, as Jackhead did?

The 'Indian' agencies are not truly so, in the sense that they are governed by provincial legislation and contemporary social work standards and often employ non-Aboriginal staff. Tensions between opposing definitions of 'expertise' — reserve experience and Aboriginality versus professional training and philosophy — remain apparent, although the gap is lessening. The history and structure of the intertribal agencies reflect top-down political aims and expediency rather than grounded community norms and aspirations. This is not to argue that the agencies are not 'cultural' but rather to reflect on the complexity of cultural claims and definitions. Child welfare is governed by the individually-directed 'best interests of the child' test while cultural claims are grounded in the interests of a community, a more diverse and ultimately oppositional claim. 'Culture' under *The Child and Family Services Act* is one factor in custodial decisions, difficult to evaluate in the individualized and unitary context of case-by-case determination, easily ignored. From the perspective of the intertribal agencies, the courts have not given cultural continuity sufficient weight. The dice remain loaded.

VI.   CHILDHOOD, CULTURE AND THE COURTS

INDIAN STATUS IS THE LEGAL RECOGNITION of a historical relationship. It may be accompanied by a variety of rights and entitlements including the right to live on reserve. It does not in itself constitute 'culture' but may be an important marker of culture. The petition of a non-status couple in *Natural Parents* v. *Superintendent of Child Welfare* (1975)[114] to adopt a status Indian child was dismissed at first instance on grounds that Indian status is an incident of birth obliterated by adoption. The British Columbia Court of

Appeal ruled that provincial adoption legislation applies to Indians except where inconsistent with the *Indian Act*. The birth parents wanted the child to be adopted by relatives in accordance with Indian custom, and appealed. The Supreme Court of Canada ruled that, as s. 88 of the *Indian Act* incorporates by reference all 'laws of general application', provincial legislation must be analysed with care: the question is whether the child 'still has entitlement to be or to continue to be registered as an Indian under s. 11 of the Indian Act'. Adoption legislation must be construed as preserving Indian status[115] and therefore cannot extinguish Indian status.

Does 'Indian status' have meaning, absent 'culture'? In *Nelson* v. *Children's Aid Society of Eastern Manitoba* (1975),[116] the Manitoba Court of Queens Bench considered the culture-nurture question.

Part of the applicants' complaint is that adoption by non-Indian parents removes an Indian child from the Indian cultural atmosphere and environment. If that is the case, these children have been abandoned for some considerable time by their parents and a complaint of this nature now is difficult to understand. In my view the Indian Act does not attempt to compel persons who are Indians to live within any particular cultural environment as a condition of retaining the status of Indian within the meaning of the Act.

This chapter surveys judicial responses to 'culture' in contested child protection cases.

The leading case on the weight to be given to culture (as 'race') is *A.N.R. and S.C.R.* v. *L.J.W.*.[117] W., a status Indian woman, voluntarily placed her six-week-old baby (the Supreme Court of Canada wrongly states that the child was 'apprehended') in the temporary care of Dakota-Ojibway agency, then in its first year of operation. The mother's husband, a violent man, denied paternity and W. feared he would kill the baby. The agency treated the case as a permanent wardship and placed the child with Metis foster parents. The baby was briefly returned to W. at the age of two, the foster parents reclaimed the child, refused further contact with her mother and proceeded with an application for de facto adoption whereby maternal consent is waived after three years. The agency gave W. no assistance and she failed to register her protest in time.[118] Demonstrations were held outside the foster home while the mother made abortive attempts at visitation. The trial judge ruled that the child had been abandoned, granted the adoption order and noted that the advantage of being raised in an 'Indian' environment in forestalling a possible identity crisis in adolescence is outweighed by the 'real possibility' of psychological damage should bonds formed with the foster parents be broken. The court recognized cultural difference between Metis and Indian but ruled that a Metis role model for an Indian child was an acceptable answer to the 'cultural identity question'.

The Manitoba Court of Appeal scrutinized trial testimony of W., elders and psychologists on W.'s culture and spirituality, and reviewed bonding and abandonment issues. There was no abandonment where the mother had not given up the child and was refused agency assistance. The foster parents wrongly refused maternal access, erred in teaching the child she was 'theirs' and gave false information to the child about her identity. Despite these errors, the child's bonds to the foster parents and the stable secure home they provided were of greatest weight. On cultural identity, Matas J.A. wrote,

[i]n an appropriate case, the court may grant a transracial order of adoption. However, I agree that a child's culture and heritage should be considered by the court as one of the factors to be weighed.... Depending on the circumstances, it is a factor which could have greater or lesser influence in the court's final decision. In the case at bar, the evidence supports the view that the factor is an important one.

O'Sullivan J.A. saw the case as a conflict between claims of 'nature and nurture' with the 'twist' that the mother is an Indian, the foster parents not, a fact of 'considerable weight' but not decisive. There is no proprietary right to a child. Custody cannot be awarded to right past wrongs. The effect of parental ties must be assessed solely in terms of the child's benefit. The weight given to the mother's claim of specific cultural identity, as opposed to a broader 'Aboriginal' one, was, however, sufficient to block the adoption order. Custody was awarded to the foster parents with maternal access still a possibility.

Wilson S.C.J. delivered the judgment of the Supreme Court of Canada.[119] It is not the function of an appellate court to reinterpret evidence. There was evidence of abandonment and in any case *de facto* adoption is not predicated on abandonment. The foster parents acted reasonably and it was inappropriate to characterize their conduct as an illegal assertion of title. The weight of the 'racial element' is inversely related to bonding.

[T]he significance of cultural background and heritage as opposed to bonding abates over time. The closer the bond that develops with the prospective adoptive parents the less important the racial element becomes.

'Race' and 'culture are irrelevant: it is a 'simple' question of two women claiming to be the mother of a child and one does not know her.

It has nothing to do with race, absolutely nothing to do with culture, it has nothing to do with ethnic background. It's two women and a little girl, and one of them doesn't know her. It's as simple as that; all the rest of it is extra and of no consequence...

Society has changed. '"Race" is of diminished importance in an interracial society.' The sole question for the courts is the parent-child relationship.

Much was made in this case of the inter-racial aspect of the adoption. I believe that inter-racial adoption, like inter-racial marriage, is now an accepted phenomenon in our pluralist society. The implications of it may have been overly dramatized by the respondent in this case. The real issue is the cutting of the child's legal tie with her natural mother ... [The court] has an obligation to ensure that any order it makes will promote the best interests of her child. This and this alone is our task.

Where the child is young, separation prolonged and bonding established, the weight given to culture is minimal. The judgment reflects the rigid 'psychological parenting' theory of Goldstein, Solnit and Freud which asserts that once a child-parent bond has formed, there must be no further interference by the state or a separated parent.[120] The theory is problematic: a child can 'bond' with a highly abusive adult, children are often closely bonded to more than one adult, it may be impossible to establish with whom the child is bonded and the theory entirely fails to address the importance and complexity of culture and kinship.

The courts may conflate culture with economic resources. The Saskatchewan Queen's Bench Court in *Mooswa* v. *Minister of Social Services for the Province of Saskatchewan* (1978), 30 R.F.L. 101 returned the child to the birth mother, a rehabilitated alcoholic, because

basic in this kind of problem is the right and need of the child to be raised, if possible, by its natural mother in its natural environment and its own cultural surroundings ... amongst people of her own race and culture.

The standard of living 'may not be considered acceptable by others' but the court should not interfere 'if those standards conform to those considered average in the particular class or group to which the parent(s) belong'. The fact that the applicant was the birth mother and the separation of only six month's duration weighed in the decision. The principle was rejected by the Manitoba Court of Appeal in *Director of Child Welfare* v. *B.B.* (1989).[121]

I do not accept as sound the principle enunciated by the trial judge that there are certain standards or norms which are acceptable for Easterville but unacceptable for the rest of the province. Economic conditions may differ but there is only one standard of care to be considered and applied.

The Supreme Court of Canada in that case disagreed, opting for a more flexible economic standard.

In *Child and Family Services* v. *B.A.B.* [1992] M.J. No. 613 (Man. Q.B.), foster parents applied for adoption, with the support of the Winnipeg agency who had placed the child with them. The child, five years old, had been in their care for exactly half her life. Awasis, the agency responsible for the child's home reserve, intervened, using expert testimony on adolescent identity problems in transracial adoption to argue for placement with an aunt who lived a traditional Indian way of life. The court rejected the argument.

This case is about culture — but it is also about relationships — and it is also about commitment. M. is entitled to be raised by those who have demonstrated, rather than simply expressed, their commitment to her.

Awasis appealed in hopes of obtaining a strong judicial mandate for culturally-appropriate case planning and inter-agency collaboration. Directive 18 of the *Child and Family Services Program Standards Manual*, Section 421, was enacted in support of the 1985 'cultural amendment' to the *Child and Family Services Act*. The directive requires mainstream agencies placing an Aboriginal child to work to provide a culturally-appropriate placement and to notify 'the appropriate Indian agency or Native organization' of the child's entry into the system. The program standard contains seven pages of instructions. The persistent failure of mainstream agencies to adhere to the policy is the issue at root of Awasis intervention and appeal.

Nurture trumps culture in the courts.[122] Nurture is now, culture is for later. Bonding always wins and cases cannot be processed quickly enough to accommodate both, where a child has been placed even 'temporarily' outside the original cultural group. Yet the evidence that Aboriginal children may experience severe difficulties in (unmediated) transracial placements is convincing. In 1992, the child whose adoption was contested in *A.N.R. and*

S.C.R. v. *L.J.W.*, was declared a dangerous offender at the age of 16 under a rarely-used provision of *The Young Offenders Act*. Her name and photograph were published when she and a boyfriend forced their way in to a rural house at gunpoint, stole money and cut telephone lines. 'We wanted to go public because we consider these people to be highly dangerous', a Royal Canadian Mounted Police spokesman said.[123]

Children may display interest in their original cultures which adoptive parents are under no obligation to accommodate. Nor are adoptive parents legally required to divulge to a child the fact of Indian status and entitlement.[124] Failure to divulge status is involuntary enfranchisement. This fundamental constitutional (and Treaty) problem has not moved Canadian courts to break ties with prospective adopters for proposed kith or kin placement, however safe. Ideas about adoption confidentiality tailored to 'like' placements and infertile couples in an era of cultural imperialism and a unitary vision of childhood continue to dominate adoption law and policy.

The courts justify the commodification of childhood (the 'abstraction of child from culture', in Marlee Kline's poetic phrase) in several ways.[125]

First, courts may explicitly deny the relevance of maintaining a First Nations Child's culture ... Second, courts may hold that culture is important, but treat it as an abstract category that can be filled by any First Nations culture ... Third, courts may emphasize the child's psychological bonds with her foster parents, but not consider relevant bonds with her culture. Alternatively, the courts may hold that the child needs the stability of a permanent placement, while ignoring the stability that would result from maintaining a connection to her culture.

Courts may view case plans which stress cultural continuity as separate from, or in conflict with, the child's interests. The best interests test permits almost unlimited judicial discretion. Notions of 'right to a home' stand in opposition to 'right to a native home' in agency policy. Child welfare is nowhere more problematic than in the shifting politics of neocolonialism. Whose voice is given political moment, whose rights-claim is recognized, is structured by changing ideologies of citizenship. Children are not well represented in these debates.

The Manitoba experience discloses problems with both old and new child protection agencies. The intertribal agency system has been troubled by political interference, untutored decisionmaking and, above all, by a legacy of interconnected and ultimately culturally-destructive practices addressed by case-by-case intervention. Although the intertribal agencies have come under judicial fire many times in the last decade, it cannot be shown that Manitoba Aboriginal children are worse off, physically or culturally, than under former regimes. Where cultural genocide is threatened, preservation of birth culture is the central issue, yet 'culture' can have little (positive) meaning in a context of severe abuse. The question is whether child protection can bear the burden of an absolutist view, either way.

VII. New Therapies of Freedom

RESERVES ARE FEDERAL ENCLAVES untouched until recent decades by the operations and constituent theories of provincial child welfare systems. Nineteenth-century institutional models for the induction of citizenship in 'abnormal' children were appropriated for the assimilation of Aboriginal childhood. This imperialist vision doomed Aboriginal childhood but deemed Aboriginal children salvageable, by effacing difference. Other Anglo-Canadian projects for civilizing children — child migration, the Home of the Friendless — were challenged by a professionalizing social work. Imperialist models of citizenship (enfranchisement) and normalization (assimilation) dominated Aboriginal and reserve childhood for another eighty years. The geopolitical isolation of the reserve created a time- and culture-warp bypassed by the changing technologies of childhood. The 1960s rediscovery of child abuse coincided with provincial child welfare service provision to reserves and the economies of life-or-death intervention. The consequent wholesale removal of children became a new form of assimilation, resisted by Aboriginal leaders, families and sometimes the children themselves. The residential schools are gone. Control of education has in large measure returned to Indian bands. Control of child welfare remains contested.

Euro-Canadian governance of Aboriginal childhood has had a profound impact on the lives of Aboriginal peoples. The introduction of physical and sexual abuse; the determined erosion of social structures and belief systems which minimize idiosyncratic abuse; the exacerbation of abuse by cultural disenfranchisement, poverty and despair; the displacement of thousands of children: there is little about the lives of Aboriginal peoples which has not been deeply affected by childhood intervention or special disqualification. Deep differences in culture and aspiration suggest that the assimilation of childhood on either imperialist or Anglo-Canadian social work models could never have succeeded. The control of Aboriginal childhood provided the impetus and the opening wedge in the struggle for self-government.

Will self-government be tutored by imperialism, or will it reflect older modes so distasteful to Le Jeune and nineteenth century Indian management policy: communitarian, non-punitive, non-hierarchical? Will the conditions of childhood be improved? The Manitoba experience demonstrates that change of management does not by itself solve systemic problems. Aboriginal therapies of freedom which 'align political, social, and institutional goals with individual pleasures and desires, and with the happiness and fulfilment of the self'[126] are not those of Canadian social work, paternalistic state projects of rescue or the nepotistic controls exercised under nineteenth-century patriarchal constructs of tribalism which hide the conditions of children and women.

Aboriginal therapies of freedom define child and self by connection to the generative culture. That connection is one which the peoples themselves must establish. The scientific social work of the Progressive Era focussed on maintaining and improving the family unit and removal of the child, the solution of an earlier era, was to be a last resort. This reflects the shift from individual to family therapy. Aboriginal solutions reflect a further shift, from family therapy to community therapy.

Aboriginal approaches to healing — community-based, spiritual, holistic, intimate[127] — have begun to demonstrate that therapies which embody local ethos, knowledge and control, and which recognize the cultural damage of child abuse, are the most effective in preventing abuse and healing its effects.[128] A focus of healing is the excision of the Foucauldian colonized soul and the reassertion of culture and culturally-relevant processes. Projects embodying such therapies are small-scale and local. 'The system' has to a significant extent accommodated and informed these initiatives. Most approaches draw on mainstream child protection perspectives but interpret these within an Aboriginal community context. Many judges, legal counsel, police officers and child protection workers serving Aboriginal communities have in effect become part of the resistance.[129] These community-generated and community-oriented projects stand in contradistinction to the top-down disciplinized approaches reflected in the Canadian governance of childhood. They are not readily amenable to replication or external control.[130]

A new construct of childhood is emergent in these models of transformation, in the arguments of Aboriginal mothers and intertribal agencies in child custody disputes, in legislatve and judicial discourse. Cultural continuity is now the primary competing definition of the best interests of the child. This 'cultural construct' challenges practices which fail to account for the child's interests in culture and kinship and contrasts with earlier constructs which commodified children in a moral marketplace, as acultural and infinitely transformable.

Aboriginal culture, as the House of Commons Member explained in the 1879 *Indian Act* debates, is about everyday life.[131]

They were attached to it because it was inherited from their ancestors, because it had become part of their very nature and entered, in all its ramifications, into their everyday life. They would never cease to adhere to the Aboriginal system until they ceased to be Indians.

It is this 'everydayness' of culture and experience which is fundamentally threatened by the removal of children and loss of control over childhood. Canada is the homeland of unique First Nations cultures, diverse and barely visible on mainstream cultural landscapes. Whether they are in danger of disappearing altogether cannot be shown. Effacing culture means the end of a people. Childhood is both invention and repository of culture, central in strategies of assimilation, discourses of difference, tactics of resistance, and the politics of reclamation. The Manitoba experience reflects the centrality of childhood in postcolonial policy. While children have been pawns and even cannon-fodder in these larger struggles, it cannot be forgotten that they have important stakes in an outcome which protects equally their bodies and their cultures.

Notes

* My thanks to Wendy Whitecloud, Rob McQueen, Wesley Pue, Russell Smandych, Jack London and Michael D.A. Freeman for their comments and support, to Len Kaminski for sharing his archival findings with me, and to Sheryl Rosenberg for her excellent research assistance. Research was supported in part by a grant from the Legal Research Institute, University of Manitoba. This essay is for Maia Littlestar (Uchakos) McGillivray.

A note on terminology: The term 'Aboriginal' includes the Inuit of Northern Canada; non-status Indians, descendants of those original inhabitants of what is now Canada who never registered as 'Indians' or who 'achieved' citizenship and lost Indian status, *infra* note 32; Metis, descendants of French traders and their Aboriginal partners who constitute a distinct culture ('Metis' also designates a wider European-Aboriginal descent); and 'registered', 'status' or 'treaty' Indians, constitutionally under the aegis of the federal government. I have tried to use the term 'Indian' consistently to refer to those bearing that legal status. Issues and claims of all groups often overlap.

1. M. Foucault, *Discipline and Punish: The Birth of the Prison* (Vintage, 1979) 29-30.

2. N. Rose, *Governing the Soul: The Shaping of the Private Self* (Routledge, 1989) 257.

3. Foucault, *supra* note 1 at 239, 215-6.

4. *Cultural colonialism* is the term used in B. McKenzie and P. Hudson, 'Native Children, Child Welfare and the Colonization of Native People' in Levitt and Wharf, eds., *The Challenge of Child Welfare* (University of British Columbia Press, 1985) 125. The authors reject 'traditional' social work accounts of the vast over-representation of aboriginal children in care; the explanation lies in a cultural colonialism which justifies separation and assimilation of aboriginal children. *Cultural genocide* is the term used by Judge Kimelman, Chair of the Review Committee on Indian and Metis Adoptions and Placements, to describe the effects of child welfare agency practice on the lives of Aboriginal peoples. See The Committee, Final Report, *No Quiet Place*. Manitoba Community Services, 1985 ['The Kimelman Report'].

5. Foucault, *supra* note 1 at 293 *et seq.* This carceral progression is thoroughly documented. See Manitoba, *Public Inquiry into the Administration of Justice and Aboriginal People* (1991) Volume 1 *The Justice System and Aboriginal People* [The Aboriginal Justice Inquiry]. The carceral system detailed by Foucault is Mettray, a youth correctional facility whose disciplinary regime bore striking resemblance to educational institutions for Aboriginal children and to the young offender facilities in which they are overwhelmingly represented today: six in 10 youthful offenders in Manitoba correctional facilities are Aboriginal. See also Law Reform Commission of Canada Report No. 34, *Aboriginal Peoples and Criminal Justice* (Ottawa: 1991), observing that 'From the Aboriginal perspective, the criminal justice system is an alien one ... deeply insensitive to their traditions and values; many view it as unremittingly racist. Abuse of power and the distorted exercise of discretion are identified time and again ...'. The six-volume report of the Canadian Royal Commission on Aboriginal Peoples, which found similar conditions and systemic problems, was released in 1996.

6. For an overview of cultural studies ('the organization of cultural value in the advanced capitalist world'), see J. Frow, *Cultural Studies and Cultural Value* (Oxford, 1995) and his discussion of the work of Michel de Certeau. See also Austin Sarat and Thomas Kearns, eds., *Law in Everyday Life* (University of Michigan, 1993) and in particular the essays by Sarat and Kearns and by Patricia Williams.

7. *Ibid.* at 48 *et seq.*, citing Michel de Certeau, *The Practice of Everyday Life* (1984).

8. Among Canadian First Nations scholars who have written about the effects of child welfare and residential schooling on family and culture is Patricia Monture-Angus, *Thunder in My Soul: A Mohawk Woman Speaks* (Fernwood, 1995). Most commentary on the governance of Aboriginal childhood is by non-Aboriginal scholars, consultants, the judiciary and public inquiry. On the importance of an autohistorical approach, see R. Smandych and G. Lee 'Women, Colonization and Resistance: Elements of an Amerindian Autohistorical Approach to the Study of Law and Colonialism' (1995) 10 Native Studies Review 21.

9. See Frow, *supra* note 6 at 64 *et seq.*

10. See generally A. Fleras and J.L. Elliott, *The Nations Within: Aboriginal-State Relations in Canada, the United States, and New Zealand* (Oxford UP, 1992); J.R. Miller, *Skyscrapers Hide the Heavens: A History of Indian-White Relations in Canada* (University of Toronto Press, 1989); J.R. Miller, ed., *Sweet Promises: A Reader on Indian-White Relations in Canada* (University of Toronto Press, 1991); H. Buckley, *From Wooden Ploughs to Welfare: Why Indian Policy Failed in the Prairie Provinces* (McGill-Queens UP, 1992); E.J. Dosman, *Indians: The Urban Dilemma* (McLelland and Stewart, 1972).

11. During early contact, for example, Aboriginal peoples thought European languages uncouth, requiring Europeans to learn Aboriginal languages in order to trade, treat and proselytize. The mythology of the Red Man and imaginings of his 'original' culture were enthusiastically embraced in Europe. New World trade influenced European fashion, changed European diet (and the plants of both Old and New Worlds) and inspired the philosophies of, among others, Locke and Rousseau.

12. Fleras and Elliott, *supra* note 10 at 3.

13. Scott's poetry portrays Indians as savage, wild and prone to violence. Despite his romantic involvement with the 'noble savage', he was committed to an imperialist vision of assimilation throughout his career with Indian Affairs. B. Titley, *A Narrow Vision: Duncan Campbell Scott and the Administration of Indian Affairs*

in Canada (University of British Columbia Press, 1986). The 'Indians' of Scott's poetry in fact belong to 53 Nations. The dozens of distinct dialects fall into 11 language groups. The largest language group, Algonkian, which includes at least two Cree dialects, is spoken by about 100,000 people; the smallest, Kootenay, by about 30. Huron (Central Canada) and Beothuk (Newfoundland) languages are extinct, as are the Beothuk, shot for sport by transatlantic fishermen on shore leave.

14.   Canada's is the first Aboriginal population colonized by England to do so. Fleras and Elliott, *supra* note 10 at 3, 4. European contact brought typhoid, diphtheria, plague, measles, tuberculosis, scarlet fever, influenza and a variety of venereal diseases to which Aboriginal peoples had no immunity. The decimation of populations following first contact made conquest easy and fed the mythology of cultural desuetude.

15.   Infant mortality and suicide rates are twice that of the non-Aboriginal population; the violent death rate is three times that of the non-Aboriginal population. Indian Affairs, *Highlights of Aboriginal Conditions 1981-2001, September 1989.*

16.   Averaging about 550 members per band. The figures are provided by Indian Affairs, Manitoba Region, accurate to 30 December, 1993. Lands reserved for Indians constitute .2 per cent of Canadian land for two per cent of the population; four per cent of United States land is reserved for .5% of the population. Buckley, *supra* note 10. Reserve lands and entitlements remain under active negotiation. Population pressure on lands and services and claims of ancestral entitlements have resulted in a long series of tactical occupations of parks, roadways and Indian Affairs offices, including the 1990 Oka armed standoff in Quebec Mohawk territory.

17.   Miller, 1989, *supra* note 10 at x.

18.   The animosity with which Aboriginal peoples were regarded on the post-settlement Prairies was described in 1908 by an official in the Alberta Attorney-General's Office: 'Those with whom I have spoken are not, I would gather, very much in sympathy with the Indian, nor with the efforts to better his condition. They look upon him as a sort of pest which should be exterminated.'

19.   The focus on war as evidence of resistance in popular and academic literature obliterates the complexity of Aboriginal resistance to assimilation. First Nations relations with British-Canadian governments were characterized by 'legalization' rather than confrontation. Using law and legal process (represented in the west by the North-West [Royal Canadian] Mounted Police and earlier, and unofficially, the Hudson's Bay Company) rather than waging war was a clear political choice. On the law enforcement role of the Hudon's Bay Company, see generally the work of

Russell Smandych and Rick Linden. On colonial legal relations in Upper Canada during this period, see S.L. Harring, ' "The Liberal Treatment of Indians": Native People in Nineteenth Century Ontario Law' (1992) 56 Sask. L.R. 296-371. Harring concludes that the courts tempered the paternalism of the *Indian Act* by according full individual rights to Indians but failed to come to terms with 'the political rights of the Indian people as tribes, or with the broader concerns of Indian culture and social life'.

20. Miller, 1989, *supra* note 10 at 95. Miller characterized the shift as from non-directed to directed cultural change. 'On the whole, the adoption of European goods had not meant profound changes in the values, rituals, and beliefs of the Indians before the nineteenth century'.

21. Miller, 1989, *supra* note 10 at 21.

22. Miller, 1989, *supra* note 10 at 191.

23. *An Act Providing for the Organization of the Department of the Secretary of State of Canada, and for the Management of Indian and Ordinance Lands*, S.C. 1868, c.42, 1867, 30 & 31 Victoria, c.3 (U.K.). The *Indian Act* R.S.C. 1970, c. 1-6 governs Indian status. A Registrar determines who is an Indian. Originally entitled to be registered as 'status Indians' are the descendants of charter groups designated in the 1868 Act as 'all persons of Indian blood, reputed to belong to a particular tribe, band or body of Indians ... and their descendants'. Later amendments granted status to wives and to the illegitimate children of status Indian women, unless it was shown that the father was not an Indian. This no longer applies and 'Bill C-31 Indians' account for a large proportion of reserve returnees. Enfranchisement or deregistration was originally the means whereby Indians gained voting rights at the cost of status. By majority vote, a band may be enfranchised. A per capita share of band funds and annuities is paid on enfranchisement.

24. Debates of the House of Commons, 31 March, 1879.

25. 'The department's policy has, therefore, been gradually to do away with the hereditary and introduce an elective system, so making (as far as circumstances permit) these chiefs and councillors occupy the position in a band which a municipal council does in a white community ... . The provisions ... have not been taken advantage of as speedily or extensively as desired.' Deputy Indian Affairs Superintendent Smart, 1897 Indian Affairs Annual Report, quoted in Indian Affairs, *Indian Government under* Indian Act *Legislation 1868-1951* (1983). The 1982 Indian Affairs report *Strengthening Indian Band Government* observed that band councils are 'more like administrative arms of the Department of Indian Affairs than they are governments accountable to band members'. This strategy,

at least, was successful.

26. Miller, 1989, *supra* note 10 at 189.

27. In making the point that assimilationist was commanded but resisted, Miller quotes *Henry IV, Part 1*: '*Owen Glendower*: I can call spirits from the vasty deep. *Hotspur*: Why, so can I, or so can any man; But will they come when you do call for them?' J.S. Miller, 'Owen Glendower, Hotspur and Canadian Indian Policy' in Miller, 1991, *supra* note 10.

28. Miller, 1989, *supra* note 10 at 207.

29. Bowles *et al.*, *The Indian: Assimilation, Integration or Separation?* (Prentice-Hall, 1972) at 71-2.

30. 'The Dismantling of the Department of Indian Affairs and Northern Development, the Restoration of Jurisdictions to First Nations Peoples in Manitoba and Recognition of First Nations Governments in Manitoba: Framework Agreement', December 7 1994. Between 60 First Nations in Manitoba ... as represented by the Assembly of Manitoba Chiefs ... and Her Majesty the Queen ...'.

31. Manitoba Chiefs rejected the initial plan on grounds of lack of community consultation and consultation with women. There is disagreement within Aboriginal communities about the meaning and wisdom of 'devolution'. Breakaway Aboriginal women's groups have their origins in confrontations with the Assembly. Manitoba has taken a route to self-government rejected by all-chiefs' associations across Canada. Its conferral as a relatively easy fulfilment of a federal Liberal 'Red Book' election promise suggests a certain political expediency. In the history of imperialist and neocolonialist policy, however, there is no doubt of the historic significance of this act.

32. Tactics of resistance included the secret observance of forbidden traditional ceremonies (rain dance, potlatch); refusal to comply with minor regulatory schemes; revision of social, economic, political or cultural norms and redefinition of group boundaries. The post-1960s pan-Indian movement crossed lines of traditional enmity, language, status, culture (plains, coast, northern, south, agrarian, migratory, rural and urban) in recognition of the shared experience, spiritual roots and resistance to marginalization of these cultures. See J. Nagel and S. Matthew, 'Ethnic Reorganization: American Indian Social Economic, Political, and Cultural Strategies for Survival' (1993) 16 Ethnic and Racial Studies 203-235; and R. Jarvenpa, 'The Political Economy and Political Ethnicity of American Indian Adaptations and Identities' (1985) 8 Ethnic and Racial Studies 29-48. Manitoba Dene visiting the Navajo in the 1980s discovered a common language,

suggesting how little still is known of pre-colonial relations between Aboriginal peoples.

33. Miller, 1989, *supra* note 10 at 191.

34. The pass system was instituted to control movements during the summer of 1885 in the wake of the North-West Rebellion and was virtually unenforced by 1893 but the petty power it gave federal Indian Agents has long been a sore point. Control over band membership, reserve access and use of alcohol on-reserve are now governed by band by-law.

35. Delegitimation creates resistance. The custom of the potlatch, for example, died out as a cultural practice in Alaska, where it was not prohibited, long before it died out in Canada, where it was illegal.

36. Stone describes four views of the nature of the child which had emerged by the mid-nineteenth century, 'the adoption of each of which profoundly affects the way [the child] is treated': born in Original Sin and requiring total subordination of will to adult authority (the 'religious' view); born *tabula rasa*, entirely malleable (the 'environmental' view); born with character and potential predetermined but somewhat susceptible to improvement through education (the 'biological' view); born good and corrupted by society (the 'Utopian' view, crystallized in Rousseau's *Emile*). L. Stone, *The Family, Sex and Marriage in England 1500-1800* (Pelican, 1979) 254. These competing visions of childhood are all visible in nineteenth-century childhood discourse and protection policy.

37. Rose, *supra* note 2. See R. Dingwall *et al.*, 'Childhood as a Social Problem: a Survey of the History of Legal Regulation' (1984) 11 J. Law and Society; M.D.A. Freeman, *The Rights and Wrongs of Children* (Pinter, 1983). The difference for late nineteenth-century child welfare is one of degree.

38. J. Donzelot, *The Policing of Families* (Hutchinson, 1980). Donzelot's observation that the changing governance of childhood improved conditions for children and women is not born out to any great degree in this study of Aboriginal childhood.

39. Rose, *supra* note 2 at 186.

40. J. Ursel, *Private Lives, Public Policy: 100 Years of State Intervention in the Family* (Women's Press, 1992). The new interest in the regulation of childhood and the statutory augmentation of state powers is seen in England, France and the United States, with remarkable similarities in provisions and justifications.

41. Kelso was a key figure in the development of the Canadian foster care system, Children's Aid Societies, statutory powers of apprehension and the juvenile court. See J. Bullen, 'J.J. Kelso and the "New" Child-savers: The Genesis of the Children's Aid Movement in Ontario' (1990) 82 Ontario History 107. The need for new legislation was publicized in the New York 'Mary Ellen' case, in which a child houseworker was removed from abusive guardians under animal protection legislation, there being no other legal grounds for her apprehension.

42. D.E. Chunn, *From Punishment to Doing Good: Family Courts and Socialized Justice in Ontario 1890-1940* (University of Toronto Press, 1992); Ursel, note 36; L. Gordon, *Heroes of Their Own Lives: The Politics and History of Family Violence, Boston 1880-1960* (Penguin, 1988); C. Hooper, 'Child Sexual Abuse and the Regulation of Women: Variations on a Theme' in C. Smart, ed., *Regulating Womanhood: Historical Essays on Marriage, Motherhood and Sexuality* (Routledge, 1992).

43. Bullen, *supra* note 41 at 157-58. Children were placed on farms, given a bare education, subjected to 'many obvious injustices' and 'condemned to a working-class world that offered few opportunities for personal development and social mobility'.

44. Chunn, *supra* note 42 at 36.

45. See J. Korbin, *Child Abuse and Neglect: Cross-Cultural Perspectives* (University of California Press, 1981). The 'norm' is also heterosexually biased and omits family formations which do not include children.

46. M. Eichler, *Families in Canada Today: Recent Changes and their Policy Consequences* (Gage, 1983). Eichler calls this the 'monolithic bias'. Closely linked is the 'conservative bias' which includes 'a tendency to either ignore children altogether, or to see them merely as objects to be acted upon, rather than as active participants in family life'.

47. M. Valverde, *The Age of Light, Soap and Water: Moral Reform in English Canada, 1885-1925* (McClelland & Stewart, 1991). Valverde establishes linkages between hygiene (cleanliness, moral reform, social and racial purity); Canadian nativism (anglo-protestant patriotism which sought to identify a 'native' Canadian identity in the British Empire); and the 'unabashed' interventionism of social work. 'Nativism' was most strident on the Prairies, 'fantastical' in view of the fact that Western Canada was neither administratively nor in its general population 'white', until late in the nineteenth century (107-8).

48. *Ibid.* at 54, citing Canadian Methodist minister Samuel Dwight Chown, one of the first of the proto-professionals to attempt the reconciliation of social science and religious values.

49. An estimated 11 per cent of the Canadian population may be their descendants. The last group left England in 1967. See P. Bean and J. Melville, *Lost Children of the Empire: The Untold Story of Britain's Child Migrants* (Unwin Hyman, 1990). The movement was both 'welfarist' and 'instrumentalist' according to J. Eekalaar, '"The Chief Glory": The Export of Children from the U.K.' (1994) 4 J. Law and Society 487. For a Canadian perspective, see K. Bagnell, *The Little Immigrants* (Macmillan, 1980).

50. 'The Departure of the Innocents' in Bean and Melville, *ibid.* at 59.

51. Untrue, given the children's farm or domestic placement and lack of skills, but effective in the enactment of Canadian child labour laws which tended to benefit adults rather than children.

52. For depictions of Manitoba 'Barnardo boys' in fiction, see R.J.C. Stead, *The Bail Jumper* (Briggs, 1914) and E.A.W. Gill, *Love in Manitoba* (Musson, 1911). In both novels, the 'Barnardo boys' are ill-treated, of problematic morals and all but nameless. Gill, a cleric with St. John's Cathedral Winnipeg on leave from England, also wrote *A Manitoba Chore Boy: Letters from an Emigrant* (London Religious Tract Society, 1908), a glowing account of a year on a Manitoba farm aimed at juvenile readers and overt propaganda for child migration.

53. The economic value of child labour was vitiated by child labour laws and by political and economic change. Exploitation of the 'Home' children was apparent by the turn of the century and lack of follow-up by British child export agencies was strongly criticized by Canadian observers. Imperialism shaped child welfare until the 'Great War' changed Canada's relations with England and ended colonialist aspirations. The Depression coincided with 'The Dirty Thirties' of Prairie drought and deep poverty.

54. *Home of the Friendless Report of the Investigating Committee, 1926* (Manitoba Sessional Paper No. 47). The Home's purpose, according to its Articles of incorporation, was 'sheltering, relieving, assisting, reclaiming or otherwise dealing with the fallen, helpless, destitute and afflicted, or other person, whether male or female, needing help, protection or assistance including children'. Its religious agenda was protected by the provision that that 'No person shall hold the office of directress or manager unless she shall be an Evangelical Protestant'. The Home could contract for an 'absolute and uninterrupted custody of and control' of children 'which shall be upheld by all courts'. Control of girls would cease at 18,

of boys at 16. As the 1926 Report noted, the provisions were 'in obvious conflict with both the spirit and the letter of general provisions of The Child Welfare Act' of 1922; s.188 of that Act exempted the Home from its general provisions, permitting only a right of inspection. This was a 'bare right' according to its Directress. The Articles were based on those of the Winnipeg Children's Home, incorporated in 1887. S. 188 was amended effective 23 April, 1926, in consultation with Crouch, to authorize the public inquiry. The evidence points strongly to a spy on the Fletcher committee, alerting Crouch to 'surprise' Home inspections. I am grateful to Dr. Len Kaminski, University of Manitoba, for sharing this important archival research with me and for his helpful discussions on the implications and aftermath of the Report.

55.   L.R. Bull, 'Indian Residential Schooling: the Native Perspective' (1991) 18 (Supplement) Canadian Journal of Native Education 3 at 14-15. On residential schools, see also note 10 generally; J.R. Miller, 'Owen Glendower, Hotspur, and Canadian Indian Policy' in Miller, 1991, note 10; Aboriginal Justice Inquiry, note 9; N.R. Ing, 'The Effects of Residential Schools on Native Child-Rearing Practices' (1991) 18 (Supplement) Canadian Journal of Native Education 65; Cariboo Tribal Council and University of Guelph, 'Faith Misplaced: Lasting Effects of Abuse in a First Nations Community' (1991) 18 Canadian Journal of Native Education 161; J. Gresko, 'White "Rites" and Indian "Rites": Indian Education and National Responses in the West, 1870-1910' in D.C. Jones *et al.*, *Shaping the Schools of the Canadian West* (Detsilig, 1979) at 84.

56.   Reverend John West, First Priest of the Church of England in the Red River Settlement in the Years 1820 to 1823, *The British North West American Indians with Free Thoughts on the Red River Settlement* (typescript copy of the original diary manuscript, St. John College Library, University of Manitoba). 'In my appointment as Chaplain to the [Hudson's Bay] Company, my instructions were to reside at the Red River Settlement; and under the encouragement and support of the Church Missionary Society, I was to seek the Instruction and to ameliorate the condition of the native Indians.' West embarked 27 May, 1820 at Graves End on the company ship Eddystone. His diary records many instances of the care taken by Indian parents of their children 'of whom they were passionately fond' (yet 'they brutally lend their daughters of tender age, for a few beads, or a little tobacco'). He returned 10 September, 1823 with a disappointing letter from Governor Simpson which elicited the observation that 'the resolves of Council in Hudson's Bay relative to the amelioration of the condition of the Indians, and promoting morality and religion in the country, were like the acts of the west Indian legislatures passed professedly with a view to the promoting of religion among the slaves — *worse than nullities*.' Costs of his 'Establishment' must fall to Mission charity. I am grateful to Russell Smandych for bringing the manuscript to my attention.

57.   The mother, a widow who refused to entrust her daughters to West, secretly took her sons away amid rumours that West would 'cut off the ears of one of them for leaving the school without leave'. West makes mention of the jealousy of 'the Catholics' of his 'Native Indian School Establishment', with the inference that this was the source of the rumours: 'The attempt is made to prejudice the minds of the Indians against giving their children, insinuating that I wish to collect them, with the intention of taking them to England'. The mother's decampment was occasioned by preparations of West's ally Chief Pigewis [Peguis] to make war on her people, the Sioux. West's hopes of addressing Peguis' tribe on educating their children were frustrated: 'Oh! what faith, and patience, and perseverance are necessary lest the mind should grow weary in the arduous work of seeking to evangelize the Heathen' (*ibid.*, 30 March, 1823).

58.   Based on Armitage, *supra* note 10 at 107 *et seq.*

59.   Miller 1989, *supra* note 10 at 196.

60.   Arnold referred to the 'effacement' of the Welsh language, a unique branch of Gaelic. When English state education was enforced in Wales in 1880, Welsh was outlawed from the schools and children were punished for speaking it, a point of pride for many. The anglicization project backfired, leading to the late-nineteenth century renaissance of Welsh literature and culture. English schooling for Wales was fuelled by the Commissioners' horror at the lack of religious knowledge of children interviewed, who were probably pulling their collective leg. J. Morris, *The Matter of Wales* (Oxford, 1984) 239. The difference for Aboriginal children is most notably the removal from family and village systems of support and the imposition of a much more alien system. On the 'invention' or 'rediscovery' of Welsh culture (with parallels yet to be explored for Aboriginal cultural rediscovery), see P. Morgan, 'From a Death to a View: The Hunt for the Welsh Past in the Romantic Period' in E. Hobsbawm and T. Ranger, *The Invention of Tradition* (Cambridge, 1983).

61.   These included beating, head-shaving, isolation and ridicule. Restrictions were eventually relaxed. Children in later decades learned rudiments of their own languages from other students and were exposed to other Aboriginal cultures, an experience which later played a strong role in the pan-Indian movement (*supra* note 32) and the strategies of self-government.

62.   Miller 1989, *supra* note 10 at 196.

63.   Miller, 'Owen Glendower', *supra* note 27 at 332.

64.   Bull, *supra* note 55.

65. Miller, 1989, *supra* note 10 at 213.

66. Conversation of the author with a Cree student, April 1994.

67. A. McGillivray, '*R.* v. *K.(M.)*: Legitimating Brutality' (1993) 16 Criminal Reports (4th) 125; Stone, *supra* note 36.

68. Conversation of the author with a former Alberta residential school student, October 1993, who planned to form a victim collective for male survivors of residential school discipline. He is searching for the nun, now in her 80s, who acted as discipline officer, in order to sue the Catholic Church for damages. Officials have confirmed that she is still alive, but will not say where she now lives.

69. Kimelman Report, *supra* note 4 at 201.

70. Aboriginal Justice Inquiry, *supra* note 5 at 514-515. See Ing, *supra* note 55 for accounts by former pupils. But see Cariboo Tribal Council, *supra* note 55 at 180, suggesting that 'The type of school attended by the respondents' mothers did not seem to affect family life, while respondents whose fathers had attended residential school had somewhat different experiences from those whose fathers had attended non-residential school.' While perhaps the majority of Indian children did not attend residential school, studies and personal accounts suggest far-reaching effect on the quality of family life and community cohesion where even one family member, especially a father, did so. The picture is complex. Christian corporal punishment values even without the residential school experience have suggested to elders that the birch switch is somehow part of traditional Aboriginal values, while domestic violence and child sexual abuse in 'closed' stressed communities can spread rapidly. 'Culture' may deny as well as protect.

71. Miller 1989, *supra* note 10 at 199. Miller also cites state parsimony as a cause of the failure of the system.

72. On Saskatchewan Indian child welfare control and the adoption crisis, below and see A. McGillivray, 'Transracial Adoption and the Status Indian Child' (1986) 5 Canadian Journal of Family Law 437-67. Seventy-five per cent of Canadian bands have full control of education.

73. On a more hidden level are goals of consolidation of political power through control of the federal dollars attached to each on-reserve body.

74. Child abuse is 'a political concept designed to attract attention to a phenomenon which is considered undesirable or deviant'. Definition 'varies over time, across cultures, and between different social and cultural groups'. R. Gelles, 'A Profile of Violence Toward Children in the United States' in Gerbner et al., eds., *Child Abuse: An Agenda for Action* (Oxford, 1980) at 83. See A. McGillivray, 'The Reconstruction of Child Abuse: Western Definitions and Non-Western Experience' in Freeman and Veerman, eds., *The Ideologies of Children's Rights* (Martinus Nijhoff, 1992) and 'The Criminalization of Child Abuse' (LL.M. Thesis, University of Toronto, 1988).

75. Aboriginal Justice Inquiry, *supra* note 9, Ch. 14. For an example of the history of service provision in a culturally mixed community, see M.H. Richards, 'Cumberland House: Two Hundred Years of History' (1974) 27 Saskatchewan History 108. The island community includes status and non-status Indians descended from the 'Home Indians' (Swampy Cree who traded at the Fort), Metis refugees from the Red River Rebellion and non-Aboriginal people. Health needs were attended to, in various measure, by Hudson's Bay Company factors, missions and provincial nurses stationed at Cumberland House.

76. Canadian Welfare Council and Canadian Association of Social Workers, *Joint Submission to the Special Joint Committee of the Senate and the House of Commons Appointed to Examine and Consider the Indian Act* (Ottawa: The Council, 1947) 3. Custom adoption is legally recognized for Inuit children and Canada's ratification of the United Nations *Convention on the Rights of the Child* demurred from the requirement of state approval, for that reason. Custom adoption is not recognized for other Aboriginal children even where tradition is equally strong. Cree custom in some places encourages the giving of a first-born child to the maternal grandmother to raise and mothers in may Aboriginal cultures give infants to infertile sisters. A Cree student born in Vancouver was raised by his grandmother at Nelson House, Manitoba, under this custom. Conversation with the author, September 1994.

77. On jurisdiction, see E.F. Carasco, 'Canadian Native Children: Have Child Welfare Laws Broken the Circle?' (1986) 5 Canadian Journal of Family Law 111; S. Bull, 'The Special Case of The Native Child' (1989) 47 Advocate 523; and C. Davies, 'Native Children and the Child Welfare System in Canada' (1992) 30 Alberta Law Review 1200. On federal attempts to shift Indian responsibilities to the provinces as a cost-cutting measure, see Fleras and Elliot, note 10 at 50. For a review of constitutional and statutory considerations in restructuring Indian child welfare services, see D.R. James, 'Legal Structures for Organizing Indian Child Welfare Resources' [1987] 2 C.N.L.R. 1, proposing use of band by-law powers for reserve child welfare control.

78. H.B. Hawthorn, ed., *A Survey of the Contemporary Indians of Canada: A Report on Economic, Political, Educational Needs and Policies* (Ottawa: Canada Department of Indian and Northern Development, 1966) at 327. See also H.P Hepworth, *Foster Care in Canada* (Canadian Council on Social Development, 1980); P. Johnston, *Native Children and the Child Welfare System* (Lorimer, 1983); McKenzie and Hudson, *supra* note 4.

79. Saskatchewan child care workers visiting reserves during this era hid their cars in the bushes to avoid having their tires slashed and windshields broken, and literally ran in, grabbed the child and ran out to avoid personal attacks. McGillivray, *supra* note 72.

80. Social worker cited in McGillivray, *ibid*. Children living with extended family members were seen as abandoned; impoverished living standards and rashes caused by dirty water were interpreted as neglect; language and communication problems complicated evaluation. Ethnocentrism, middle-class standards and a bias favouring the nuclear family were evident in apprehension decisions, as were visibly and seriously damaged and endangered children.

81. Indian Affairs, *supra* note 15.

82. McGillivray, *supra* note 72 at 448-49.

83. Transracial adoption was a rarity in North America until the late 1960s. A Canadian study conducted in the late 1950s reported 115 such adoptions in a 12-year period; 92 per cent of those children were part 'white'. The North American transracial adoption movement began with the Montreal Open Door Society which was founded in 1959 to find homes for Montreal Black children. In collaboration with the Montreal Child Services Centre, the Society had by 1963 placed 201 children of mixed and minority (mostly Black) backgrounds; 95 per cent of these children were transracially adopted. McGillivray, *ibid*.

84. Hepworth, *supra* note 78 at 120.

85. *Cf.* Saskatchewan Social Services which ran aggressive ad campaigns for transracial adoption from 1966 to the early 1980s. 'AIM-Adopt Indian and Metis' was replaced in 1972 with 'REACH-Resources for Adopting Children' which included Aboriginal children in the same 'hard-to-adopt' category as disabled and older children and sibling groups, with the observation that 'race' is 'a factor which severely limits placement opportunities'.   By 1975, the ratio of Saskatchewan Indian children adopted by non-status parents to those adopted by status Indian parents was 19:1. The Canadian average was 5:1. Between 1962 and 1971, 167 status children were adopted by non-status parents and 26 by status

parents. Between 1972 and 1981, 722 status children were adopted by non-status parents and 120 by status parents, a ratio of 6:1. (Adapted from Social Services Saskatchewan, Planning and Evaluation, *Services to Children Under the Family Services Act, 1975* and Indian and Northern Affairs Canada, *Indian Social Welfare, Social Security, National Programs*, v. 7, 1982. The Canadian average is from Hepworth, *ibid.*, 117.) Collaboration between Saskatchewan Social Services and Federation of Saskatchewan Indian Nations to recruit status Indian adoptive parents began in March 1984. See McGillivray, *supra* note 72.

86.   Kimelman Report, *supra* note 4; Aboriginal Justice Inquiry, *supra* note 5 at 520.

87.   Many Aboriginal children placed out-of-province were older and more difficult to place, but the attractions of sunny southern climes with free trips for workers with each placement also played a role at this stage of Manitoba child welfare. Sources confidential by request. Repatriation, the movement to return adoptees to their home reserves, has not been well documented. In one well-known case, a 14-year old girl adopted by an Alberta couple was returned to her Manitoba home reserve where she was shunned and ridiculed. She was finally returned to Alberta after being raped by three reserve youth. See The Kimelman Report, *supra* note 7, on the transracial adoption experience; see also *infra* note 123.

88.   On Aboriginal child welfare in other provinces, see W. Warry, 'Ontario's First Peoples' in Johnson and Barnhorst, eds., *Children, Families and Public Policy in the 90s* (Thompson, 1991); J.A. MacDonald, 'The Child Welfare Programme of the Spallumcheen Band in British Columbia' in Levitt and Wharf, *The Challenge of Child Welfare, supra* note 4; A. Armitage, 'Family and Child Welfare in First Nation Communities' in B. Wharf, ed., *Rethinking Child Welfare in Canada* (McClelland & Stewart, 1993) profiling the innovative Winnipeg Ma Mawi Wichi Itata Centre; M. Sinclair et al., 'Aboriginal Child Welfare In Canada' in Bala *et al.*, eds., *Canadian Child Welfare Law: Children, Families and the State* (Thompson, 1991) at 171.

89.   *The Child and Family Services Act* R.S.M. 1985, c. C-80 s. 6(1): 'Any 3 or more persons over the age of 18 years, who desire to associate themselves together for the purpose of providing child and family services, may make an application to the minister for incorporation as an agency in a prescribed form'. The provision is a holdover from the Humane Society era of nineteenth-century child welfare and is now without counterpart in Canadian child protection legislation.

90.   The Agreement was extended to December 1986 by joint accord 26 November, 1985. An additional Tripartite Master Agreement was entered into by Canada, Manitoba and Manitoba Keewatinowi Okemakanac, tribal council for northern reserves, in 1983, to establish Awasis Child and Family Services. The agreements

are continued yearly on an *ad hoc* basis while attention is focussed on constitutional negotiations which may render them redundant.   See text accompanying note 30, *supra*.

91.   Six intertribal agencies serve Manitoba reserves. Awasis serves 26 bands covering the entire northern half of the province (1984, head office in Thompson); Dakota Ojibway, which began operation as a non-mandated agency in 1981 under a special funding agreement with Indian Affairs, serves eight bands in the southwest (Brandon); West Region serves eight bands in the west-central area (1985, Dauphin); Anishinaabe serves five bands in the centre of the province (1986, Ashern); Intertribal serves four bands (1980, Peguis Reserve, also Head Office of the Assembly of Manitoba Chiefs); and Southeast serves eight bands (1983, Winnipeg). Several bands are not associated with an intertribal agency; services are provided by non-mandated agencies and mainstream agencies are called in when a child is to be apprehended. Ma Mawi Wi Chi Itata, a Winnipeg agency which by choice is not mandated, employs 67 social workers, all Aboriginal (most have university degrees) and provides a range of family support programs.

92.   Ss. 6(14) of the *Child and Family Services Act, supra* note 89, allows bands and tribal councils, together with the government of Canada, to apply for agency incorporation. Although individual bands can apply for incorporation, the province maintains its policy of dealing only with intertribal councils.

93.   Kimelman Report, *supra* note 4 at 276.

94.   P. Hudson and S. Taylor-Henley, *Agreement and Disagreement: An Evaluation of the Canada-Manitoba Northern Indian Child Welfare Agreement*, 1987. The authors' interviews with members of Keewatinowi Okemakinac Tribal Council disclosed widespread belief that the intertribal agencies were a step toward self-government. Other warning signs of systemic problems are seen in J. Isitt and B. Roberts, *An Assessment of Services Delivered under the Canada-Manitoba-Indian Child Welfare Agreement* (Coopers & Lybrand, 1987) for the First Nations Confederacy/ Southeast Resource Development Council. Political interference, overburden and worker incompetence are apparent in the study but the authors minimize the implications for child protection.

95.   Giesbrecht, P.C.J. *The Fatalities Inquiries Act Report: An Inquest Respecting the Death of Lester Norman Desjarlais*. Brandon, Manitoba, 31 August, 1992.

96.   Kimelman Report, *supra* note 4 at 86-87.

97. Both reports recommended appointment of a Child Advocate independent of the Ministry of Family Services, reporting directly to the legislature. In 1993 the office of 'Child Advocate', a ministry staff member reporting directly to the Minister, was established under the *Child and Family Services Act*.

98. Banishment — the revocation of reserve residence privileges by band council resolution pursuant to s. 81 of the *Indian Act* — is called 'BCRing'. Teachers and workers have been BCRed, fired, threatened and attacked for reporting child abuse.

99. 'A licence to abuse, sex attacks ignored'; 'Point fingers and get fired'. *The Winnipeg Sun*, 22 December, 1991.

100. The child was finally examined at age 11 by Winnipeg doctors specializing in child sexual abuse symptomology. She remains at home, reportedly well. Sources confidential by request.

101. 'The bogeyman' was convicted of the sexual assault and sodomy of three children. A fourth conviction was overturned by the Manitoba Court of Appeal on grounds that the victim's diagnosis of multiple personality disorder, brought on by abuse, had not been sufficiently proven; without this understanding of his testimony, guilt was not established beyond reasonable doubt. The appeal court refused to order a new trial in view of the trauma he had suffered. The victim was angered by the decision not to retry his abuser and by lack of understanding of his condition by the Court of Appeal. Source confidential by request.

102. 'Incest', widespread child sexual assault, is not unique to this reserve. The 1987 report, *A New Justice for Indian Children* by S. Longstaffe, Winnipeg Children's Hospital Child Protection Centre, described multigenerational sexual abuse in small reserve communities and recommended intervention and protection options for protection and healing. No action was taken. The incidence of sexual abuse in geopolitically isolate communities (including ghettoized urban populations) is so high that one senior worker asked me whether this might be a part of 'original Indian culture'. It is not, nor has any culture been known to thrive under regimes of widespread sexual use of children and in particular of female children. Tribal cultures have established complex rules for ensuring marriage does not take place within a much broader range than provided in Canadian *Criminal Code* incest provisions. Dakota rules, for example, prohibit marriage within all degrees of consanguinity.

103. Reviews include a 1984 evaluation of Dakota-Ojibway CFS; the 1985 Kimelman Report; a 1986 review of Manitoba West Region and Southeast CFS; a 1987 review of Awasis CFS; the 1991 Aboriginal Justice Inquiry; the 1992 Giesbrecht Report and the 1993 Report of the First Nations Child and Family Task Force.

Issues and recommendations, whether positively put forward or couched within the text, are remarkably consistent: abuse is a problem, political interference is a problem, control should reside in the bands. The *New Justice* report (submitted to Manitoba Grand Chief Phil Fontaine, the Manitoba Family Services Minister and the Manitoba Regional Director of Indian Affairs, in that order) reflects deadlock between Task Force members, each chosen for representation of a political constituency. It glosses over the extent and severity of child abuse, makes only brief mention of political interference and borrows language from the Giesbrecht Report (children are pawns; put children first) while ignoring the recommendations for more accountability and less political interference. The Report recommended a five-year decentralization plan leading to local reserve control.

104. *Winnipeg Free Press*, 30 September, 1993.

105. 'Chief charged', *Winnipeg Free Press*, 16 February, 1996. This was a 'nationalistic' statement about agency jurisdiction, rather than a personal family matter. Source confidential by request.

106. *Cf.* J.A. MacDonald, 'Child Welfare and the Native Indian Peoples of Canada' (1985) 5 Windsor Yearbook of Access to Justice 285. MacDonald enthusiastically endorses the Manitoba intertribal model.

107. The ratio reported in Johnston, *supra* note 72. Animus Research Consultants, *Aboriginal Justice Inquiry Report on Manitoba Child and Family Services*, AJI Research Paper Number 3, March 1991. Statistics were available for Indian children in care of Aboriginal agencies (31 per cent) but mainstream agencies keep no data identifying Aboriginal children; it is estimated that 30 per cent of children in care of mainstream agencies are Aboriginal. Given the concerns about record-keeping expressed by Johnston, Kimelman (*supra* note 4) and Giesbrecht, it is surprising that this information is not collected.

108. Animus, *ibid.* at 10, using Manitoba Community Services statistics for 1986 and 1989.

109. Interview, Wayne Helgeson, Executive Director, Ma Mawi Wi Chi Itata Centre, Winnipeg, June 1993.

110. Winnipeg murder trials in 1995 included a foster mother convicted of smothering a 2-year-old child with fetal alcohol syndrome; and a foster mother acquitted in the death of an abused disordered 5-year-old (ingestion of antihistamines was the explanation for the brain swelling which killed him but how the child got the medication, and the cause of his severe bruising, were not explained). Three sexually abused preadolescent girls resident in a Winnipeg 'special needs' foster

home were raped by their foster father; he took them to hospital when they began having nightmares and waited at the open examining room door. His bail was paid by the Social Services check for that month. Source confidential by request. The victims in these cases are all Aboriginal, as are two of the three foster homes.

111. Kaye Dunlop, legal counsel to Awasis Child and Family Services. Conversation with the author, December 1995.

112. Interviews, Margo Buck, staff psychologist, Winnipeg Children's Hospital Child Protection Centre and Heather Leonoff, legal counsel, Winnipeg Child and Family Services, August 1993.

113. McKenzie and Hudson, *supra* note 4.

114. *Re Birth Registration No. 67-09-022272* [1974] 1 W.W.R. 19 at 21, 13 R.F.L. 244 at 247 (B.C. S.C.); [1974] 3 W.W.R. 363, (1974) 4 R.F.L. 396, (1974) 44 D.L.R.(3d) 218 (S.C.C.), (sub. nom. *Re Adoption Act*) (sub. nom. *Re Birth Registration No. 67-09-022272* [1976] 1 W W.R. 699, (1975) 60 D.L.R. (3d) 148, 21 R.F.L. 267, [1976] 2 S.C.R. 751, 6 N.R. 491 (S.C.C.).

115. The petitioners argued on appeal that the Act discriminated on the basis of race, *contra* ss. 1(b) of the Canadian *Bill of Rights*, in that adoptive parents of status Indian children are deprived of the 'right' to have the child's ancestry and family ties obliterated by the adoption and the child is similarly deprived of that 'right'. The argument was properly rejected.

116. [1975] 5 W.W.R. 45, 56 D.L.R.(3d) 567, 21 R.F.L. 222 (Man. C.A.), [1974] 5 W.W.R. 449, 46 D.L.R.(3d) 633 (Man. Q.B.). The five Nelson children were apprehended in 1970 and, with parental consent, became permanent wards of the state. The two youngest children were placed in adoptive homes. In 1974 the parents applied for custody of the other three, still in foster care and by then aged 10, 12 and 13.

117. *A.N.R. and S.C.R* v. *L.J. W.* (1984) 37 R.F.L. (2d) 181 (Man. Cty. Ct.), *Re. W.; W.* v. *R. and R.; R. and R.* v. *W. (sub nom. A.N.R. and S.C.R.* v. *L.J.W)* (1983), 32 R.F.L. (2d) 153, [1983] 2 C.N.L.R. 157, 19 Man. R. (2d) 186 (Man. C.A.), reversed 36 R.F.L. (2d) 1 (S.C.C.). See McGillivray, *supra* note 72, basing this discussion.

118. When Dakota-Ojibway received its mandate under tripartite agreement, this case was viewed by the agency as a test of its legal power to place children. Sources confidential by request.

119. *A.N.R.* v. *L.J.W.* [1984] I W.W.R. 1, 36 R.F.L. (2d) 1, (sub. nom. *L.J.W* v. *A.N.R.*) I D.L.R. (4th) 193, (sub. nom. *Woods* v. *Racine*) 48 N.R. 362, 24 Man. R. (2d) 314 (S.C.C.).

120. *Beyond the Best Interests of the Child*, 2d ed. (Macmillan, 1979).

121. *Director of Child Welfare* v. *B.B.* (1988), 14 R.F.L.(3d) 113 (Man. C.A.); *B.B.* v. *Director of Child and Family Services* (1989), 62 Man. R.(2d) 233, [1989] W.D.F.L. 967 (S.C.C).

122. A case in which culture and nurture coincided outside the context of (parental) child abuse involved a custody dispute between a Manitoba Island Lake Aboriginal woman and her Scottish ex-husband. An affidavit dated 7 February, 1994 was submitted by an Anglo-Canadian academic authority on child abuse and law, to the Scotland court. The affidavit dwelt on 'skin tents' and other 'horrors' of reserve life, and concluded that 'I have little doubt that the prospects for life, health and happiness of a young child in the south-west of Scotland are infinitely preferable to those of a young child reared on an Indian reservation [sic] in Manitoba'. The court awarded the mother custody anyway. A letter to the academic from the Island Lake Tribal Council, 23 February, 1994, pointed out that 'none of your arguments took into consideration the value of culture and the ongoing struggle of our communities to fight the kind of bias evidenced in your document'. The letter concluded that 'little separates the discriminatory conclusions of your "evidence" from the pious and righteous beliefs held by those who established residential schools and other institutions designed to achieve cultural genocide'. There are no 'skin tents' in evidence in Manitoba, although canvas ones do appear at pow-wows and summer camps. While averages tell a harsh tale, a great many Aboriginal families and reserves conduct their lives and care for their children in an exemplary fashion.

123. 'Teens wanted in rural house jacking', *Winnipeg Free Press*, 24 October, 1992. The child was severely abused and neglected by her adoptive parents, despite their affirmations to the courts. Sources confidential by request. Two Manitoba adoptees murdered their adoptive parents following years of abuse. Cameron Kerley, adopted at the age of 11 by a United States man who beat and raped him, returned at the age of 19 in a state of extreme intoxication and beat him to death with a baseball bat. He was sentenced to 15 years to life but was permitted to serve his sentence in Manitoba. Ronald Kishlicky, adopted as a baby by a United States couple and sexually abused by his stepfather, is serving a 15-year manslaughter sentence in Virginia for killing his adoptive mother with a butcher knife when he was 16. His Manitoba family wants to bring him back to Canada. 'That killer is my son', *Winnipeg Free Press*, 3 December, 1995. Carla Williams, adopted by a Netherlands couple at age 5, bore two children to her abusive adoptive father. Her

return to her home reserve was arranged by Anishinaabe agency. 'Compensation sought for disastrous adoption', *Winnipeg Free Press* 9 November, 1989. Her lawsuit did not go forward due to her ill health.

124. Lack of onus on either state or adoptive parent to inform the child of Indian status poses a serious constitutional problem. See McGillivray, *supra* note 72. The Indian Affairs booklet *Adoption and the Indian Child* (1993) states at 12, 'Our concern is with the Indian child, registered as a status Indian who has rights and is eligible for benefits *which may not be obtained unless adoptive parents are aware of them*'; and at 15, 'When an adopted Indian child reaches the age of 18, the Registrar will provide him or her with a registry number, and the name of the Indian band to which he or she may be registered. This is done only upon request.' This is the only mention of the need to protect Indian status after adoption. Agencies now stress with prospective adopters the importance of Aboriginal culture and Winnipeg provides support groups, pow-wows and other activities designed to maintain cultural links for adopted children. There is also a support group for adoptive parents of Aboriginal children with fetal alcohol syndrome; these children form a large percentage of children presently available for adoption. Participation is by choice of adoptive parents.

125. M. Kline, 'Child Welfare Law, "Best Interests of the Child" Ideology, and First Nations' (1992) 30 Osgoode Hall L.J. 375 at 396. See also M. Kline, 'The "Colour" of Law: Ideological Representations of First Nations in Legal Discourse' (1994), 3 Social and Legal Studies 451.

126. Rose, *supra* note 2. Tutorial regimes of the 'psy' disciplines are not a strong part of Aboriginal parenting, nor is it expected that they would be. The counsel of elders, roles of the grandmother and older sister, legends and traditions, circle and communitarian approaches, developments in 'sister' indigenous cultures, are rich sources of parenting 'advice' which may shape the 'new' therapies of freedom.

127. Dakota-Ojibway Child and Family Services, focus of the Giesbrecht Inquiry, plans a treatment centre to serve the 12,000 residents of its eight reserves for those recovering from addiction, community suicides, sexual and physical abuse and 'residential school syndrome': 'In order to heal our people, we must go beyond counselling'. A holistic combination of traditional and non-traditional therapies, education and skills training is planned. Clergy and Indian Affairs officials have agreed to participate in the residential schools counselling program. 'Healing First Nations' wounds', *Winnipeg Free Press* 15 April, 1994. At the time of publication of this essay, there has been no further development of the plan.

128.   A small group on Hollow Water Reserve succeeded after many years in persuading the community to take joint action against child sexual abuse. The 'holistic' approach developed on Hollow Water combines traditional spirituality with agency expertise to treat offender, victim and family while ensuring independent protection for the victim. The approach is premised on the fact that victims and abusers will continue to live in the same intertwined communities. If the common law system is for a community of strangers, then Aboriginal law must be the opposite, with unaccountable ramifications. In *R.* v. *S.(H.M.)* [1989] M.J. No. 273, the accused pleaded guilty to the sexual abuse of his foster child; the court set terms of probation to fit the decision of the Hollow Water healing circle. Aboriginal communities 'have led the way in the treatment of offenders,' according to Margo Buck, staff psychologist, Winnipeg Children's Hospital Child Protection Centre. 'The models that they have come up with are far better than models white agencies produce. Hollow Water is light years away from our understanding.'

129.   The Hollow Water project, *ibid.*, is led by agency-trained reserve residents. The lead case for 'circle sentencing' is *R.* v. *Moses* (1994) 11 C.R.(4th) 357, [1992] C.N.L.R. 116 (Yukon Terr. Ct.), concluding that 'circle [community-based] sentencing' avoids 'the futility, destruction, and injustice left behind in the wake of circuit courts' by returning offender responsibility and rehabilitation to the community. A study of alternate sentencing in Manitoba and Saskatchewan reserve communities highlights judicial activism and support by prosecution, police, probation and child protection agency personnel; community empowerment is the most frequently-stated outcome. See R.G. Green, *Aboriginal Sentencing and Mediation Initiatives: The Sentencing Circle and Other Community Participation Models in Six Aboriginal Communities* (LL.M. Thesis, University of Manitoba, 1995). But appeal courts have overturned community-guided sentences, making renegades of judges who approve sentences departing from provincial sentencing tariffs. The Canadian Criminal Code s. 170 was amended in 1996 to stress the desirability of alternative measures in sentencing offenders, with particular attention to the needs of Aboriginal offenders; a Manitoba judge has raised 'constitutional' problems with the provision. *Winnipeg Free Press*, 5 October, 1996.

130.   The development of community-oriented holistic therapies illustrates a central characteristic of First Nations agencies: a sense of obligation to strengthen families and communities', a matter of agency discretion under the *Child and Family Services Act*. Flexibility in funding is necessary to the development of programs, in view of the high ratio of 'special needs' children (sibling groups, children with fetal alcohol syndrome or effect, children with behaviour problems due to sexual abuse) and the lack of treatment facilities on reserve. West Region, an agency with low staff turnover and strong support from its Chiefs, was 'block-funded' on a trial basis by Indian Affairs, with some success; see B. McKenzie, *Evaluation of the*

Pilot Project on Block Funding for West Region Child and Family Services, July 1994.

131. Cited *supra* note 24. See also text accompanying notes 6 to 9, *supra*.

VI

Domesticating Reason:
Children, Families and Good Citizenship

ALICE HEARST

I. THE FAMILY AND THE POLITICAL ORDER: LOCATING THE FAMILY CRISIS

T HE RITUAL INVOCATION of a 'crisis of the family' has long been a staple of American political rhetoric. Challenges to the privileged position of the traditional nuclear family undermine a favorite fantasy, in which well-fed, rosy-cheeked children move from an orderly suburban world of neatly manicured lawns into an efficient and equally orderly world of full employment. In that universe of the Protestant imagination, the family is a private and autonomous institution that nonetheless works hand-in-hand with the state: the welfare and stability of the family is essential to the welfare and stability of the political order. Indeed, the family is the glue that holds the social order together in a liberal regime. It converts the needs of dependants into a private, rather than a public, responsibility (Fineman, 1995), while at the same time imbuing its members, particularly children, with those values essential to operating successfully in the social and political worlds outside of the home (Dailey, 1993). Without a private family to perform those functions, it would be impossible to theorize a public sphere where equal and rationally self-interested individuals interact.

But the relationship between the family and the state in the United States, like the relationship between individuals in real-world families, is fraught with tensions. In a liberal state, the family is as much a threat to the political order as it is essential to it; family loyalties may impede allegiances to the political order (Benn, 1988; Pateman, 1980). Families may inculcate values at odds with those most conducive to perpetuating established structures of authority in the public sphere (Guttman, 1987), and thus may frustrate the state's interest in assuring that individuals will grow into the kinds of sober and responsible citizens who can be trusted to operate within existing structures of authority. Reason may be clouded by familial attachments (Pateman, 1980), or, far worse, the family may not inculcate in its members 'right' reason (Mehta, 1992).

In the United States, the procreational family[1] has traditionally enjoyed considerable support and protection from third party interference. Despite a tradition according that family a certain degree of privacy, however, the family has not been immune from state intervention (Dailey, 1993; Olson, 1986). The family has been carefully molded: the state has had considerable input in defining who could claim status as a family, in defining what rights, privileges and liabilities attached to that status, and in defining the relationships of individuals within the family. Through this structuring of social relations emerged a family that could be relied upon to absorb the costs of dependency and to properly socialize its members.

This essay inquires into the socializing functions of the family, and how those functions have been defined in American constitutional discourse. Embedded in that discourse about socialization lies an image of good citizenship: as Steven Shiffrin has pointed out, there has rarely been any question of *whether* the state could intervene in the family or other social relations; rather the question has been *what kind* of citizen the state may seek to reproduce (Shiffrin, 1991). The movement for children's rights over the last three decades has generated anxiety — manifested in political rhetoric about the crisis of the family, if not in constitutional discourse — about the extent to which the family can continue to be trusted to adequately socialize its members.

The current discourse of good citizenship and socialization through the family is deficient, however, in several respects. First, the language of citizenship reflected in constitutional discourse about the family often represents a cramped vision: the 'goodness' of families is defined in terms of whether they produce sober and law-abiding citizens, without attention to other qualities that contribute to robust citizenship. Second, the constitutional discourse assumes an association between family and citizenship that inquires little, if at all, into what values the family actually imparts and how those values are related to good citizenship. The third concern flows directly from the second: in articulating a vision of citizenship, the law draws on images of individuals as autonomous and rational actors that form the grounding for liberal political and legal theory in general, which is peculiarly unsuited to understanding how the family might be regulated in relation to child rearing. Both constitutional discourse in the United States and the liberal political theory upon which that discourse draws lack any coherent theory of the child, except as an imperfect adult whose rational capacities are impaired. Thus, treatment of the child in the family tends to be entirely future-oriented: is the family raising a child who is likely, in the future, to exhibit the qualities that mark a good citizen? That loose theoretical stance leads the law to focus on reinforcing parental authority, or, in extraordinary cases, transferring that authority to a state agent, in ways that ignore the needs of children and fundamentally misunderstand the functions the family performs in reproducing citizens.

The problems that such an approach creates are manifested in much of the current debate over family values. Critics of children's rights, in increasingly shrill rhetoric, have argued that the current turn toward rights for children threatens the unity of the conventional family: Unsettling the authority of parents or the privileged position of the procreational family unsettles ideals of good citizenship and reason itself (Hafen, 1983; Glendon, 1991). When questions of children's rights are considered in the law, the focus is often upon how mature a particular minor is, as in the abortion rights cases, or how much a child might be expected to benefit from an extension of rights typically accorded adults, as in cases dealing with the rights of juvenile offenders.

As political theorist Nancy Rosenblum recently observed, many of 'the moral and political values necessary for liberal democratic citizenship' can be learned outside of the family — justice, tolerance, and a host of others — notwithstanding the fact that in a perfect world, those values might *also* be learned in the family (Rosenblum, 1995, at 12). Rosenblum continues:

What we get *exclusively* from the family is love, and the capacity to form intimate attachments. ... Emotional security does not lead inexorably to good character or good citizenship, but insecurity interferes with the formation of *every* social connection in which moral awareness is sharpened and translated into responsibility. It increases the chance that we will react to others with avoidance, fear, anger [and] hostility (*ibid.*).

Anne Dailey similarly argues that the law has failed to articulate a model of family justice that reinforces 'affective virtues', as part of her thoughtful approach to re-imagining the family and its role in producing good citizens (Dailey, 1993, at 1024). Building on that thesis, this essay argues that the law must develop not only a concept of family justice, but a concept of the child that recognizes the child in the here and now, and not simply as a future citizen or autonomous-being-in-progress.

II. PROMOTING THE SOBER CITIZEN: REINFORCING STRUCTURES OF AUTHORITY

THE PROCREATIONAL FAMILY presumably inculcated in its members 'industry, frugality, temperance, moderation, and the whole lovely train of republican virtues' (Grossberg, 1984, at 10; Teitelbaum, 1985). Those values assured that the refined and sedate individuals who emerged from the family would understand not only the potential of, but the limits to, individuality. The family protected in the law *domesticated* the reason of its members — pruning it to reflect a particular understanding of citizenship. Despite the widely held belief that the American legal regime followed a 'tradition of non-interference in the family' (Schneider, 1985), that doctrine never significantly limited the power of the state to regulate the family, as numerous commentators have observed (Dailey, 1993; Minow, 1987; Olsen, 1986). Early U.S. Supreme Court cases sanctioned state concern with drawing a heterogeneous immigrant population into the mainstream as much as they occasionally carved out a space for the exercise of parental prerogatives (Minow, 1987). 'Normal' families operated with little overt intervention, but states routinely regulated the family under the aegis of their police power authority to promote public health, welfare and morals. Control was maintained by simply defining out of existence those social units that did not conform to the family ideal (Grey, 1980; Olson, 1986).

Most importantly, the state's authority to supervise child rearing was essentially unquestioned: even the most conventional family could not refuse to educate its children, for example, and 'deviant' families, like those of the poor, could erect virtually no barriers to state intrusion (Grossberg, 1984; Minow, 1987). In some cases, however, the privacy of the family was real: the law paid little attention to imbalances of power within the family once the external forms were met. By refusing to recognize the rights of individual members within the family for matters like abuse, the law drew a circle around the family, creating a sort of black hole of densely packed relationships.

Until the mid-1960s, this concept of family privacy — setting up the family form and then turning a blind eye to the operation of the family once those forms were met — was found largely in a variety of common law doctrines rather than in the Constitution, although it was indirectly rendered in a few early Supreme Court cases that referred to fundamental rights to rear one's children without undue interference.[2] Even in those cases, the scope of the right hinged directly upon the parent's overarching *duty* to prepare the child for 'additional obligations' of citizenship.

This approach to regulating the family was inscribed in liberal thought itself. As Uday Mehta recently pointed out in a wonderfully insightful book, traditional liberalism rests upon a fairly limited concept of reason, with good citizenship defined more by habits of submission, self-control, and obedience than by the exercise of critical thought.[3] '[I]n Locke[,] rationality and the means for its inculcation ... are deployed to construct, consolidate and impose a norm of "normality" ' (Mehta, 1992, at 11). Moreover, because 'reason, self-discipline, and virtue are the products of an early immersion in the disciplinary and hierarchical matrix of the family' (*ibid.*, at 140), controlling the family form was integrally related to controlling the manner in which reason itself would be reproduced.[4]

In 1965, however, the family was expressly constitutionalized. By recognizing a substantive due process right of privacy in *Griswold v. Connecticut*, the Supreme Court for the first time gave real substance to the concept of family privacy, and undercut the conventional justification — protecting public morals — advanced to support regulation of the family. In significant ways, that change closed the door to the family by limiting the grounds upon which state regulation of the family could be justified.

Almost concurrently, the Court recognized equally important substantive due process rights of individual privacy, in *Eisenstadt v. Baird*, couched in terms of personal autonomy.[5] These changes opened up the family by enabling individual family members to transcend the traditional boundaries of family privacy and challenge the authority of those holding power within that relationship.

As the debate over the meanings of privacy and autonomy has taken shape in constitutional discourse — especially cases touching on the status of children — two clearly distinct ideologies of citizenship have emerged. On one hand, good citizens are defined as individuals who are generally tractable and willing to accept established modes of authority. At the same time, a dissenting voice has consistently urged a broader understanding of how the law ought to regulate the family, an approach that is more attentive to the ways in which families shape the citizenship — and hence autonomy — potential of their members, and focuses on the state's role in securing the conditions necessary for the development of citizenship. That latter approach holds potential for thinking about the future needs of children, but continues to replicate the problem of understanding children *as* children.

The idea that the reasoning citizen could develop only within the milieu of a carefully delimited family constellation was deeply ingrained in the Court's earliest treatments of the family. In the American context, concerns with imposing a set of normalizing values arose first in the context of conflicts between parental authority and the common school system, where the state had a strong interest in homogenizing what was perceived to be a heterogeneous immigrant rabble (Woodhouse, 1993; Rubin, 1986).[6] The Court was always at pains to note the state's legitimate interest in 'promot[ing] civil development ... in order to improve the quality of its citizens, physically, mentally and morally ...'. As Barbara Woodhouse points out in her detailed historical analysis of *Meyer v. Nebraska*, 262 U.S. 390 (1923), and *Pierce v. Society of Sisters*, 268 U.S. 510 (1925), the Court was strongly motivated by concerns for 'Americanizing the immigrant' into accepting dominant cultural values (Woodhouse, 1993; Minow, 1987).

In *Prince v. Massachusetts*, 321 U.S. 158 (1944), the Court talked explicitly about the nature of the state's interest in children. In *Prince*, the issue was whether the child labor laws of Massachusetts prohibited a woman from allowing her legal ward to distribute Jehovah's Witnesses religious tracts on the public streets. The Court initially noted that Massachusetts had a strong and legitimate interest, both on behalf of the child and the community, in assuring that 'children be both safeguarded from abuses and given opportunities for growth into free and independent well-developed men and citizens' (*ibid.* at 165). The Court then went on to observe that

the family itself is not beyond regulation in the public interest ... Acting to guard the general interest in youth's well being, the state as *parens patriae* may restrict the parent's control by requiring school attendance, regulating or prohibiting the child's labor and in many other ways ... [T]he state has a wide range of power for limiting parental freedom and authority in things affecting the child's welfare.

* * *

Among the evils most appropriate [for state regulation] are the crippling effects of child employment, more especially in public places, and the possible harms arising from other activities subject to all the diverse influences of the street [even when the child is accompanied by an adult] (*ibid.* at 165-66; 168).

The language in *Prince* raised a suggestion that the state had an interest in enhancing a child's options as a future citizen in the face of overbearing familial indoctrination. Certainly, the reasoning suggests, ordinary citizens did not allow their children to hawk religious literature in the public streets, and it therefore seemed obvious that children might need protection from the fanatical zeal of a parent whose religion countenanced no loyalties competing with loyalty to God.

As the dissent points out, however, the case turned not on concerns about the child's welfare *per se*, but upon concerns about the non-conformity of Jehovah's Witnesses as a group, and the kind of socialization to which a child in such a family might be subjected.

[T]here is not the slightest indication in this record, or in sources subject to judicial notice, that children engaged in distributing literature pursuant to their religious beliefs have been or are likely to be subject to any of the harmful 'diverse influences of the street'. Indeed, if probabilities are to be indulged in, the likelihood is that children engaged in serious religious endeavor are immune from such influences. Gambling, truancy, irregular eating and sleeping habits, and the more serious vices are not consistent with the high moral character ordinarily displayed by children fulfilling religious obligations.

* * *

[T]he Jehovah's Witnesses are living proof of the fact that even in this nation, conceived as it was in the ideals of freedom, the right to practice religion in unconventional ways is still far from secure. Theirs is a militant and unpopular faith, pursued with a fanatical zeal. They have suffered brutal beatings, their property has been destroyed; they have been harassed at every turn by the resurrection and enforcement of little used ordinances and statutes (*ibid.* at 175-176).

The Jehovah's Witnesses again caused consternation in the controversial flag salute cases that reached the Court in the early 1940s. While family authority is discussed only indirectly, it is important to understand the dynamic conflict between family and state that lay beneath the surface in these cases in order to understand how the Court cast the relationship of the state and the family with respect to child rearing and citizenship.

In *Minersville v. Gobitis*, 310 U.S. 586 (1940), two children were expelled from the public schools of Minersville, Pennsylvania, for refusing to participate in a daily pledge of allegiance to the national flag, and were therefore compelled to attend a private school. Their father brought suit, claiming that the requirement denied his family's religious freedom and as well as his children's entitlement to a free public education. The children had been raised 'to believe that such a gesture of respect for the flag was forbidden by command of Scripture' (*ibid.* at 592).

The Court upheld the school board's requirement. Justice Frankfurter wrote the majority opinion, which focused upon the nature of the state's interest in acculturating children, and the tensions between parental and public authority when those aims diverged.

[W]e are dealing here with the formative period in the development of citizenship ... What the school authorities are really asserting is the right to awaken in the child's mind considerations as to the significance of the flag contrary to those implanted by the parent. In such an attempt the state is normally at a disadvantage in competing with the parent's authority, so long ... as parents are unmolested in their right to counteract by their own persuasiveness the wisdom and rightness of those loyalties which the state's educational system is seeking to promote ... (*ibid.* at 599).

Justice Frankfurter went on to describe the ways in which the family and the state were interdependent.

The preciousness of the family relation, the authority and independence which give dignity to parenthood, indeed the enjoyment of all freedom, presuppose the kind of ordered society which is summarized by our flag. A society which is dedicated to the preservation of these ultimate values of a civilization may in self-protection utilize the educational process for inculcating those almost unconscious feelings which bind men together in a comprehending loyalty, whatever may be their lesser differences and difficulties (*ibid.* at 600).

Moreover, the danger posed by the refusal of the Gobitis children to salute the flag went beyond a simple problem of one or two children simply standing quietly in a classroom without taking a pledge of loyalty; an exemption for 'dissidents ... might introduce elements of difficulty into the school discipline, might cast doubts in the minds of the other children ...' (*ibid.*).

In *Gobitis*, the Court set family and state at odds: state concerns for promoting national unity could certainly override 'lesser' religious differences. Only three years later, however, in *West Virginia Board of Education v. Barnette*, 319 U.S. 624 (1943), the Court reversed itself, holding that state legislatures could not compel a child to salute the flag. The West Virginia legislature had enacted a statute labeling the failure to engage in a 'stiff-arm' salute, raising the right hand with the palm upward, as an act of insubordination (*ibid.* at 628). The Jehovah's Witnesses sought an injunction to avoid having their children expelled for 'failure to conform' (*ibid.* at 629), and then be subjected to delinquency proceedings for being unlawfully absent from school.

The reversal was dramatic, if only because reversals are rare and this one followed so closely upon the heels of the *Gobitis* case. In fact, the holding did not suggest any significant diminution of state authority to inculcate patriotic impulses in children. According to the Court, the state continued to have wide latitude to educate children into citizenship.

[N]ational unity as an end which officials may foster by persuasion and example is not in question ... [T]he State may 'require teaching by instruction and study of all in our history and in the structure and organization of our government, including the guaranties of civil liberty, which tend to inspire patriotism and love of country' (*ibid.* at 631).

Nonetheless, the state could not '[compel] ... utterance ... forc[ing] an American citizen to publicly profess any statement of belief or to engage in any ceremony of assent to one' (*ibid.* at 634).

In marked contrast to *Gobitis*, the Court in *Barnette* sidestepped any discussion of the tension between the family and the state. Rather than acknowledging the issue of parental influences on the child's behavior and values, thus construing the dispute, as it clearly was, as a contest between the state and the family for control over the child's loyalties, the decision spoke only in terms of individual rights to freedom of conscience. That approach simplified the issue, and foreshadowed the emergence of a jurisprudence of children's rights that tried to envision the child as individual whose actions are unconnected to the web of intimate relations in which he or she is enmeshed. Moreover, the Court exhibited a tolerance for minor deviations from the state's efforts to induce conformity. 'We can have intellectual individualism and the rich cultural diversities that we owe to exceptional minds only at the price of occasional eccentricity and abnormal attitudes' (*Barnette, supra*, at 641-642).

Overall, however, the cases revealed strong support for the state's authority to imbue children with fealty to extant structures of authority, and were cognizant of the alliance between the state and the family with regard to crafting citizenship. Families that seemed abnormal were distrusted; even those families like the Jehovah's Witnesses, with admittedly 'high moral character', achieved only limited success when their claims ran counter to state interests in assuring that children could transcend familial ties in favor of 'those almost unconscious feelings which bind men together in a comprehending loyalty' in a nation of ordered liberty.

III. INCURSIONS INTO THE ALLIANCE: REDEFINING FAMILIES AND CITIZENSHIP

WHILE THE EARLY CASES were relatively clear about the kinds of families that would be privileged, the image of citizenship lurking in the background was not clearly articulated until 1972 in *Wisconsin v. Yoder*, 406 U.S. 205 (1972). In that case, Justice Burger waxed eloquent about the connections between good families and good citizens in granting an exemption from compulsory school laws to Amish parents wishing to protect their children from worldly influences thrust upon them by attendance at a public high school. As noted earlier, Justice Burger extolled the ideal family — tied tightly into a small and homogeneous community, self-contained and austere — that produced the ideal citizen — an individual who was self-reliant, law-abiding, politically disengaged and not prone to question authority.

But not all of the justices in *Wisconsin v. Yoder* agreed with Chief Justice Burger. Three of the Justices in the majority echoed the sentiments, expressed in the dissenting opinion of Justice Douglas, that the state had an independent obligation to the child to maximize the child's life options through the provision of an adequate education. The dissenting and concurring opinions highlighted the jarring tensions that would become increasingly apparent in the cases discussing children's rights and the socializing functions of the family in general: tensions between assuming that parents always represented children's interests and recognizing that the family was uniquely able to submerge those interests, as well as tensions over the definition of what constituted adequate acculturation overall.

The dissent in *Yoder* suggested that the emerging substantive due process right of privacy and autonomy might be important in considering the position of children.[7] By 1980, the language of autonomy was commonplace in constitutional discourse, but defining what capacities were necessary to assert an autonomy right were highly contested matters.

The rights revolution of the 1960s initially appeared to indicate a groundswell of support for recognizing children's rights. With *In re Gault* in 1967, and *Tinker v. Des Moines Independent School District* in 1969, the Court accepted without question the idea that children can hold rights as individuals distinguished from the rights of the family as a group. Those initial cases, however, did not significantly alter the superior authority of parents or the state in regard to children: children by and large remained anchored to family authority.

In re Gault, 387 U.S. 1 (1967) involved a challenge to the structure of the juvenile justice system. Fifteen-year-old Gerald Gault was accused of making a harassing phone call. Finding that Gerald had disturbed the peace by making the telephone calls and that he was 'habitually involved in immoral matters' (*ibid*. at 9), a juvenile court judge confined him to a juvenile detention facility for the remaining six years of his minority. An adult committing the same misdemeanor would have been subject to a fine and up to 60 days in prison.

The Court opened its opinion with a discussion of the juvenile justice system and the nature of the state's authority as *parens patriae*. The Court explained that traditionally

a child unlike an adult, has a right 'not to liberty but to custody'. He can be made to attorn to his parents ... [i]f his parents default in effectively performing their custodial functions — that is, if the child is 'delinquent' — the state may intervene. In doing so, it does not deprive the child of any rights, because he has none (*ibid*. at 17).

The Court then noted that the denial of basic procedural rights worked a serious hardship on children, holding that the juvenile judge had abused his power, and observing that 'the condition of being a boy does not justify a kangaroo court' (*ibid*. at 28). The Court concluded that juveniles were entitled to a number of basic procedural rights, such as notice of the charges, right to counsel, and rights to a transcript and review.

While *In re Gault* broke ground by recognizing children as individuals in their own right, *Gault* did not significantly displace traditional structures of authority. One of the points the Supreme Court made was that the juvenile proceedings reflected an utter disregard for the traditional parent/state partnership, harking back to the notion that a child's parents would be best suited to restrain and mold him into an obedient citizen.

[U]nder traditional notions, one would assume that in a case like that of Gerald Gault, where the juvenile appears to have a home, a working mother and father, and an older brother, the juvenile judge would have made a careful inquiry and judgment as to the possibility that the boy could be disciplined and dealt with at home (*ibid.* at 28).

Shortly after *Gault*, the Court recognized that juveniles might have other constitutionally guaranteed rights. *Tinker v. Des Moines Independent School District*, 293 U.S. 503 (1969) was a challenge to the suspension of three teenagers who wore black arm bands to school to protest the United States' involvement in the Vietnam War. School authorities argued that the arm bands created a disruption in the school.

In language that has been widely repeated, the Court held that '[n]either students or teachers shed their constitutional rights to freedom of speech or expression at the schoolhouse gate' (*ibid.* at 506). The Court dismissed the school's assertion that the children's acts created a risk of disruption: '[t]he Constitution says we must take this risk, and our history says that it is this sort of hazardous freedom — this kind of openness — that is the basis of our national strength and of the independence and vigor of Americans who grow up and live in this relatively permissive, often disputatious, society' (*ibid.* at 508-509).

The language was bold, and suggested an active vision of citizenship: 'The classroom', according to Justice Fortas, "is peculiarly the 'marketplace of ideas'." The Nation's future depends upon leaders trained through wide exposure to that robust exchange of ideals which discovers truth 'out of a multitude of tongues, [rather] than through any kind of authoritative selection' (*ibid.* at 512).

Justice Black argued, in dissent, that the case posed a threat to established modes of order, sanctioning '[u]ncontrolled and uncontrollable liberty ... [t]he enemy to domestic peace'.

[t]he schools of this Nation have undoubtedly contributed to giving us tranquility and to making us a more law-abiding people ... School discipline, like parental discipline is an integral and important part of training our children to be good citizens — to be better citizens ... One does not need to be a prophet or a son of a prophet to know that after the Court's holding today some students in Iowa schools and indeed in all schools will be ready, able and willing to defy their teachers ... [and all public schools may be subjected to] break-ins, sit-ins, lie-ins, and smash-ins ... Turned loose with lawsuits for damages and injunctions against their teachers as they are here, it is nothing but wishful thinking

to imagine that young, immature students will soon believe it is their right to control the schools ... (*ibid*. at 524-525).

Yet, in context, Justice Black's argument seems to be overkill. The students who refused to obey the school district's rules ranged in age from eight to 15, and their parents, one a Methodist minister working for the American Friends Service Committee and another active in the Women's International League for Peace and Freedom, were deeply involved in anti-war activism. As Robert Burt has noted, there is little reason to believe that the children were engaged in anything more than parroting their parents' ideas, and thus they were not stepping out of the conventional orbits of authority.

[T]he *Tinker* Court erred ... in its failure to acknowledge the potential educational and constitutional relevance of the facts in the case suggesting that the children's arm bands reflected more their parents' convictions than theirs. The Court ignored the possibility that school officials might exclude parental political views from school in order to free children to think through these questions for themselves. ... The *Tinker* Court should have acknowledged that the constitutional question would have changed complexion if the school officials had convincingly argued that they were acting not to impose their political views on students, but rather on behalf of the root values of the first amendment — tolerance, diversity of thought, individual autonomy — against parental impositions on children (Burt, 1975 at 314).

Nor was the precedent set in *Tinker* extended very far. In *Bethel v. Fraser*, 478 U.S. 675 (1986), the Court sustained the school's authority to discipline a student whose nominating speech for a candidate for a school government position was offensive in its use of sexual metaphor, and in *Hazelwood School District v. Kuhlmeir*, 484 U.S. 260 (1988) decided two years later, the Court allowed school officials to censor a story in a school newspaper discussing teenage pregnancy.

The Court continued to extend procedural rights, but in a limited manner: in *Goss v. Lopez*, 419 U.S. 565 (1975) for example, the Court held that a teenager suspended for misconduct in school was entitled to notice and an explanation of the charges, as well as the right to present his own case, but in only the most informal manner. Similarly, the Court rejected the claims that students had constitutional rights that prohibited schools from applying any form of corporal punishment in *Ingraham v. Wright* in 1977, 430 U.S. 651.

Thus, while children's rights have been recognized, they have not been fashioned in ways that substantially alter the distribution of power between parents, children, and the state. As other scholars have noted, the Court has continued to reinforce traditional structures of authority: parental authority in a traditional family, or, in the absence of an adequately functioning family, the state as *parens patriae* (Burt, 1979; Rubin, 1986).

A more interesting case was *Parham v. J.R.*, 442 U.S. 584 (1979), examining the scope of procedural rights due to children when their parents, or the state, if they were in state custody, sought to admit them to a state mental institution. The Court held that the children, who admittedly had 'substantial liberty interests' at stake, were nonetheless adequately protected against the abuse of parental authority by the normal review provisions conducted by medical personnel at the institution.

The majority characterized the dispute as one between parents and the state over who had authority to render a final disposition on a child's hospitalization. As Burt points out in his review of *Parham*, the Court did not hold that

parental authority as such warrants respect. Rather, *the authority over children that commands constitutionally mandated respect is that which is backed by force clearly promising effective control over children's destructive influences.* On this view, parents occasionally embody such force. But when parents in fact fail to control their child, then their authority no longer commands respect in principle. Parents whose effective authority has failed can rehabilitate themselves and their claim to constitutionally mandated respect only by invoking some extra-familial authority to buttress their weakened force — a psychiatrist who will institutionalize their child, a teacher who will paddle their child, a judge who will rule their child (Burt, 1979, at 328).

Overall, the children's rights cases since 1967 have not moved far toward inquiring into whether the conventional construction of children in the law is connected to producing responsible citizens. While children have become visible as individuals who *may* hold and exercise rights independent of the family, the scope and meaning of autonomy-oriented rights has to date received little amplification, largely because they continue to be viewed as incomplete or imperfect adults. And yet, those concerns seem to be the critical ones in understanding the family/state relationship: what happens to children in families that is most critical to their ability to function as citizens as they grow to independence?

IV. AFFECTIVE TIES AND REDEFINING THE CHILD

AS NOTED EARLIER, the affective bonds that children develop in attachments to primary caretakers are critical to the development of stable and healthy individuals. In recent years, the Court has declined several times to take advantage of an opportunity to expand the meaning of autonomy rights for children, in ways that are attentive to children's potential for autonomy (Minow, 1989), but to their status *qua* children. From *Smith v. OFFER*, 431 U.S. 816 (1977), a case in which foster parents sought procedural protection against arbitrary termination of relationships with foster children, to *Michael H. v. Gerald D.*, 491 U.S. 111 (1989) in which a putative father sought to establish a parental right over the child with whom he had been living (admittedly sporadically) during the child's first three years of life, the Court has been reluctant to acknowledge the importance of affective ties.

In *Smith*, the Court held that foster parents were not deprived of substantive or procedural due process rights when denied the opportunity for an administrative hearing to determine whether foster children who had been in their care for a year or more could be removed, either to be reunited with their parents or placed in other foster homes. The foster parents claimed that

when a child has lived in a foster home for a year or more, a psychological tie is created between the child and the foster parents which constitutes the foster family the true 'psychological family' of the child. That family, they argue, has a 'liberty interest' in its survival as a family protected by the Fourteenth Amendment (*ibid.* at 839).

Responding to these claims, the Court first observed that

the importance of the familial relationship, to the individuals involved and to the society, stems from the emotional attachments that derive from the intimacy of daily association, and from the role it plays in 'promot[ing] a way of life' through the instruction of children. ... No one would seriously dispute that a deeply loving and interdependent relationship between an adult and a child in his or her care may exist even in the absence of blood relationship ... [In situations of long term care at least] it is natural that the foster family should hold the same place in the emotional life of the foster child, and fulfill the same socializing functions, as a natural family (*ibid.* at 844).

The Court held, however, that the foster family did not acquire 'family rights' because it was a state-created unit[8] from the outset, with a specific and limited mission.

The quick dismissal of the foster family may seem odd if, as I have suggested, the Court has traditionally deferred to the most conventional family form: foster care tends to be provided by middle to lower middle class married couples who would be expected to provide fairly conventional socialization. Perhaps the result can be explained by the fact that the case presented a number of compelling — and competing — stories: biological parents often surrendered children into state care under less than voluntary circumstances, with the express understanding that the family could be reunited, and recognizing the rights of a psychological family set the stage for conflict with the biological and often pre-existing emotional ties that children had with natural parents; the guardian *ad litem* independently appointed to represent the children in foster care argued that there were already sufficient safeguards to protect foster parents' interests. Moreover, the lengthy decision was attentive to the ways in which a state child protection service could be invoked to the disadvantage of all of the parties concerned, coercing the sometimes arbitrary removal of children from poor families for reasons that were merely a pretext for race and class bias, wrenching children from a variety of affective bonds, and encouraging foster parents to distance themselves from children who were in desperate need of emotional attention.

For purposes here, however, *Smith v. OFFER* was noteworthy because the Court gave short shrift to the importance of any the emotional bonds that might develop between particular foster parents and foster children, articulating instead a blanket rule precluding claims based upon the importance of the psychological family. Despite the Court's express recognition that those affective bonds might be critical in a given case, depending upon the length of time in foster care, the conditions of the entry into the system, and the particular relationship between the members of the foster family, the Court barely considered the concrete impact of its decision, being preoccupied instead with the competing interests of foster and natural parents.[9] The lower court's findings that foster children might be subjected to 'the trauma of separation' or 'the harmful consequences of a precipitous and perhaps improvident decision to remove a child' — were discussed only by a concurring justice with reference to the fact that 'not all grievous losses fall within the ambit of the Due Process clause' (*ibid.* at 858).

One of the most compelling examples of a disregard for the importance of affective ties in non-traditional families was the Court's decision in *Bowen v. Gilliard*, 483 U.S. 587 (1987). At issue in *Gilliard* was the constitutionality of a provision of the Deficit Reduction Act of 1984, requiring the pooling of income received by all family members for purposes of determining levels of benefits under the Aid to Families with Dependent Children program. The statutory change in effect lowered benefit levels for families receiving AFDC funds if there was a child in the family for whom the custodial parent was receiving child support: child support was considered family income where prior to the change, that income (and the child for whom it was intended) had been excluded from the benefit calculation. The statute left families receiving AFDC benefits with a Hobson's choice: child support could be refused, thus making all of the children eligible for AFDC; the child support could be accepted and assigned to the state, entailing a significant cut in overall benefits, or the child receiving benefits could move out of the house.

The Court upheld the statute, largely in an attempt to privatize the costs of dependency. There was a conscious disregard for the impact of the decision on a family's ability to maintain emotional bonds. The language of the opinion was couched in largely abstract terms respecting state authority to place reasonable conditions on the receipt of welfare benefits and finding its interest in cutting the budget deficit to be eminently reasonable.

The dissenting opinion of Justices Brennan and Marshall reflected a different picture of the impact of the legislation. First, the dissenting opinion sorted out the claims of the benefit recipients and those of the children receiving private support, which the majority had lumped together. The children's claims, the dissent noted, 'were *not* that the Government had unfairly denied them benefits, but that it ha[d] intruded deeply into their relationship with their parents' (*ibid.* at 609).

[T]he Government has told a child who lives with a mother receiving public assistance that it cannot both live with its mother and be supported by its father. The child must either leave the care and custody of the mother, or forgo the support of the father and become a Government client. The child is put to this choice not because it seeks Government benefits for itself, but because of a fact over which it has no control: the need of *other* household members for public assistance. A child who lives with one parent has, under the best of circumstances, a difficult time sustaining a relationship with both its parents. A crucial bond between a child and its parent outside the home, usually the father, is the father's commitment to care for the material needs of the child, and the expectation of the child that it may look to its father for such care. The Government has thus decreed that a condition of welfare eligibility for a mother is that her child surrender a vital connection with either the mother or the father (*ibid.* at 610).

After a lengthy discussion of the ways in which the provision of child support provided a means of maintaining a bond with an absent parent, the dissent then turned to evidence establishing that the children in the class action suit had been deprived of a significant bonds with either their mothers or fathers through the operation of the statute. In one of the cases, a father discontinued both child support and visitation with his seven year old child when the mother assigned the benefits to the state as required by the statute, because he objected to his son being on welfare. The dissenters observed that

Sherrod, of course, has no control over any of this, but nonetheless must suffer the loss of his father's care:

Sherrod is very upset that this father no longer visits him. He frequently asks me why his daddy does not come to see him any more. Since the time his father has stopped visitation, Sherrod has begun to wet his bed on a frequent basis. Also since the visitation stopped, Sherrod has become much more disruptive, especially in school. Furthermore, his performance in school seems to have declined.

The financial and emotional cost of losing this connection with the father may be too much for the child to bear. If so, the only way to avoid it is to leave the custody of the mother (*ibid.* at 621).

The dissenters discussed another instance where a mother gave up custody of her daughter, Karen, in order to retain support for her other three children.

Karen may now keep her $200 in child support, and her mother may now obtain AFDC for herself and her other children. They may no longer, however, live in the same household. The burden of their choice hardly requires elaboration. (*ibid.* at 623)

* * *

Contemporary life offers countless ways in which family life can be fractured and families made unhappy. The children who increasingly live in these families are entitled to the chance to sustain a special relationship with both their fathers and their mothers, regardless of how difficult that may be ... A child cannot be held responsible for the indigency of its mother, and should not be forced to choose between parents because of something so clearly out of its control. No society can assure its children that there will be no unhappy families. It *can* tell them, however, that their government will not be allowed to contribute to the pain (*ibid.* at 633-634).

In *Michael H. v. Gerald D.*, 491 U.S. 119 (1989) the Court ducked the issue of affective ties by recognizing the family rights of a marital couple in the face of a claim of biological parenthood by a third party. The Court dismissed both the claims of Michael and his alleged daughter, Victoria, who sought to continue a filial relationship.

The case raised a challenge to California's then extant law creating an irrebuttable presumption of paternity in the husband of a woman whose child was conceived during the course of a valid marriage. Victoria was conceived as the result of an adulterous relationship between Michael and Carole while Carole was still living with her husband, Gerald. After Victoria was born, her mother moved out of the marital home, and she and Victoria lived off and on with Michael for three years. During that time, Michael held himself out as Victoria's father, and she called him Daddy. Some time during that three year period, Michael underwent DNA testing revealing with virtual certainty that he was Victoria's biological father. Eventually, Carole resumed her relationship with Gerald, and thereafter refused to let the relationship between Victoria and Michael continue.

The bulk of the decision addressed Michael's claim that the California statute deprived him of a substantive due process right to maintain a relationship with his daughter. Michael had claimed that his established relationship with Victoria, coupled with the fact of biological parentage, gave rise to a substantive due process right to continue that relationship. The evidentiary presumption, however, precluded even the possibility of Michael making such a showing: his authority to challenge Gerald's presumptive paternity was irrebuttably barred.

The majority characterized the legal issue as a contest between a conventional and a non-conventional family: '[The recognition of parental rights] rest[s] upon the respect — indeed, sanctity would not be too strong a term — traditionally accorded to the relationships that develop within the unitary [marital] family' (*ibid.* at 123). Thus, the legal question, the opinion asserted, was

whether the relationship between persons in the situation of Michael and Victoria has been treated as a protected family unit under the historical practices of our society ... We think it impossible to find that it has. In fact, quite to the contrary, our traditions have protected the marital family against the sort of claim Michael asserts (*ibid.* at 124).

The majority opinion then dismissed Victoria's distinct claim in a single paragraph.

[Victoria] claims a due process right to maintain filial relationships with both Michael and Gerald. This assertion merits little discussion, for, whatever the merits of the guardian ad litem's belief that such an arrangement can be of great psychological benefit to a child, the claim that a state must recognize multiple fatherhood has no support in the history or traditions of this country. Moreover, even if we were to construe Victoria's argument as forwarding the lesser proposition that, whatever her status vis-a-vis Gerald, she has a liberty interest in maintaining a filial relationship with her natural father, Michael, we find that, at best, her claim is the obverse of Michael's and fails for the same reasons (*ibid.* at 130-131).

In each of these cases, the Supreme Court had an opportunity to look into both how the law could reinforce affective bonds and how the existence of such bonds was likely to affect the various childrens' growth and development. Its reluctance to do so is not surprising: it is extraordinarily difficult to fix on an adequate theory of the child that does not simply label the child as something less than a rational adult. Yet accommodation of children's needs for care and affection might move the Court toward some such theory. At the very least, the discussion of such a set of ideas should not be foreclosed by refusing to accept children's needs as a legitimate object of constitutional concern.

V. CONCLUSION

THESE KINDS OF DECISIONS REVEAL a marked refusal to take into account children's sensibilities and experiences. The difficulty in attempting to articulate a vision of the child as a legal subject leaves children at risk in a system where parents' rights or state interests can always trump their concerns, and impedes a more carefully nuanced discussion of the assumptions built into the concepts of reason, autonomy and citizenship upon which the law's regulation of the family is built. More thoughtful approaches, echoes of which are apparent in a number of the dissenting opinions in the cases discussed above, open the door to ways in which discussions of children's rights can be recast to protect those interests of children in security and stability that will affect their future as citizens. The problem with those dissenting voices, however, is that they place perhaps too much emphasis on children's *potential* as autonomous individuals, and insufficient attention to the *immediate* needs of children for the care and attention that will enable them to form solid human relationships. As Jennifer Nedelsky (1988) points out, autonomy — a central value of citizenship — is a process that continues across a particular individual's life path. Nedelsky argues, for example, that human autonomy must be seen as a process, not an end alone. Individual autonomy grows and changes over time. Indeed, she argues, the experience of a child moving through time provides a better paradigm for understanding the nature and limits of autonomy than the model of autonomy which currently permeates liberal and especially liberal-legal thinking (Nedelsky, 1989). Moving toward a theory of the child in the law requires careful thinking about how citizenship and autonomy develop.

As long as constitutional debate stays mired in questions of whether the family is falling down on its obligation to raise good citizens without either examining closely what a good citizen looks like and what citizenship values derive from the family a good citizen comes from, the law will remain unresponsive to the importance of affective ties. Recasting the discourse — and the nature of the rights recognized — has significant potential for moving toward a more complex, but ultimately more beneficial, approach to understanding the connections between autonomy, family and socialization for children.

Notes

1.   Michael Grossberg refers to that family as republican (*Governing the Hearth* (University of North Carolina Press, 1985)), Eva Rubin as traditional (*The Supreme Court and the American Family* (Greenwood Press, 1986)), and Martha Fineman as sexual (*The Neutered Mother, the Sexual Family, and other Twentieth Century Tragedies* (Routledge Press, 1995)). I prefer to utilize the term 'pro-creational' since much of the regulation of that unit has centered on the family's childbearing/child rearing activities, and is largely concerned with how that unit absorbs the costs of dependency and produces adequately socialized children.

2.   *Meyer v. Nebraska*, 262 U.S. 390 (1923), *Pierce v. Society of Sisters*, 268 U.S. 510 (1925), and *Prince v. Massachusetts*, 321 U.S. 158 (1944). In each of these cases, the scope of parental authority or privacy was narrowly construed.

3. Contemporary rights theorists articulate a broader understanding of reason (Jeremy Waldron, 'When Justice Replaces Affection: The Need for Rights' 11 Harvard Journal of Law and Public Policy 625). While that work is significant in understanding the theoretical connections between rights, law and reason, that discussion is beyond the scope of this work.

4. Mehta's argument (*The Anxiety of Freedom* (Cornell University Press, 1992)) is particularly fascinating as it illuminates the connections between the exercise of familial authority and a conscious fashioning of individual reason. In Locke's writings on education, Mehta notes, great emphasis is placed upon teaching a child to submit to the force of authority at a very early age, preferably before the age of three, which typically demarcates the boundaries of conscious memory. As Mehta points out, Locke's 'pedagogical project ... attempts to mold or homogenize individual reason', but then — and this is the subtle turn — 'makes natural law [in The Second Treatise] contingent on human reason ...' (1992 at 142).

5. At the same time, the Court began to recognize children's rights, although it did not go so far as to recognize a child's *substantive* due process right to autonomy or care and affection.

6. Eva Rubin notes, for example, of two models of the public school system: the first envisioned the school as the extension of the family, where the state stepped in as *parens patriae*, while the second saw the school in competition with parents, working to inculcate democratic values (Rubin, 1986).

7. For an interesting discussion of *Wisconsin v. Yoder*, see R. Arneson and I. Shapiro, 'Democratic Autonomy and Religious Liberty: A Critique of *Wisconsin v. Yoder*' Nomos 34, eds. R. Hardin and I. Shapiro N.Y.U. Press.

8. The marital unit is state-created as well.

9. One justice, in a concurring opinion, noted that while he would reject outright any claim that the harms claimed here were losses 'invok[ing] the protection of the Due Process Clause', he disagreed with the Court's decision not to distinguish between the claims of the foster parents and the foster children, stating that 'it is by no means obvious that foster parents and foster children have the same interest in a continuation of their relationship'.

References

Arneson, Richard and Ian Shapiro (1994), 'Democratic Autonomy and Religious Liberty: A Critique of *Wisconsin v. Yoder*' Nomos 34, eds. R. Hardin and I. Shapiro (New York University Press).

Benn, Stanley I. (1988), *A Theory of Freedom* (Cambridge University Press).

Burt, Robert A. (1975), 'Developing Constitutional Rights of, in and for Children' 39 Law and Contemporary Problems 293.

_____. (1979), 'The Constitution of the Family' in 1979 Supreme Court Review, eds. Philip Kurland and Gerhard Casper (University of Chicago Press).

Coontz, Stephanie (1992), *The Way We Never Were: American Families and the Nostalgia Trap* (Basic Books).

Dailey, Anne C. (1993), 'Constitutional Privacy and the Just Family' 67 Tulane Law Review 955.

Fineman, Martha (1995), *The Neutered Mother, the Sexual Family, and Other Twentieth Century Tragedies* (Routledge Press).

Glendon, Mary Ann (1991), *Rights-Talk: The Impoverishment of Political Discourse* (The Free Press).

Grey, Thomas C. (1980), 'Eros, Civilization and the Burger Court' 43 Law and Contemporary Problems 83.

Grossberg, Michael. (1985), *Governing the Hearth* (University of North Carolina Press).

Hafen, Bruce C. (1976), 'Children's Liberation and the New Egalitarianism: Some Reservations About Abandoning Youth to Their 'Rights' ' [1976] Brigham Young University Law Review 605.

_____. (1983), 'The Constitutional Status of Marriage, Kinship and Sexual Privacy — Balancing the Individual and Social Interests' 81 Michigan Law Review 463.

_____. (1991), 'Individualism and Autonomy in Family Law: The Waning of Belonging' [1991] Brigham Young University Law Review 1.

Henderson, Lynne N. (1985), 'Legality and Empathy' 85 Michigan Law Review 1574.

Mehta, Uday Singh (1992), *The Anxiety of Freedom* (Cornell University Press).

Minow, Martha (1987a) 'Are Rights Right for Children?' 1 American Bar Foundation Research Journal 203.

_____. (1985), ' 'Forming Underneath Everything that Grows': Toward a History of Family Law' [1985] Wisconsin Law Review 819.

_____. (1987b), 'Interpreting Rights: An Essay for Robert Cover' 96 Yale Law Journal 1860.

_____. (1990), *Making All the Difference: Inclusion, Exclusion and American Law* (Cornell University Press).

_____. (1986), 'Rights for the Next Generation: A Feminist Approach to Children's Rights' 9 Harvard Women's Law Journal 1.

_____. (1987c), 'We, the Family: Constitutional Rights and American Families' 74 Journal of American History (3) 959.

Nedelsky, Jennifer (1989), 'Reconceiving Autonomy: Sources, Thoughts and Possibilities' 7 Yale Journal of Law and Feminism 1.

Okin, Susan Moller (1989), *Justice, Gender and the Family* (Basic Books).

Olsen, Francis E. (1985), 'The Myth of State Intervention in the Family' 18 Journal of Law Reform 835.

O'Neill, Onora (1988), 'Children's Rights and Children's Lives' 98 Ethics 445.

Pateman, Carole (1980), *The Disorder of Women: Democracy, Feminism and Political Theory* (Stanford University Press).

Raz, Joseph (1986), *The Morality of Freedom* (Oxford University Press).

Rosenblum, Nancy L. (1995), 'Family Values: Comment on S. Burtt, "The Needs of Children: Towards a New Politics of Family Structure" and I. Young, "A Critique of Pure Family Values" ' (unpublished).

Rubin, Eva R. (1986), *The Supreme Court and the American Family* (Greenwood Press).

Schneider, Carl (1985), 'Moral Discourse in Family Law' 83 Michigan Law Review 1803.

Shanley, Mary L. (1983), 'Feminism and Families in a Liberal Polity' in Irene Diamond, ed., *Families, Politics and Public Policy* (Longman Press).

Shanley, Mary L. and Minow, Martha (1995), 'Revisioning the Family in Political Theory and Law' (unpublished).
Shiffrin, Steven (1991), 'Liberal Theory and the Need for Politics' 89 Michigan Law Review 1281.

Teitelbaum, Lee E. (1985), 'Family History and Family Law' [1985] Wisconsin Law Review 1135.

Waldron, Jeremy (1985), 'When Justice Replaces Affection: The Need for Rights' 11 Harvard Journal of Law and Public Policy 625.

Woodhouse, Barbara Bennett (1993), 'Hatching the Egg: A Child-Centered Perspective on Parents' Rights' 14 Cardozo Law Review 1747.

VII

Reconstructing Childhood: Toward a Praxis of Inclusion

S H E I L A   M A R T I N E A U*

The experiences of children may be illuminated by, and in turn may challenge, our frameworks for understanding not only families and schools but also politics, work, poverty, social class, organizations, bureaucracy, urban life, social stratification, and social change.

Barrie Thorne

I. THE POLITICS OF CHILDHOOD

RECOGNIZING THE POLITICAL NATURE OF CHILDHOOD and the cultures of children means examining the connections between children's care and harm, work and play, rights and responsibilities, and protection and exploitation. The 'politics of childhood' is a framework for addressing children's issues which links the macro-concerns of childhood with the micro-cultures of children. It recognizes the potential contribution of children, *as* children, as active participants in community life. In this context, the politics of childhood advocates the age-appropriate inclusion of children in social policy, planning, and programming.[1] Through the development of inclusionary and participatory practices, we can nurture the capacities of children as political actors in the present and cultivate their potential as contributors to society.

The politics of childhood recognize that children both influence and are influenced by their social worlds. When childhood historian Neil Sutherland portrays the 'culture of childhood' in terms of children interacting in families, schools, playgrounds, and neighbourhoods (1996), he articulates a childhood historically grounded in the diverse cultural and economic conditions of children's everyday lives. Children's activities and interactions with one another form a diversity of micro-cultures, while the macro-concerns of childhood point the way to children's participation in, and contribution to, the larger social world of adults. While this is a simplistic picture, it outlines a critical perspective from which to view and review social policies, practices, and structures affecting children. Such a perspective draws on poststructuralism, which 'defines discourse and structure as something which can be acted upon and changed' (Davies 1993, 11), and incorporates the insights of sociologist Barrie Thorne (1987).

'Attention to children', Thorne asserts, 'may expand our overall notions of "the political"' (1987, 100). Indeed, the politics of childhood revisions children as political actors, not just as politically acted upon. Thorne claims that the collaborative strategies, ethical sensibilities, and political complexities of children's lives challenge the universal stages of moral development that psychologists attribute to children; these 'stages' are more probably constructed by such social practices as age-graded educational institutions (93, 99) and sex-gender socialization. Thorne's qualitative and interpretive research with school-aged children has led her to understand children as 'complex actors, strategists, performers, users of language, [and] creators of culture' (101). This perspective urges the reconsideration of childhood, child abuse, child labour, and children's rights as they are currently constructed. What follows is a preliminary sociological exploration, a bibliographic essay, toward a praxis of inclusion as an ethic for respecting and revisioning children in society.

II. CONSTRUCTING CHILDHOOD

THE CONSTRUCTION OF CHILDHOOD is an innately ambiguous process. Anne McGillivray has observed that childhood is 'a condition which varies according to social convenience and social conscience' (1992, 217). This tension results in a historically shifting concept of childhood which constructs the cultural as the natural. Here Ludmilla Jordanova makes a useful distinction.

Were these [constructions of childhood] in fact 'inventions' — that is, creations of the human mind — or were they 'discoveries' — that is, recognitions of a state existing outside the realm of ideas? If childhood and adolescence are inventions, then they may be understood in the same terms as other cultural products. If they are discoveries, 'the child' and 'the adolescent' become natural, timeless categories, waiting in the wings of history for just recognition. (1989, 10)

In the context of racism, Patricia Hill Collins identifies the social suppression of knowledge as the mechanism by which inequalities are invented and then portrayed as 'natural' and thus 'inevitable', justifying domination based on (invented) difference (1990, 5). In constructing the 'natural' child, the suppression of knowledge begins in infancy. We naturalize children — simultaneously inventing and discovering them as natural beings, based on shifting notions of what is natural — and we socialize children to conform to the natural by suppressing that which has been constructed as unnatural. This dualism embeds notions of the natural in such categories as age, sex, gender, class, ethnicity, and ability.

Through naturalization, Westerners have historically constructed children as innocent and malleable or evil and seductive (Shahar 1990). We idealize children as naturally asocial, asexual, apolitical, and ahistorical, all the while suffusing 'the natural' with cultural assumptions. The construction of the natural child is historically and culturally situated. We socialize children to conform to complex notions of the natural, use severe discipline if necessary to enforce conformity, and then classify children as naturally normal or abnormal. This is evidenced in the imposition of prescribed sex-gender roles.

Through socialization, which interacts with naturalization, children learn that diversities of age, sex, gender, class, culture, ethnicity, and ability embody differences of power and privilege. As Catharine MacKinnon put it, 'Difference is the velvet glove on the iron fist of domination' (1989, 219). The hegemonic claim that difference defines domination camouflages the co-implication that domination defines difference. Contemporary analyses of power and privilege routinely address sex-, race-, and class-based inequalities but the category of *age* — the natural-cultural age-ranges that define different phases of the life cycle — is often overlooked. Low age status typically renders children powerless and vulnerable to adult idiosyncrasies and systemic inequalities.

III. CONSTRUCTING CHILD ABUSE

TO RECOGNIZE THAT CHILD ABUSE is a social construct (Hacking 1991) is not to deny its existence. Specific forms of physical, emotional, verbal, and sexual abuse are recognized in particular times and places; extreme manifestations of child abuse include murder, torture, and incest. Child abuse is perpetrated by men *and* women against boys *and* girls, occurs across all class *and* cultural lines, and invokes relations of both power *and* powerlessness. The concept of a 'complex of abuses' recognizes that 'child abuse' does not fall into discrete categories (Martineau 1993). This analytic approach moves away from the culture of blame and shame, and emphasizes individual and collective responsibility for child abuse and for its prevention.

A brief account of the current understanding of child abuse includes the following: child abuse inflicts deliberate harm; it deprives children of potential; it perpetrates and perpetuates unresolved shock and trauma; and it is rooted, in Western parenting, in a 'poisonous pedagogy' (de Mause 1974, Hacking 1991, Hendrick 1994, Herman 1992, McGillivray 1992, Miller 1983, 1986). Child abuses affects both mind and body, irrespective of the dominant type of abuse. It is deeply sexed and gendered and takes different forms in different class and cultural contexts (Martineau 1993). When 'discipline' masks child abuse or when child abuse masquerades as discipline, a distinction between abuse and discipline may be made in terms of actions that are destructive and actions that are instructive. (The *instructive discipline* of participation in community projects is discussed below).

Perceiving child abuse purely as a social construction, as Hacking seems to do, is perilously one-sided and lacks a material analysis. Extending this to its logical conclusion, a constructionist could claim that child abuse does not 'really' exist. This perspective depends upon sustaining a polarization between essentialism and constructionism that privileges the latter. To disrupt this dualism, I draw on poststructuralism and Diana Fuss's deconstruction of the essence-construct binary in *Essentially Speaking* (1989). Fuss claims that oppositions are not only interactive but 'co-inherent' and illustrates how essentialism and constructionism (or anti-essentialism) are co-implicated. In other words, 'essentialism is *essential* to social constructionism' (1) and vice-versa. Our social constructions are based on what we identify as essential, and what we claim to be essential is socially constructed because we cannot separate the natural from the cultural. In this sense, the material and the structural co-inhere. Iris Marion Young's interpretation of Derrida's deconstructionism demonstrates that 'what a concept or category ... claims to exclude is implicated in it' (1990, 304). The essence of any (valid or useful) construction of child abuse is the real harm it causes. Although child abuse is identified differently in different contexts, 'abuse' by definition inflicts harm and trauma even if interlaced with love and care.

British childhood historian Harry Hendrick observes that abusive adults are ever-present — it is how we define and identify child abuse, in the context of public interest, that is subject to 'rediscovery' (1994, 242); Jordanova (*supra*) would call it 'reinvention'. Studies of the history of Western childhood bear this out: there has almost always been a line over which one ought not cross, yet the line is continually crossed and children brutalized in the name of love and morality (Pollock 1983, Shahar 1990). Cruelty to children in many periods of Western history has gone unquestioned or even unrecognized. This may be because 'care' and 'harm' are intimately intertwined and constructed dualisms of natural and unnatural, normal and abnormal, offer little guidance. Child abuse within families has been legitimized (and aggravated) by naturalizing patriarchal sex-gender roles and by normalizing domination based on differences of sex, age, size and ability. Child abuse or 'under-protection' is a marker of the absence of respect for children as political actors in the social world. ('Over-protection', a similar marker, is discussed below.)

Central to the reconstruction of child abuse is its recurrent appearance and disappearance. In his inquiry into four sensationalised child abuse cases which reached the law courts of Freud's Vienna in 1899, for example, Larry Wolff asks why child abuse emerges periodically, only to be buried again. He concludes that when the Viennese were confronted with child abuse, it was perceived as at once too horrible and too familiar. Abuses of children were 'excessive variations on the accepted patterns of nineteenth-century parental discipline' (1988, 193). If child abuse was too familiar, it had to be denied; if it was too horrible, someone else had to be blamed: *it could not be us*.

Child abuse is on the political agenda today because its identification as a social problem occurred in a receptive social environment (Nelson 1984, 5). This 'receptive environment' was found in a rapidly-growing middle class which upheld liberal ideals of freedom, equality, and natural rights (6-7). Victorian ideologies of childhood as a safe and sheltered time of life and the bourgeois family as a haven in a heartless world provided the 'cultural backdrop' needed to construct child abuse as a social problem (5). Public recognition of physical abuse emerged out of the 'battered child syndrome' identified by United States radiologists in the 1940s and 1950s (Hendrick 1994, 243), while feminists have called attention to the sexual abuse of female children in the 1970s and 1980s.

Modern concepts of childhood and child abuse are framed by compulsory education and prolonged childhood which co-inhere with the needs of industrialization (Nelson 1984). Hendrick places these constructs in a historical context.

The introduction and gradual consolidation of compulsory schooling confirmed the trend towards the creation of the child as a distinctive being characterised by ignorance, incapacity and innocence. This understanding of the 'nature' of childhood was then subjected to scientific scrutiny and elaborated upon through further description and explanation ... Consequently, reformers also knew what they expected of children in terms of behaviour, performance and development. These expectations, and the apprehensions on which they were based, would be broadened and deepened well into the twentieth century, but many of the fundamental stereotypes were in place around the early 1900s, and they were derived almost entirely from middle-class patriarchal and domestic ideals ... [and] would figure prominently in the construction of relevant social policies ... (1994, 37)

Hendrick is talking about England. English educational and social welfare systems were imported to Canada. The 'building of the educational state' (Curtis 1988) on the English model had an enormous impact on Canadian children. The early educational state constructed itself as moral guardian of Canadian society, but its essence was an immoral imposition of morality through the corporal punishment and emotional humiliation, especially of working class and immigrant children (Curtis 1988). Hidden in compulsory education's promise of equality was the continuation of gender, class and cultural inequality (12-15). That social control was the aim of education is apparent in the symbolic power and symbolic violence of the educational state's 'instruments of knowledge' which impose (or suppress) expressions of social reality (Harker 1990, 94-5).[2] These symbols both mirror and manifest the links between power and violence.

IV. CONSTRUCTING CHILD LABOUR

THE CONSTRUCTION OF THE EDUCATIONAL STATE in Canada, as elsewhere, thrust working-class children into the turbulent shift from an agricultural to an industrial economy, forcing them from farm to factory to school. In the context of the educational mandate of social control as moral development, '[s]tate schooling became a place for the systematic administration and reproduction of "childhood", and of the social institutions needed to sustain it, like the "family"' (Curtis 1988, 16-7). This shift prolonged middle-class childhood and motherhood, infantilising women and trivializing the social, including labour, contributions of children. At the same time, working-class children were exploited for economic gain. Although most Canadians cringe at the mention of 'child labour' because of atrocities committed during early industrialization (Parr 1982), and because of past and present atrocities in developing countries, it must be recognized that child labour has a varied history.

In today's Western world we assume that adults work and children play. But, as Thorne observes, young children do not experience a play-work dichotomy: children 'work while playing and play while working' (1987, 100). Children work at home, at school, and in the marketplace. Like the valuable social dimensions of earlier apprenticeship systems, the curricular and extracurricular activities of children are designed to turn them into contributing members of society. Children work in hunting and gathering, fishing and agricultural, and industrial and technological societies, although their contributions are not equally recognized in these different cultural contexts.

In some contexts, child labour is condemnable; in others, it is not. For example, industrial labour might brutally disrupt agricultural family life and plunge children into an environment of what can only be called torture and neglect, as it did in England, France, and Canada (Heywood 1988, Bradbury 1982). Or industrialization might conceivably bring children in from the isolation of the fields, pay them wages for their labours, allow them to work alongside other family members in a (protective) factory environment, and provide them with skills that would benefit them throughout life, as was apparently the case in Norway (Schrumpf 1993). Norwegian scholar Ellen Schrumpf describes the former account as the 'misery version' of child labour, a moral tale that views the past as primitive and the present as the culmination of 'constant progress' (222).[3] I suggest that the misery version was more than a moral tale: it carried dire material consequences for children. But Schrumpf's analysis brings into question the condemnation of *all* forms of child labour.

We do not object when 10-year-olds have paper routes, work as beta-testers, go to college, or run for city council. Nor do we usually object when children perform in theatre, film, television, or advertising commercials while attending school. We presume responsible supervision, even though many child actors have grown up to tell stories of drug abuse and disillusionment.[4] Precocious and productive children are celebrated in the media. Nevertheless, when we ban exploitative child labour, we often fail to acknowledge children's work. Jordanova recovers and revalues children's work when she counts school attendance as unpaid labour.

When we state that children no longer 'work' we mean that they no longer endure long hours of labour daily, under the control of an employer, for which they may or may not have received wages. Yet children are not now free to do as they please, and, although they do not receive payment for attending school, it certainly counts as 'work' ... (1989, 19)

Brit Berggreen identifies two ways in which children have been treated in Norway: in the first, they are integrated into the social and economic world of adults; in the second, they are segregated in nurseries and schools where certain issues and topics are censored (1988, 832-3).

These models can be generalized to other Western societies. Simply stated, the integration model is under-protective and the segregation model is over-protective. Under-protected children are 'little adults', children without childhoods who are confronted with inappropriate experiences and responsibilities.[5] Over-protected children are coddled and separated from adult cultures and occupational spheres. According to Berggreen, over-protected children are perceived as innocent and childish, reinforcing the notion that children are socially ignorant and culturally incompetent. In Taiwan, such children are said to suffer from 'greenhouse syndrome' because they do not mature to cope well with adult responsibilities.[6] We can conclude that children should no more be treated like pampered pets than they should be abused or neglected or exploited.

The extreme states of integration and segregation — under-protection and over-protection — are common sites of child abuse and neglect. Thorne observes that well-intentioned but romanticized ideologies of childhood 'mask the harsh realities of children's subordination: placing children on the pedestal of sentimentality helps obscure the ways in which adults abuse and exploit them, and government policies contribute to their growing impoverishment' (1987, 98). Replacing under-protection with over-protection subverts the possibility of respecting and revisioning children. The United Nations *Convention on the Rights of the Child* counters the conditions of under-protection with an idealization of nuclear family harmony and happiness

(Preamble, United Nations 1991), which posits over-protection. But the Convention also promotes the *child's right to be heard*, thus pointing toward a praxis of inclusion.

V. CONSTRUCTING CHILDREN'S RIGHTS

THE UNITED NATIONS *Convention on the Rights of the Child* was conceived in 1979, the International Year of the Child, negotiated over a period of ten years, unanimously adopted by the General Assembly of the United Nations in 1989, and ratified by Canada in 1991 (Lewis 1994; United Nations 1991). Responsibility for implementation is shared by Canada's federal, provincial, and territorial governments. In the province of British Columbia, the Convention is being incorporated into the *School Act*, the *Adoption Act*, the *Corrections Act*, the new *Child, Family, and Community Service Act* (Human Rights 1994, i, 65-70), and the revised *Child, Youth, and Family Advocacy Act*, among others. The Convention also informs the influential British Columbia Ombudsman's Public Report on *Fair Schools: Respect, Listening, Advocacy, Participation, Inclusion* (1995) and the *Report of the Gove Inquiry into Child Protection in British Columbia* (1995). The Society for Children and Youth of British Columbia (SCYBC) has initiated a Rights Awareness Project (RAP), funded to promote the Convention and monitor compliance with its provisions.[7]

Almost every Article in the Convention explicitly or implicitly addresses some form of what is today constructed as child abuse or neglect. We need to be cautious that the Convention is neither perceived nor promoted as a panacea for children's problems or as a license to reinforce the *status quo*. The Convention fails to address systemic poverty and privileges Western ideologies through its advocacy of 'modern teaching methods' for non-Western countries (Articles 27 and 28, United Nations 1991). The Convention needs to be problematised as a reconstruction of imperialism and colonialism, as a document which may serve the interests of global capitalism even as it promotes the rights of children.

Efforts by front-line workers daily faced with family poverty and child abuse to apply the provisions of the Convention in a community are confronted or countermanded by multi-cultural conflict, parental resistance,[8] and right-wing backlash against even the idea of children's rights (McGovern

1994). The 'religious right' in Canada fears that the Convention means that children do not have to obey their parents — for example, orders to turn off the television — or that children can now consent to sex with paedophiles (McGovern, 26-7), criminal laws notwithstanding![9] Extremes aside, for most social workers the Convention promises welcome solutions to social problems but, for many parents, the Convention represents and reinforces unwelcome intrusions into private family life. Nevertheless, the Convention stands as a powerful symbol of a new perception of childhood. It invites a reconstruction of childhood which recognizes children's needs and children's capacities.

Interpretating and applying the Convention in diverse cultural contexts is, however, problematic. Interrogating the Convention from this perspective is beyond the scope of this essay. Here I address the question of accountability, the apparent granting of children's rights without responsibilities. This is a problem of interpretation rather than substance. Responsibility is implicit in the concept of rights (McGillivray 1994). This concept needs to be explicit in teaching children's rights to children.

Thorne points out that 'children tend to be constructed as "the other"' (1987, 91), as opposite and inferior to adults. This hierarchy reifies the 'autonomy' of adults and the 'dependency' of children which, in the context of children's rights, is incoherent. It is not surprising that the Convention embodies a dualism between children and adults but it consequently reifies a polarity between rights and responsibilities. For psychologist Roger Hart,

The Convention, being more concerned with protection, does not emphasize the responsibilities which go along with rights. Children need to learn that with the rights of citizenship come responsibilities. In order to learn these responsibilities children need to engage in collaborative activities with other persons including those who are older and more experienced than themselves. It is for this reason that children's participation in community projects is so important. (1992, 7)

The Convention grants children age-appropriate rights and protections but does not address age-appropriate responsibilities for the consequences of actions, choices, and decisions exercised as rights. While Convention provisions are being incorporated into social programs and child protection legislation in the province of British Columbia, social inequalities remain largely unexamined. Which children most need to know their rights? Teaching rights-consciousness to children living in violent, impoverished, authoritarian, or over-protective family — families not likely to be receptive to children's rights-consciousness — seems ineffective. Rights that a child can only access after being apprehended by social services highlights a serious problem of access to rights and remedies provided for in the Convention. The rhetoric of children's rights fails to challenge such systemic inequalities.

To clarify the context of the argument for respecting and revisioning children, it is useful to distinguish between *natural rights* and *cultural rights* while recognizing their co-inherence. All children have natural rights —to food, clothing, shelter, emotional care — and the rights and entitlements of any human being. Cultural rights represent a continuing negotiation of age-appropriate rights attached to age-appropriate responsibilities which vary according to culture and historical situation. Cultural rights and responsibilities are interrelated and reflect cultural diversity. Children's responsibilities in Canada at present might include being honest, playing safely, trying their best at school, respecting the rights of others, and so on (Rights Awareness Project 1995). More mature responsibilities might include taking responsibility for the consequences of one's actions and making reparation, financial or otherwise, for injury and damage caused to others.

Carol Gilligan has shown that rights and responsibilities are complementary. If we use Fuss's model, we see that they are also co-implicated: rights attend to sameness, equality, and an ethics of justice; responsibilities attend to difference, equity, and an ethics of care (Gilligan 1982). A children's rights framework which idealizes over-protection as a corrective to under-protection (as does the Convention, on its face) does not ultimately respect or revision children. By making responsibilities integral to the negotiation of cultural rights, over-protected children would become less segregated from adult society.

From an educational perspective, the 'talk' of rights and the 'walk' of responsibilities go hand-in-hand.[10] If we do not attach responsibilities to cultural rights, we invite children to make increasing, and perhaps increasingly hostile, demands upon the state and to engage in adversarial relations and retaliations through the legal system. I have met parents who embed cultural rights in developing children's autonomy, responsibility, family contribution, and community participation, fostering mutual respect between their children and adults. I have witnessed the introduction by middle-class social services personnel of the concept of children's rights to disadvantaged youth in state care. These youth (perhaps understandably) totalized 'rights' as a license to make extreme economic demands upon those in positions of authority. There were no principles taught, or mechanisms in place, for addressing personal responsibility or community participation in relation to this 'talk' of rights. Conversely, there are now several youth groups working closely with government and non-government agencies, thereby incorporating community participation with the right to be heard. These scenarios are pedagogically complex.

We cannot assume that legislating rights for children will eliminate abuse, nor can we 'add children and stir' as the corrective to systemic inequity and economic inequality. We need to ask questions about teaching rights and accessing rights. Which children might abuse rights-claims through need or manipulation or misunderstanding? Which children might be abused and humiliated for demanding their rights? Which children will have access to rights and which will not? Children do not live lives which are ahistorical, acultural, apolitical. Children live, work, play, and learn within social structures in Western and non-Western cultures which reinforce inequality and trivialize children.

In promoting children's rights, and in promoting respect for children and their abilities, the participation of children in family and community projects must be addressed. How can cultural rights separated from a meaningful concept of responsibility nurture children's capacity to act in the larger world? Where is the appropriate compromise between under-protection and over-protection? Corporal punishment, for example, is properly condemned as a disciplinary measure but it has yet to be widely replaced with discipline in its true sense of inculcating responsibility.[11] New understandings of discipline are required. How can children become contributing members of society, responsible rights-bearers, if they are neither engaged in instructive forms of self-discipline nor respected and revisioned as participating members of their families and communities?

VI.   CHILDREN'S PARTICIPATION

CHILDREN'S PARTICIPATION IN COMMUNITY PROJECTS and policy-making processes is not a new concept. Examples can be drawn from the traditions of precolonial indigenous cultures in the Americas and elsewhere.[12] Such participation is new, however, in the contemporary Canadian context. The United Nations *Convention on the Rights of the Child*, the *Gove Report on Child Protection in British Columbia*, and the Ombudsman's *Report on Fair*

Schools all point toward the desirability of children's participation in public arenas. The Society for Children and Youth of British Columbia, and its Rights Awareness Project, advocate and practice child participation. Such participation could be valued as children's work.[13]

Integral to respecting the child's right to be heard is the fostering of children's participation in the development and implementation of policies and projects which affect children. A continuum of participation — a guide to what children's participation in community affairs might be — is seen in the table below.

CONTINUUM OF CHILDREN'S PARTICIPATION

NON-PARTICIPATION			DEGREES OF PARTICIPATION				
1	2	3	4	5	6	7	8
manip-ulation	decor-ation	token-ism	assigned but informed	children consulted and informed	adult-initiated, decisions shared with children	child-initiated and directed, adult super-vision	child-initiated, shared decision making with adults

Source: Adapted from Roger Hart's vertical 'Ladder of Participation' (1992, 9).

At the first level, children are exploited to support adult 'childhood' causes, without understanding the issues, while the adults pretend the 'causes' are inspired by children. At the second level, children are used to bolster a cause in an indirect and ornamental way, although the adults involved do not pretend that the cause is inspired by children. At the third level, children are given a 'voice' but little or no choice about the subject or style of communicating and little or no opportunity to formulate their opinions (Society 1995, 3).

Genuine participation does not begin until the fourth level, when children are assigned to projects and informed of their roles. At the fifth level, children act as consultants to projects designed and run by adults and are informed of the outcomes of decisions made by adults. At the sixth level, projects are initiated by adults and decision-making is shared with children. These increased levels of participation employ the principle of instructive discipline. At the seventh level, projects are initiated and directed by children under the supervision of adults. At the highest level of participation, projects are initiated by children and decision-making is shared with adults (Society 1995, 3). Hart points out that children need not always operate at the highest levels.

Different children at different times might prefer to perform with varying degrees of involvement or responsibility. ... [P]rogrammes should be designed which maximize the opportunity for any child to choose to participate at the highest level of his [or her] ability' (1992, 12).

Teaching children the relationship between rights and responsibilities has long-term implications for age-appropriate participation in community projects. Recognizing children's rights means looking through the lenses of the politics of childhood and the cultures of children. It means constructing cultural rights in a context of community participation, shared power, and mutual respect in adult-child relations. It means that children must be given a real voice in claiming rights and resolving systemic inequities. It means that children have not only a right to expression but a right to be heard and, ultimately, a right to be recognized as contributing members of society.

Linking cultural rights with responsibility and participation is not explicated in the Convention. There are tensions between rights ideology and praxis in the hierarchical and exclusionary social structures in which children live. Bare talk of rights reflects a 'blue-box' recycling mentality where a change at the consumer level makes it appear that a much larger problem is being solved, when little has in fact changed.[14] For Foucault, 'a way of teaching and *saying* [is] a way of learning and *seeing*' (1975, 64). Thus, children's natural and cultural rights will be perceived precisely as they are constructed through discourse (Foucault, 1990). This discourse, to have the meaning and effect presumably intended by the drafters of the Convention, requires the participation and voice of children.

VII. RESPECTING AND REVISIONING CHILDREN

THE POLITICS OF CHILDHOOD recognizes the capacity of children to act in the social world. In constructions of childhood, we see that essentialism informs constructionism — perceptions of the natural are essential to constructions of the cultural — and that social convenience does indeed permeate social conscience. We see the co-inherence of care and harm and understand that a material essence of real harm underlies our shifting constructions of child care and child abuse.

Re-evaluating child labour as children's work means noticing that children's work and play are interactive and acknowledging that children can be involved in adult society in a dynamic balance between extremes of under- and over-protection. As children need to become more involved in the adult world, so adults need to become more involved in the child's world. The construction of cultural rights must intersect with age-appropriate responsibilities in order to respect and revision children and provide opportunities for public participation which recognize children as political actors in the larger society.

Not elaborated in this essay, but integral to the concerns raised, is the primacy of children's safety and of children's recreation as a natural right (SCYBC). If there is such a right, for example, as freedom of expression, this needs to be further explored in the context of the philosophy outlined here. We need to learn and to teach how to express productive anger and appropriate aggression (Rich 1976, Gould 1981); to avoid polarizing nurturing as natural to females and aggression as natural to males (Ashe and Cahn 1994); to acknowledge the joy *and* the rage of child rearing (Pollock 1983, Thorne 1987); and to realize the powerful roles both women and men play in gender socialization. We need to shift from ideologies of isolated and possessive parenting to family, community, and workplace networks which accommodate child care. 'Mothering' needs to be rethought as child rearing in which men and women participate, enriching men's experiences in private life and enhancing women's experiences in public life (French 1985, 533). Marilyn French posits that sex-gender dualism represents 'not an expression of natural differences between the sexes but a suppression of natural similarities' (533-34).[15] Recalling the co-implication of difference and domination, we need to remain cognizant of similarities and differences in a parallel age-analysis of expressions and suppressions in power relations between children and adults.

We need to pursue flexible working arrangements, through work hours, job-sharing, home-based work stations, and workplace daycare facilities, allowing adults to interact with children in a variety of contexts. We need co-operative work/ study programs for children. We need to confront the facts of child abuse and neglect, not at the margins of society, but at the core of our culture. We need to understand that the ideal of children's natural rights in a class society is contra-indicted by government cutbacks to social services, and how to make the point that this is a central disjunction of a 'family values' social agenda. These cutbacks are occurring despite Canada's ratification of the *Convention on the Rights of the Child* and in the face of *Campaign 2000* (Popham 1994), the 1989 House of Commons resolution to end child poverty in Canada by the year 2000 (Canadian 1995). We need to confront that about our construction and governance of childhood which is both too horrible and too familiar.

One way to see ourselves is to look to other cultures. The African proverb that 'it takes a whole village to raise one child' retains its challenge to Western child rearing structures.[16] In pre-colonial African villages, children had many mothers and were taught to 'tell everyone' if anybody tried to hurt them (Ubochi 1990).[17] In some urban African-American (and Canadian Black) communities today, children have both 'bloodmothers and othermothers' (Collins 1990, 119). Children in traditional Inuit societies had a strong sense of belonging with, participating in, and contributing to, the whole tribe when life was 'lived in the bush' (Wadden 1991); this sense is not lost even where economies have changed. Aboriginal healing circles in Canada bring abused and abusers together through a praxis of individual and collective responsibility (Fontaine 1991).[18] In such precolonial South American Indian tribes as the Bari of Columbia, children had a voice in consensus decision-making on issues directly affecting them, such as relocation of the household. Reaching unanimous agreement reflected Bari principles of mutual respect, shared power, and individual autonomy nurtured by communal parenting (Buenaventura-Passo and Brown 1980). A common theme of children's lives in indigenous and peasant societies was 'learning by living' (Heywood 1988).

What might it mean to adapt the best of collective practices and indigenous philosophies to dominant Canadian, North American, and Western European contexts? If this is what the praxis of children's rights suggests, how does cross-acculturation resonate with the monoculturalism seemingly inscribed in the *Convention on the Rights of the Child*? In our present construction of childhood, child abuse, children's work, and children's rights, we are well-advised to consider Thorne's compelling insight that

experiences of children may be illuminated by, and in turn may challenge, our frameworks for understanding not only families and schools but also politics, work, poverty, social class, organizations, bureaucracy, urban life, social stratification, and social change (1987, 99).

Children's rights challenge our understanding of macro-social structures. Thorne draws on the politics of childhood and the cultures of children to provides a manifesto for respecting and revisioning children.

In this exploratory essay, I have proposed a praxis of inclusion. This entails rethinking perceptions of childhood. Responsibility is central in constructing children's cultural rights and inseparable from advocating children's participation in society. Combining these concepts into a rights-complex requires analysis of the ethics, equity, efficiency, and operating principles of a *gestalt* of children's equality. Constituting a children's rights-complex is intimately connected with how we live and how we constitute ourselves as a society.

From a poststructural perspective, there is much to be done in recognizing children's rights in a multicultural context. Developing policies and strategies around a rights-complex model which acknowledges the politics of class and cultural diversity as it advocates responsibility and participation is a central issue. Professional mentorship programs can be structured as inclusionary practices involving children, families and communities. Participation can be fostered by curriculum changes in the education system which allow children to earn credit by collaborating in community projects. Children's work can contribute to rebuilding community infrastructures through apprenticeship-participation programs in the 'third sector' of volunteerism (Rifkin 1995). Most important, children can be included in projects in which their interests and the interests of their communities are involved. The praxis of children's rights advocated here may not prevent child abuse or the exploitation of child labour. Such a praxis can, however, facilitate children's agency by nurturing their present capacities as political actors and thus cultivate their potential as future contributors to society.

Notes

*   I would like to thank Anne McGillivray for her helpful comments and generous editorial assistance.

1. References to 'children' in this essay include youth. The category 'children' refers to three approximated age groups: first, infancy to the age of reason (children to the age of seven, 'infants, toddlers, and children'); second, the age of reason to puberty (eight-12, 'children and juveniles'); and third, puberty to maturity (13-18, 'adolescents and young adults'), leaving the definition of 'maturity' open to interpretation. This reflects the literature on the history of childhood in the West rather than the 'age grades' of developmental psychology.

2. Harker draws on Pierre Bourdieu and Jean Claude Passeron, *Reproduction in Education, Society, and Culture* (Sage, 1977).

3. Although Schrumpf identifies significant differences in time, in that Norway was industrialized between 1850 and 1910, after England, France, and Canada, she does not view Norway as a different case. If difference in time accounts for the Norway experience, then the 'misery version' cannot be dismissed as a Progressive Era perspective. It must be seen as an accurate description of sociospecific conditions of early industrialization. It is conceivable that there were always children who preferred working in the factory to attending school. In any event, the Norwegian perspective offers possibilities for respecting and revisioning children.

4. A contemporary example is child star Macaulay Culkin, emotionally and educationally neglected in the midst of economic excess. His movie career has earned him $50 million and Culkin is the object of his parents' bitter divorce and child custody battle. Judy Bachrach, 'A Star is Torn' in *Vanity Fair Magazine* (February 1996): 54-68. Some former child actors have straightened themselves out with therapy and drug rehabilitation and now mentor the new generation of child actors.

5. Studies on children's 'risk and resiliency', coming out of developmental psychology and 'adolescent psychopathology', address the plight of the 'distressed child' (for example, see Luthar and Zigler, 'Vulnerability and Competence: A Review of Research on Resilience in Childhood', 1991). Children living under distress — poor health or disability; child abuse or neglect; recent immigrant or refugee status aggravated by poverty and discrimination; or conditions of war, crime, pornography, or prostitution, to name a few — become little adults, children without childhoods.

6. A Taiwanese friend introduced me to this useful concept.

7. RAP is funded by the Vancouver Foundation, the Law Foundation of British Columbia., and the Federal Department of Canadian Heritage. The committee addresses three areas: child abuse and neglect, children's play and recreation,

and juvenile justice. RAP is 'pioneering' the Convention in British Columbia by disseminating information to city, school, social service, and other child service agencies through the provision of presentation materials and comprehensive information kits. The Legal Research/ Education Advisory Group, a RAP sub-committee, is mandated to identify provincial policies not in compliance with the Convention. Currently in the planning stages is the involvement of local and regional youth groups in community education on the Convention.

8. Reported by family counsellors at a RAP conference in January 1996.

9. Foucault argues for 'consensual incest', an 'inconsequential pleasure', in *The History of Sexuality, Volume I: An Introduction* (1990). See Vikki Bell's *Interrogating Incest: Feminism, Foucault and the Law* (1993). While it is difficult to agree that a child could consent to incestuous relations with an adult, we can imagine that some sibling incest, for example, might be construed as consensual. Equally problematic is Bell's reification of 'Father-Daughter' incest, restricting incest to heterosexual intercourse between adult men and young girls and ignoring multiple forms of incest. See my Review of *Interrogating Incest* (1996) 11 Canadian Journal of Law and Society 1.

10. From the saying, 'You can talk that talk, but can you walk that walk?'. This does not deny the child's entitlement to rights, natural or otherwise, but rights do not ensure equality. In Canada, 42 per cent of young families — in which the oldest member is below the age of 30 — live in poverty (Statistics Canada, 1995). Deeply entrenched inequities and inequalities mean that at least 1.3 million children, if not considerably more, live in poverty. The poverty level is set by the Bank of Canada.

11. Corporal punishment was theoretically 'abolished' in Canadian schools in the nineteenth century but, if so, it remained 'indispensable' (Curtis 1988). Such violence was 'inherent to the system of public education'. Increasing regulation of corporal punishment suggests that it must have been regularly used or threatened (330-31). In a rigid environment of moral discipline, the supposed elimination of corporal punishment did not eliminate the humiliation of children in the name of pedagogy. The British Columbia Education Act permitted corporal punishment in the public schools until 1972, to be used as a 'last resort'; the province has now abolished it. Proposed abolition of the Canadian Criminal Code disciplinary excuse to assault has generated strong backlash. See generally John E.B. Myers, ed., *The Backlash: Child Protection Under Fire* (1994); see also the author's interviews with social workers on the abolition backlash in British Columbia (1995), on file with the author. The ancient agrarian admonition 'He who spares the rod hates his son, but he who loves him

disciplines him promptly' (Proverbs 13:24) cited by right-wing groups to justify corporal punishment is better read as a reference to the metaphor of the shepherd's staff as the rod of wisdom and guidance.

12.   See e.g. Paula Gunn Allen, *The Sacred Hoop: Recovering the Feminine in American Indian Traditions* (1986); Mona Etienne and Eleanor Leacock, eds., *Women and Colonization: Anthropological Perspectives* (1980); Geoffrey York, *The Dispossessed: Life and Death in Native Canada*, (1989); Marie Wadden, *Nitassinan: The Innu Struggle to Reclaim Their Homeland*, (1991). The issue is whether indigenous practices can be adapted to urban societies. The indigenous model of inclusion has at least two dimensions. First, those affected by particular decisions are included in the decision-making processes. Second, children and adults work interdependently as a means of transmitting skills, culture, and knowledge. These practices require a philosophy of mutual respect and shared power that transcends what the dominant culture experiences as a 'generation gap'.

13.   For example, a young advocacy consultant in Vancouver is promoting youth involvement and the *employment* of youth as active participants on community boards.

14.   People are willing to believe environmental problems will be solved if everyone takes a (blue) plastic box of bottles out to the corner every week for collection: as long as you recycle, you need not be concerned with the larger issues. Karl Marx might have viewed blue-boxing as a modern-day 'opiate of the people'.

15.   French cites Gayle Rubin's classic essay on the sex-gender system, 'The Traffic in Women: Notes on the "Political Economy" of Sex' in *Toward an Anthropology of Women*, Ed. Rayna Rapp Reiter (1975, 180).

16.   Hillary Rodham Clinton's anecdotal work *It Takes a Village: And Other Lessons Children Teach Us* (1996) takes the proverb as its *motif*. Rodham Clinton discusses her years of legal representation of children's issues and tells stories of people helping children in their communities. On Oprah Winfrey's 'Child Alert', Rodham Clinton said, 'Every individual and every institution has a role to play in society. ... Everyone can do something for a child' (22 January, 1996).

17.   Brigitte Ubochi is an American-educated African woman who grew up in a remote African village where life was relatively little-affected by colonialism.

18.   Grand Chief Phil Fontaine, Manitoba Assembly of First Nations, took part in a community healing circle as both abuser and abused. His public admission of his sexual victimization as a child opened the door for Aboriginal men to seek healing.

References

Allen, Paula Gunn (1986), *The Sacred Hoop: Recovering the Feminine in American Indian Traditions* (Beacon Press).

Ashe, Marie, and Naomi R. Cahn, (1994) 'Child Abuse: A Problem for Feminist Theory' in *The Public Nature of Private Violence: The Discovery of Domestic Abuse*, eds. Martha Albertson Fineman and Roxanne Mykitiuk (Routledge) 166-94.

Bell, Vikki (1993), *Interrogating Incest: Feminism, Foucault and the Law* (Routledge).

Berggreen, Brit (1988), 'Infantilization of Children As an Historical Process' in *Growing Into a Modern World: An International Interdisciplinary Conference on the Life and Development of Children in Modern Society*, eds. Karin Ekberg and Per Egil Mjaavatn (The Norwegian Centre for Child Research)Vol. 1, 829-42.

Bourdieu, Pierre and Jean Claude Passeron (1977), *Reproduction in Education, Society, and Culture* (Sage).

Buenaventura-Passo, Elisa and Susan E. Brown (1980), 'Forced Transition From Egalitarian to Male Dominance: The Bari of Columbia' in *Woman and Colonization:* Canadian Social Welfare Policy. Annual Conference. University of British Columbia, June 1995.

Anthropological Perspectives, eds. Mona Etienne and Eleanor Leacock (J.F. Bergin) 109-33.

Clinton, Hillary Rodham. Oprah Winfrey. 'Child Alert'. *The Oprah Winfrey Show*. Harpo Productions, Inc. BCTV, Vancouver, B.C., 22 January, 1996.

Clinton, Hillary Rodham (1996), *It Takes a Village: And Other Lessons Children Teach Us* (Simon & Schuster).

Collins, Patricia Hill (1990), *Black Feminist Thought: Knowledge, Consciousness, and the Politics of Empowerment* (Routledge).

Curtis, Bruce (1988), *Building the Educational State: Canada West, 1836- 1871* (Althouse Press).

de Mause, Lloyd (1974), 'The Evolution of Childhood' in *The History of Childhood*, ed. Lloyd de Mause (Harper & Row) 1-73.

Etienne, Mona and Eleanor Leacock, eds. (1980), *Women and Colonization: Anthropological Perspectives* (J.F. Bergin).

Fontaine, Phil, Grand Chief, Assembly of Manitoba Chiefs (1991), 'Perspectives on Native Family Violence'. Inaugural Lecture, Conference on Native Health, University of Toronto, 22 October 1991.

Foucault, Michel (1975), *The Birth of the Clinic: An Archaeology of Medical Perception*, trans. A.M. Sheridan Smith (Random House).

_____. (1990), *The History of Sexuality, Volume I: An Introduction*, trans. Robert Hurley (Vintage Books).

French, Marilyn (1985), *Beyond Power: On Women, Men, and Morals* (Ballantine Books).

Fuss, Diana (1989), *Essentially Speaking: Feminism, Nature & Difference* (Routledge).

Gilligan, Carol (1982), *In a Different Voice: Psychological Theory and Women's Development* (Harvard University Press).

Gould, Stephen Jay (1981), *The Mismeasure of Man* (Norton).

Gove, Thomas J. (1995), *Report of the Gove Inquiry Into Child Protection in British Columbia: Matthew's Story (Vol. 1), Matthew's Legacy (Vol. 2), Executive Summary* (Gove Inquiry into Child Protection).

Hacking, Ian (1991), 'The Making and Molding of Child Abuse' 17 Critical Enquiry 253.

Harker, R.K. (1990), 'Bourdieu — Education and Reproduction' in *An Introduction to the Work of Pierre Bourdieu*, eds. R.K. Harker, C. Mahar, and C. Wilkes (MacMillan) 86-108.

Hart, Roger A. (1992), *Children's Participation: From Tokenism to Citizenship* (UNICEF International Child Development Centre).

Hendrick, Harry (1994), *Child Welfare: England 1872-1989* (Routledge).

Herman, Judith Lewis (1992) *Trauma and Recovery* (Basic Books).

Heywood, Colin (1988), *Childhood in Nineteenth-Century France: Work, Health and Education Among the 'Classes Populaires'* (Cambridge University Press).

Human Rights Directorate (1994), *Convention on the Rights of the Child: First Report of Canada* (Department of Canadian Heritage).

Jordanova, Ludmilla (1989), 'Children in History: Concepts of Nature and Society' in *Children, Parents and Politics*, ed. Geoffry Scarre (Cambridge University Press) 3-24.

Judy Bachrach (1996) 'A Star is Torn' in *Vanity Fair Magazine* (February) 54-68.

Lewis, Stephen (1994), 'Reflections' Speech given at Parks and Recreation Conference, Vancouver, B.C., 6 May 1994.

Luthar, Suniya S. and Edward Zigler (1991), 'Vulnerability and Competence: A Review of Research on Resilience in Childhood' 61 American Journal of Orthopsychiatry 6.

MacKinnon, Catharine (1989) 'Sex Equality: On Difference and Domination' in *Toward a Feminist Theory of the State* (Harvard University Press) 215-34.

Martineau, Sheila (1996), 'Review of *Interrogating Incest: Feminism, Foucault and the Law*' 11 Canadian Journal of Law and Society (in press).

_____ (1993), 'Mainstream Madness: Child Abuse As Gender Socialization in the Middle Class' (unpublished).

McGillivray, Anne (1992), 'Reconstructing Child Abuse: Western Definition and Non-Western Experience' in *The Ideologies of Children's Rights*, eds. Michael Freeman and Philip Veerman (Martinus Nijhoff) 213-36.

_____(1994), 'Why Children Do Have Legal Rights: In Reply to Laura Purdy' 2 International Journal of Children's Rights 243.

McGovern, Celeste (1994), 'Social Engineers Get a New Tool: Ottawa Turns to a U.N. Treaty to Promote Greater State Control of Families' 8 August *British Columbia Report* 26-9.

Miller, Alice (1983), *For Your Own Good: Hidden Cruelty in Child-Rearing and the Roots of Violence*, trans. Hildegarde and Hunter Hannum (Farrar, Straus, Giroux).

_____ (1986), *Thou Shalt Not Be Aware: Society's Betrayal of the Child*, trans. Hildegarde and Hunter Hannum (Meridian).

Myers, John E.B., ed. (1994), *The Backlash: Child Protection Under Fire* (Sage).

Nelson, Barbara J. (1984), 'Child Abuse As a Social Problem' in *Making an Issue of Child Abuse: Political Agenda Setting For Social Problems* (University of Chicago Press) 1-19.

Ombudsman, Office of the (1995), *Fair Schools: Respect, Listening, Advocacy, Participation, Inclusion* (Province of British Columbia).

Parr, Joy (1980), *Labouring Children: British Immigrant Apprentices to Canada, 1869-1924* (McGill-Queen's University Press).

Pollock, Linda A. (1983), *Forgotten Children: Parent-Child Relations from 1500 to 1900* (Cambridge University Press).

Popham, Rosemarie (1994), *Investing in the Next Generation: Policy Perspectives on Children and Nationhood* (Child Poverty Action Group).

Rich, Adrienne (1976), *Of Woman Born: Motherhood As Experience and As Institution* (Norton).

Rights Awareness Project (RAP). Committee for Monitoring the United Nations *Convention on the Rights of the Child*. Society for Children and Youth of British Columbia. 1994-96.

Rubin, Gayle (1975), 'The Traffic in Women: Notes on the "Political Economy" of Sex' in *Toward an Anthropology of Women*, ed. Rayna Rapp Reiter (Monthly Review Press) 157-210.

Schrumpf, Ellen (1993), 'Attitudes Towards Child Work in Industry: An Argument Against the History of Misery' 2 Norwegian Journal of History 220.

Shahar, Shulamith (1990), *Childhood in the Middle Ages* (Routledge).

Society for Children and Youth of B.C. (1995), *The Right to be Heard: Convention on the Rights of the Child Newsletter*, Series 4 (Rights Awareness Project).

Sutherland, Neil (1996), *Growing Up: Childhood in English Canada From the Great War to the Age of Television* (in press).

Thorne, Barrie (1987), 'Re-Visioning Women and Social Change: Where Are the Children?' 1 Gender & Society 85.

Ubochi, Brigitte (1990), 'Introduction to Women's Studies' (unpublished).

United Nations (1991), *Convention on the Rights of the Child* (Department of Multiculturalism and Citizenship Canada).

Wadden, Marie (1991). *Nitassinan: The Innu Struggle to Reclaim Their Homeland* (Douglas & McIntyre).

Wolff, Larry (1988), *Postcards From the End of the World: Child Abuse in Freud's Vienna* (Atheneum).

York, Geoffrey (1989), *The Dispossessed: Life and Death in Native Canada* (Lester & Orpen Dennys).

Young, Iris Marion (1990), 'The Ideal of Community and the Politics of Difference' in *Feminism/Postmodernism*, ed. Linda J. Nicholson (Routledge) 300-23.

Afterword

Governing Children, Imagining Childhood

MARTHA MINOW

Imagination and fiction make up more than three quarters of our real life.

Simone Weil[1]

I wasn't used to children and they were getting on my nerves. Worse, it appeared that I was a child, too. I hadn't known that before; I thought I was just short.

Florence King, on her first day in kindergarten[2]

T HE IDEAS AND ILLUSIONS human beings hold powerfully shape how we see one another and how we see ourselves. The essays in this book each examine how shifting ideas about children implicate and support particular views of adults, of natives and foreigners, of 'us' and 'them', of nature and science and of order and disorder. Inflected by and in turn shaping images of race, class, and gender, ideas of childhood have served and also themselves been enforced by expressions of governmental power. How does it come to pass that members of a society realize the degree to which their picture of children is just that, a picture, a construction that has human architects and perhaps then can be renovated? How do recognitions of the social construction of childhood still leave limitations on what can be changed — due either to continuing confinements of vision or more material constraints on human choice? To consider these questions, knowing well that they will still remain elusive queries, I will use the rich insights of the essays collected in this volume which travel across several centuries and around Europe, England, the United States and Canada.

I also hope to retain some sense of the irony expressed by Florence King, when recalling her first day of kindergarten: adults could try to check their understandings of children by consulting children themselves who, after all, have conceptions of themselves; but these are invariably influenced profoundly by the views of the adults around them. Always already framed by language and inherited views, children nonetheless are embodied, sticky, ticklish, intense beings who change and grow. No wonder they become repositories of societal fears as well as hopes, regulations as well as dreams.

I. PICTURING CHILDHOOD

AT TIMES SYMBOLS OF EVIL AND CRIME, at times evocative of sex and seduction, or innocence and promise, children in some societies stand for all of these in the minds of adults. Striking in the chapters here is not only the shift in such conceptions over time and place, but also the moments when particular societies, or at least some of their members, acknowledged the social choices involved in the treatments of children. Rather than presuming that the governance of children reflects facts of nature or institutional practices immune from change, reformers and critics have at times challenged prevailing practices and conceptions of children that made such practices seem natural and inevitable. In no small way, this entire volume represents at least its authors' endorsement of the moments and the insight that permits them.

Thus, in 'Law, Labour and the Spectacle of the Body', Sylvia Schafer takes us to late nineteenth century France for a vivid study of shifting legal, as well as institutional and political, treatments of children. The adoption of three child protection laws in 1874 altered a prevailing conception of natural paternal authority and reflected growing skepticism toward religion or natural law when compared with democratic rule. Schafer powerfully locates a precursor for these laws in the limited exceptions to parental authority adopted in the Napoleonic civil code: state regulation of parents of children charged with crimes and punishments of parents implicated in the prostitution of their own children. These exceptions opened a toehold for arguments that other children also required protection by the state against or as substitutes for their parents. Indeed, these exceptions permitted people to question the presumed chain linking biological connection, natural affection, private protection and children, and state exclusion from the parent-child relationship.

Schafer shows how these openings in the otherwise presumed natural arrangement of parental authority and state passivity became destinations for anxieties about immigrants. As a result the 1874 reforms focused in part on immigrant child street performers. Unlike children engaged in industrial work, which contributed to the glory and wealth of the country, travelling performers were not respectable. That their children should seem in need of state protection becomes understandable in light of suspicions about foreign, travelling parents and more general discomfort with changes in the populace. The French people came to understand that the parental bond does not naturally assure children's well-being, at least when immigrant child entertainers entice and disturb the viewing public. Seeing through the shield of biological ties, the polity could choose to regulate parents and children.

Colomy and Kretzmann consider the early era of the juvenile court's history in the United States by reviving the story of Judge Ben Lindsey in the 'Gendering of Social Control'. By their account, Lindsey tried to resist then-dominant views of 'wayward' girls as dangerously-sexual bad girls, by portraying sexual precocity as normal. He condemned those who blamed sexually active teen-aged girls in moral terms and instead urged the view that these girls made correctable mistakes. The authors usefully demonstrate how many more charges against girls were brought by family members compared with charges against boys, which were more likely to have been brought by police or school officials. While desires to control conduct motivated charges, the familial role in charges against girls suggested efforts to invoke state power to reinforce roles expected by families. Finding a figure such as Judge Lindsey who resisted this family moralizing, the authors demonstrate a temporarily open debate about definitions of delinquency, relations between state and family, and female sexual conduct.

In 'Achieving the Promise of Justice for Juveniles', Janet Ainsworth returns to the creation of the Juvenile Court in Chicago, Illinois, in 1899 as a moment comfortably wedged in prevailing beliefs that sharply distinguished children from adults. The institution was new but it grew from established conceptions of children as morally, physically, and emotionally different enough from adults to warrant their own governmental setting for responding to deviance from public norms. That conception stands in relief against views gathering strength at the end of the twentieth century in the United States, views that at least contest the assumption of sharp difference between children and adults while pressing for 'adult' treatment of juvenile offenders.

As reforms make juvenile court itself look more and more like adult courts in terms of procedures and punishments, they also fuel arguments to unify the court systems and eliminate the distinct treatment for young people. Ainsworth carefully argues that a resulting unitary court need not itself be the 'adult' court but could instead bring aspects of the juvenile court for some adults. To make this argument, Ainsworth must highlight and challenge the strong tendency of political actors to portray juvenile offenders as members of groups, such as ghetto dwelling African-Americans, despised by powerful constituencies. This comment is a sobering challenge and anticipates how people in the future will look back upon this moment when the construction of childhood seems contestable and, indeed, expressive of racial attitudes as well as moral panic.

Michael Freeman's 'The James Bulger Tragedy', a study of the *cause célèbre* in England over the murder of a toddler by two ten-year-old boys, suggests not a moment of debatable images of children but instead a time of deliberate manipulation of images to advance a particular political agenda. The judge's decision to release the names of the minors fed the panic over crime which itself was fuelled, according to Freeman, at least in part by a conservative government and the press that served it. Depicting dangerous children in need of tough governmental responses could distract attention from a failing economy and potentially help the conservative government regain support with its core constituents.

Freeman provides the reader with an alternative possibility by turning to a remarkably similar incident, again in England, but some 130 years previously. There the incident was viewed as a tragedy rather than a sign of barbarous times. There the two young accused boys were viewed as lacking the capacity for moral understanding which is the predicate for the most serious penal sanctions. What changed in the intervening years? Was it the rise of psychology and psychiatry as fields authorizing experts to answer whether individuals can be held responsible? Was it a cycle of hope preceding disappointment with practices of rehabilitation? Freeman suggests, beyond these possibilities, the deliberate use of public fears by the Tories. He uses the historical contrast to create a moment for revealing the ideas, not the facts, that shape societal responses to children.

Looking at Canada, Anne McGillivray's 'Therapies of Freedom' explores political and social contests over Aboriginal child welfare. Any barriers to

state intrusion seem already weak in the face of a persistent view that
Aboriginal adults were themselves like children, incapable of governing
themselves or others. The care and education of Aboriginal *children*, for
nineteenth and twentieth century Euro-Canadians, seemed an appropriate
governmental task regardless of their parents' desires. Civilizing children,
civilizing the Indian: the two tasks converged to justify removal of children
from their homes for schooling in the late-nineteenth century. Analogous
removals occur more recently in the name of child protection.

Besides rupturing family and cultural ties, these practices further exposed
the children to remarkably high risks of physical and sexual abuse and even
death. An evangelical childsaving institution dealing with a variety of young
people persisted in its devaluation of cultural backgrounds and abusive
practices even in the face of more general reforms extending state powers in
the child welfare field. Further reforms in the 1960s and 1970s exposed the
appalling consequences of prevailing policies but promoted out-group
adoption of Aboriginal children rather than preservation of their families.
Recognizing some human choice in the treatment of these children did not
expose to view the full range of choices. Even as advocates built arguments
for preserving native cultures — and thus Aboriginal families — courts
continued to find particular conceptions of child welfare, abstracted from
culture, more persuasive. A language of psychological — *ergo* scientific —
reality trumped other ways of viewing Indian children and their families.

Alice Hearst finds in United States constitutional law a longstanding
acknowledgment of state interests in civilizing its members, including (or even
especially) children. In 'Domesticating Reason', she discloses, in a stream of
Supreme Court decisions that span nearly a century, a self-aware deployment
of law's power in the search of good citizens, not natural families or children's well-being. Thus, the reasoning and results of contested cases show
what the highest judges of the nation believed: the state could and indeed
should instil in children a loyalty toward authority and toward the nation;
parents should be respected when teachers of these ideas but not when their
interests undermined state purposes.

Seeing the state's regulation of families as persistent should expose how
much the family itself is not beyond human will but is indeed defined and
shaped by social choice. Sometimes those choices reflect efforts to help
children, but sometimes those choices reflect state concerns for order and
control. Losing frequently are arguments about children's actual ties and
affections. Instead, Hearst argues, the Supreme Court more often chooses to

picture children as vehicles for social purposes, especially the promotion of disciplined relations.

Sheila Martineau reminds us that real, embodied children lie behind the images proffered through language, political parties, experts, legislatures, courts and international conventions. Thus, in 'Reconstructing Childhood', she points out that, however much the particular notions of what counts as child abuse may shift through time and place, there are material practices that injure children; however much child labour may be framed and reframed through time, there are children who still use their bodies under the direction or orders of adults to produce goods and services. This extends of course to the very notion of childhood: perhaps invented, certainly viewed differently in different cultures and different times, where childhood still stands for palpable differences and constructed dualities between the youngest members of the species and those older ones who are bigger and heavier, more knowing and more dangerous. In teaching rights to children, Martineau advocates a contextual and experiential pedagogy involving a praxis of children's inclusion, of community participation and personal responsibility, of respect for the abilities of children as children. Teasing out the complex relationships among the 'palpable realities' of childhood, and the ways people apprehend them, is indeed both a purpose and an accomplishment of the essays here, even as they underscore the elusive qualities of a reality that can only be grasped by people, in cultures, using language and preconceptions.

That preconceptions can come to seem just that, and to seem false necessities now open to challenge and change, is an article of belief held not only by the authors in this collection but also by so many of their subjects. To see relations among parents, children, the state, and others not as a function of nature but instead as social choices invites exploration and exercise of choices. Yet so many of the authors here show the socially constructed nature of childhood as a function of forces, historical or political or economic, not as voluntary choices. Anxieties about disorder, about economic downturn, about immigrants and about native peoples figure more largely in debates about childhood than does the deliberate assessment of alternatives. Even when one recognizes choices can be made, constraints on those choices include forces of these kinds as well as the limitations of one's own understanding. The next section explores such limitations with the help, again, of the essays collected in this volume.

II. Confining Frames

Demonstrating the socially constructed nature of particular human relationships does not reshape those relationships. Limitations persist in what becomes possible. One source of limits stems from the partial nature of our understandings: we do not easily or well understand what casts shadows over our own thoughts. We may come to think that something can be altered that cannot and that something cannot be changed that indeed could be.

Some of the limitations of our imagination bear the marks of the categories through which we think. Ainsworth discusses the work of cognitive theorists who explore templates for thoughts. It could be that the theorists' own images are constrained by their culture and experience, but intriguing work suggests that we construct prototypes of categories such that we treat some members as more typical than others, and yet group a range of diverse members together.[3] The six-foot tall adolescent can be viewed as childish, then, when seeking power to make decisions about his own life, or viewed as an adult, when charged with the kind of violent offense that sustains the punishment structure of the criminal justice system.

Limits, as well as reaches, of our thought reflect our embodiment in bodies;[4] our experience of moving through time with the past as our reference point; our tendency to respond to what we see and to whom we hear even if those who are absent are absent due to our own choices. Limited conceptions of childhood in particular grow from the fact that children are socialized by adults who have particular conceptions of them. I will elaborate these thoughts before concluding.

A.   Reflecting Embodiment and Past Experience

Even though the Napoleonic Code opened up the possibility for regulating parent-child relations, as Schafer demonstrates, it also bequeathed a conception of law bound by formal, sharp distinctions. Boundary crossing in this conception seems difficult, if not unimaginable. The distinction between public and private, for example, takes on the status of a natural fact, preventing state involvement in the private lives of families. This familiar pattern of an invented dichotomy that nonetheless seems immutable may grow from the human experience with two hands and two feet: we divide the world in twos and then think the twoness is in the world.[5]

The pattern produces anomalies and collisions. Hearst examines, for example, the conflict between a right to privacy protecting families from the state and a right to privacy protecting individuals from families. It is as if the imagination has a map with only two positions, although the landscape is more fluid and complex than that. If the individual is a child, are the parents with it, against the state, or is the state with it, against the parents? A map forcing such choices fails to depict how children are related to parents and others, even as public and community practices and rules support and confine these relationships. It neglects what it takes both to nourish relationships and to protect individuals within them from danger.

B. The Absence of Children

Due to their absence as political players, conceptions of children proceed often with little sense of children's variety, fun, stubbornness, or simply, sentient experience. Where are young people in the debate over whether to treat juvenile offenders in a separate or unified court? What would groups of young people — both those accused and those victimized by crime — say they prefer or they fear, and how would that affect adult discussions? We do not know and we do not usually think to ask: our discussions proceed accordingly with limitations we can only dimly make out. Where are Aboriginal children in controversies over where they belong, with parents or foster parents, adoptive parents or residential schools? How can we get hold of children's sentiments — and do we as adults want to do so?

Paul Peterson has written what he entitles an 'immodest proposal' for children to vote, or to have adults cast votes on their behalf.[6] He compares children's welfare in the United States with the welfare of the elderly and finds startlingly worse rates of poverty, public expenditures, and expressions of care and concern. The practical problems with his recommendation are obvious to him and to others, but the thought balloon it launches could cast new shadows which reveal the limitations of our ideas about children.

How might this book be different if it included chapters written or dictated by children, or transcripts of children's voices? How would the conferences we academics attend differ if we made children a frequent topic, and had children present as commentators, audience and interruptions? Again, I suggest these not necessarily because I think they are advisable, but because they lie beyond our expectations and thus might press the edges of how we imagine children, and ourselves.

C.   Children and Adults: Interconnections

Talking with children and gleaning their views and desires does not free us from adults' preconceptions of children. Children are socialized largely by adults; children's circumstances are created by adults. Sexual abuse? Street performance? Religious martyrdom? Pressure into early study of music or chess? Gang turf fights? Anti-war protests? Children participate in such experiences in relation to and reaction to adults. Adults may look on and pretend not to be implicated.

Children learn lessons about how adults and the state view them, trust and distrust them. Those views are themselves offered to justify treatments of children whether conventional or new. Those who seek more autonomy for, and self-determination by, children may imagine children as capable of making choices or learning to do so. Adults with these views become invested in them but this does not make the views more real or true than contrary views of children's incapacities or needs for control.

Perhaps we can at most hope to de-naturalize our thoughts about children, to make them seem contingent on our past and our desires. Becoming more self-conscious about the assumptions we take for granted would include learning to examine the structures of our categories, what we suppress with them, how we carve dichotomies or sharp lines where perhaps there are only interconnections.

The idea I have used to structure this essay — that there are moments described by authors when ideas about children could change, but there are limitations even on these possibilities — no doubt reflects assumptions I have not myself considered fully. Yet this moment that permits me to make these comments seems not fully exploited, just yet. If it seems possible to point to alternative ways to understand childhood, then what assumptions about children remain unexplored in criminal law, tort law, contracts, antitrust law, cyberlaw? What assumptions about children undergird psychology, identity politics, macroeconomic planning?   What ideals and fears of government, especially along the axis of protection and paternalism, betray unexamined and alterable views of children?

Asking questions about how we think about children involves looking at the most intensely governed group of people while stretching the possible range of views about them. This book is an invitation to do just that. Perhaps it will inspire a long moment.

Notes

1. *Gravity and Grace* (Routledge and Kegan Paul, 1952).

2. *Confessions of a Failed Southern Lady* (St. Martin's Press, 1985, 1990).

3. See Ulric Neisser, *Cognition and Reality* (W. H. Freeman and Company, 1976).

4. Mark Johnson and George Lakoff, *Metaphors We Live By* (University of Chicago Press, 1980).

5. Some think this is a Western phenomenon to be contrasted with Eastern conceptions of oneness.

6. Paul Peterson, 'An Immodest Proposal' (1992) 121 Daedalus 151.